Not to Believe

∞

From Auschwitz to a New Jersey Chicken Farm

Gorham Street Books
www.gorhamstreetbooks.com
www.not-to-believe.com

ISBN: 978-0692205020

For my parents Godel and Brandla
and my wife Rhonda

"Not to believe" was my father's favorite expression
for describing behavior or events that he felt were incredible;
he often used the expression with wry or bemused humor.

His survival for more than two years at Auschwitz
was miraculous. That he never lost his faith
and still found joy in the world and its creatures
were wonders that still brighten my days.

Acknowledgments

I want to give special thanks to:
- Susan Pollack, my editor, for her guidance and support
- Lynn Whittemore for designing this book, for her long-term support of my writing efforts, and for her love and friendship

I also want to thank:
- Kelly Messier who proofread the memoir
- The Catskills Institute and its President, Dr. Phil Brown, Professor of Sociology and Health Sciences at Northeastern University, for selecting one of the chapters, *Forgiving God in the Catskills,* as the winner of their non-fiction writing contest: "The Catskills and the Holocaust"
- Susan T. Landry and Melissa Shook for their help editing and publishing another chapter, *Making Eggs,* in their *Portrait* magazine
- Susan Freireich, Sue Katz, Marion Kenneally, Barbara Kivowitz, and Fiona Maazel for their support and feedback on early versions of several of the chapters

Contents

Kibud Av

∞

And at the fall of night
The night benighted by nightfall
The gypsies with their smithies
Were forging suns and arrows.

Federico García Lorca
Romance de la Guardia Civil

Why is it that some people fear the gypsies, while others love them?
Why do some despise them, and still others pretend they do not exist?
As a teenager I wondered how people who knew me as a son could
ever truly know me. Indeed, they rarely knew my mind and perhaps
never will. I am not a gypsy, but I am from a tribe that has wandered,
and I am unsettled within that tribe. Like blacksmiths, the people who
surround me coax the flames below me, their history a firestorm that
sears my flesh. Stretched across their anvil, their tongs hold me as I
twist from side to side in a futile attempt to escape the hammer's blows.

Some Holocaust survivors have been reluctant to talk about their
experience, but my mother and father were always ready to tell their
sons stories about what they endured to survive. As a child I did not
want to hear them. I dreaded the documentaries that we watched on

1

TV that showed scenes of emaciated men and women in striped uniforms and small children holding their parents' hands as they walked
from the trains to the crematoriums. The images filled me with terror
and disbelief. When I finally found the courage to ask my father about
the tattoo on his arm, he described the selection process as he entered
the Auschwitz camp. Those chosen to work were lined up alphabetically,
after which their clothes and undergarments were removed and their
heads and pubic areas shaved. Those who were to die immediately went
elsewhere. He went to the tattoo area where a man took his arm and in
a couple of minutes inked a triangle into his flesh to mark him as a Jew,
followed by the number 83193. The tattoo marked his life…and mine.

Sometimes at night, as I lay in my bed, the evil closed in around
me. I thought of my father in his striped uniform eating his potato
gruel in the concentration camp and of my mother trapped and
shivering in a cold underground bunker in the Polish woods. My bed
was warm, but I was tormented by icy demons hiding in the dark. One
night and then another, I found myself in a black barren cave, dead
souls creeping in the shadows. In my dreams, I shivered in the cold,
waiting for the warmth to return after the winter solstice. Yet, even in
that tortured darkness, something within me reached out for holiness,
searching the ether for some magic to bring forth the gods. I yearned
for a warm light to bask in, magic to break the cycle of life and death,
a spiritual fervor that might help me stretch beyond death's chilling
grip.

My parents' stories were a terrible burden. They told me I was the
reason that they had survived and I had to work hard and be a good
boy to make them proud. As a child I just wanted to be like the kids
I saw on Saturday morning TV. I had a collie just like Timmy on *Lassie*,
and as I wandered around the farm with my dog, I felt luckier than
Timmy, the poor orphan boy. I had both my parents, but I also carried
their history. My parents called me their little prince. They told me
how lucky I was to be growing up in America, to have food and a warm
place to sleep, but if I was a young prince, I was born to a troubled
kingdom. The fates had conspired against me. My parents had suffered,
but I too had been grievously wronged. Too much was expected of me.

My mother would smile whenever I came into the room and try to hug me, pulling me toward her ample bosom, but if I made her angry, she might scream at me in Yiddish, "Hitler tried to kill me! Now you will finish the job!" It wasn't fair. How could I argue with my parents? How could I be good enough? Why did I have to go to bed with images of Jews packed into cattle cars and withered boys in striped pajamas, their eyes too big for their heads?

Looking back, I see myself as I was: a middle-class brat, overfed, overeducated, self-indulgent, but as a young man my relative comfort did little to blunt my frustrated rage. My father had lived through Auschwitz. My mother had spent the war with Jewish resistance fighters hiding from the Nazis in the Polish forests. It was not some game of cops and robbers that children play, but a battle for survival. Not a theoretical exercise, but a horrible ongoing reality. Their intimacy with death, with the extremes of human behavior, their courage and strength weighed on me. Their survival was an overwhelming achievement. In some ways, I was like any other child pushing back against his parents and trying to establish his own identity, but how could I make room for a self that was separate from their legacy? Sometimes I judged them harshly when they argued with each other over trivial things or appeared jealous of people who were richer and not stuck on a chicken farm. Over time I came to understand that my parents were miracles who could still smile and laugh after living through a nightmare, but they were still stuck inside their own lives, still trapped in their Orthodox Jewish morality and their peculiar ideas about child rearing. Were they twisted by war, or did my yearning to assimilate into American society make their European manners seem out of place? It was not only my family that conspired against me. At my Jewish grade school, and later my yeshiva high school, the rabbis badgered me with threats of eternal damnation. They hammered away, telling us we were the chosen people. We had a special obligation to God. We were chosen for what? For extermination? As I grew older, the urge to rebel against my parents, against my religion, became stronger, but I maintained the pretense of being obedient. I earned good grades, wore *tsitsis* (religious tassels on a four-cornered garment), and felt guilty.

I carried their burden, but the weight seemed onerous. I traveled through those early years with well-meaning parents and their God, a God whose severe demeanor and dreadful anger reflected life's horrors.

I was born in Munich, Germany. My parents say I spoke Yiddish and German first, but I quickly became as American as any boy who wore a yarmulke and *tsitsis;* attended Hebrew day school in Lakewood, New Jersey; and spoke Yiddish at home. I went to Ebbets Field to see the Brooklyn Dodgers play baseball. I watched up to three hours a day of 1950s TV. Every week I took a trip to the public library where I burned through all the literature set aside for teens and preteens. The books had red-orange jackets that wiped clean if I accidentally set them down on my open-faced peanut butter sandwich. I read biographies of Ben Franklin and Thomas Jefferson and novels by Mark Twain. I lived in the American dream, but I also lived in my father's nightmares chased by men in black boots and swastikas. I had that special guilt of a child who believes his parents when they tell him he will never suffer like they have. *Kibud Av* is the duty a Jewish son has to obey, love, and honor his parents. Writing this memoir has been, at least in part, an attempt to fulfill that commandment.

Coming to America

∞

We came to America in 1952, on a U.S. Navy cargo ship. I was two years old. My parents were in their early thirties. Refugees, displaced people, survivors—so many names for the homeless—they were Polish Jews who had lost their families in the well-ordered madness of genocide and the chaos of war. My mother, Bronia, who had fought with the Jewish resistance, was just over five feet tall. A buxom woman, she carried me pressed against her breasts like a trophy into New York Harbor. A flush rose to her cheeks and her heart hammered as she waded through customs and immigration. My grandfather, her father, was waiting for her at the dock. (She had never met the man. He had abandoned his family to escape from military service in World War I.

When I asked my father, Godel, about coming to the United States, he always began his answer with stories from the "good life" he left in Munich. He came out of the camps naked, but in just two or three years he established a thriving business selling watches and trading currency in postwar Munich. I will tell you more about Dad, his business partner Felix Messer, and the Jewish mafia later.

My parents met in Munich in 1948. I had heard the story many times. Godel and Bronia would smile at each other when they told it. Mom had just enough money to maintain her "independence." Like the girl with pin money on a date with a new guy, she had just enough to take a cab if things went badly. When Dad told her to spend her money on her trousseau, she hesitated. She went to her cousin Adam for advice. Adam was the main reason she survived the war. Adam took her with him into "the woods" to join the Jewish resistance group that he led. When my mother told the story, she said that Adam had counseled her, "Trust this boy. If he said it will be, it will be." Still, she had kept a little money, just in case.

"So Mom was ready to get married when you asked her?" I asked.

Dad laughed. "She was ready yesterday. I told her to go make a couple of dresses, one for the wedding and one for the party. But she was worried about spending the money, and she asked Adam, 'What should I do?' He told her: 'If he says to get a dress made, you can trust him.'

"We were married on January 16, and a year later, on the 13th of January, you came out. We had a German maid, Greta. She had a white maid's hat. She raised you. In Jewish, they say, 'Your real mother is not the mother who gave you birth, but the one that raised you.' You hated it when you lost sight of her. We went on a train to the mountains once, and she went to get some coffee in the next car, and you were exactly 18 months. You screamed, *'Greta, verlasse mich nicht* (Greta, don't leave me)!'"

In 2003 I joined my parents to celebrate their 54th anniversary. After lunch my 86-year-old father went off to rummage in his office and came back with a couple of documents he thought I should have before he lost track of them. Because it was warm in the house, he had rolled up his sleeves. His Auschwitz tattoo showed clearly through the white hair on his forearm: 83193. Below his number was a triangle pointing downward: 83193 Delta. In the plain envelope he handed me, I found a copy of my German birth certificate dated 1950.

The German *Geburtsurkunde* listed my place of birth as Richard Wagner Strasse. I saw the name and thought of New York's Mayor Robert Wagner, and then, with eyes that felt like they were coming into focus after several pirouettes, I stared at the birth certificate. It was an old copy with white text on a black background. Both my parents were listed as *Israelitisch*. A German label marked them as Jews just as clearly as the yellow patches they had worn in the ghetto, but after the

My mother, Greta and me in Munich

war, the Germans could not bring themselves to use the label *Juden*—Jews—because it had been a death sentence for so many.

"Your mother wanted to go to the United States," my dad said. "I didn't want to go. Her father was in America. She had never seen him. When I went to the Jewish Federation for help getting visas, they said to me, 'You are a speculator (a smuggler), you can't get papers.'" But he did.

"She couldn't sleep. She was obsessed with getting to America to see her father. She wrote to her friends, and eventually someone sent papers."

"So then you went right away?" I asked.

"No, I dragged my feet for a year. I didn't want to go. I had a good life, a rich life. I didn't want to leave. I paid a few dollars each time to the officials, and they changed the visa dates, one extension and then another.

"I thought I was a rich man. What's the rush? Maybe we go to Israel?

"Even after I came to America, my partner Felix was still in Germany, and he wrote me a letter: 'We can make some business. Come back to

Godel and Bronia in Munich

Munich. We'll make a business. Come, stay for a while.' Mom would not hear it. She didn't want to go, and she didn't want me to leave her with her young child to go away on a long trip.

"We were living in the Bronx, the South Bronx, and I saw this guy, and he asked me, 'What are you doing here?' Then I recognized him. I had sold watches to him in Munich. His name was Mandel, a Jewish soldier, an American. He had helped us with the police in Munich. I met him in Germany, and now I ran into him in the Bronx. We became good friends. His sister lived near us. I was trying to figure out what to do with my few dollars. He took me to look at a rooming house that I could buy as an investment. He took me to an agent on 72nd Street. I'll never forget. They were asking almost $30,000 for the building. I put down a $3,000 deposit.

"The rooming house was on 74th between West End and Broadway, 14 rooms for sale, less than $30,000. Felix's wife, Sally, said, 'Wait, wait, wait. I'll take you to my uncle.' She took me to her uncle. He had a house on the East River. He was supposed to be a *maven*. He looked at the property we were buying and said, 'It's an old house—don't do it.' So I took back my deposit. I could have bought two or three in the same area." A *maven* is an expert, from the Hebrew "one who understands," but my father's intonation made it clear that he had become skeptical of this *maven's* mastery of the New York real estate market.

"How much is that place worth now?"

"It's worth $3 million now. I was stupid, but I tell you, if I had stayed in New York, I would be dead now. I have a quiet life here. New York City, it's a helluva town. Here it's quiet. I used to sing when I was in Florida for the winter. I used to sing in Yiddish: 'I want to be back home, in my own little town where I lived in comfort and quiet.'" A big smile appeared as my dad tilted his head from side to side and sang.

"Our boat came to the States on Friday; your grandfather came the next day, Saturday. He was a rich man." Dad paused for a moment to make sure I understood he was being sarcastic. "He came to us with $300 he had borrowed from a friend. He thought his daughter would need money.

"You know, I was bringing jewelry from Germany for a fellow whose family had already come to the States. He gave me a few hundred dollars, and we brought $8,000 to $9,000 worth of jewelry. Bronia wore the jewelry, gold and diamonds and everything.

"And you were dressed like an angel, like a prince. Your grandfather saw the jewelry. He was speechless.

"You know it was August, so hot. All my stuff was still in customs. He took us down to Orchard Street. I wanted to buy a couple of shirts. He was pointing out the red lights and the traffic. 'You don't go when it is a red light.'

"I told him I knew about these things. I had an auto in Germany. He was amazed. He said, 'You had an auto?'" He laughed. Dad was five feet six inches tall and his father-in-law just over six feet tall. I think he enjoyed poking fun at the bigger man.

"You had a car? What kind?" I asked. I was surprised, too.

"An Opal.

"Your grandfather never had any money. He ran away from Poland, from the draft at the beginning of the First World War. He was also running from your grandmother. He got her pregnant and agreed to marry her, but not to stay with her and raise your mother. He came to the States and caught a new girlfriend, then he sent divorce papers back to Poland.

"Mom's passport says she was born in 1917, but I figured out it must be 1914 or 1915, when her father left. So she must two or three years older. I never tell her nothing. I never talked to her about it.

"He thought I would be like other refugees, that I would be a poor guy like him. That first day on Orchard Street, I picked out a few shirts. They cost $8. I pulled out a $20 bill to pay, and he was stunned. 'You have green dollars?' I came 40 years after him. It was different world, but we both came from small towns. We had outhouses in the fields behind the house. The first time I saw indoor plumbing was at Auschwitz."

Both of my parents were seasick on the freighter that took them to New York City. My mother was excited about getting to see her father even though he had abandoned her as a child. My father was more cautious; he worried that someone would steal some silver or china from the six large wooden crates that rode in the ship's hold. My father was an Orthodox Jew with a number tattooed on his forearm. Over the years I came to understand him as someone who could be the subject of a Buddhist dharma talk. His parents, his brother, his sisters, his nephew were all victims of the Holocaust. Dad barely survived as an inmate at Auschwitz. He taught his family to see suffering clearly, but he also taught us to try to live life with joy—and a little mischief.

The stories he told me from the small town where he grew up in Poland, from the ghetto, from the camps, made me part of his world. I remember the stories. They are embedded in me; they are part of my DNA.

The stories about the camps were the hardest to fathom. When our New Jersey neighbors set out their Christmas lights, Dad was reminded of his Christmas experiences in the camps. We had just finished dinner when he told us his Christmas story:

"I had already been in Auschwitz for almost two years. It was 1944. Most of the people were coming in from Hungary. It was just before Christmas. A capo grabbed me and said, 'You are stealing!' How did he know? I looked too good. I still had some flesh on my bones. 'I will send you someplace you won't live too long.' He was sending me to some work he thought would kill me. They took me down to the gate. You know the one, the *Arbeit macht Frei* gate."

Yes, I knew the gate. As a child I had seen pictures in books and I had seen it in the documentaries we watched on TV. Years later, as an adult, when the family visited Auschwitz, I held my father's hand as we stood beneath that sign. *Arbeit macht Frei* means "Work will make you free." It is a noble sentiment that for most of the poor souls who walked through that gate became a cynical epitaph.

I came to understand that you needed to be lucky to survive, but you also needed to be fearless. Would I have had his courage, his determination? Would I have found a way to live from day to day? Dad pressed his lips together and shook his head as he relived the moment.

"I'm standing there waiting to be picked up for my next work. It was the day before Christmas, and the soldiers were walking around happy. They already had their Christmas presents. They had wine, salamis. Short story, I stood there the whole day and nobody came for me. I was lucky.

"But I still needed someplace to go." Dad explained that if you did not have work, you went to the gas chambers. "I went to one block where I had friends, but they were sick in the block, typhus. They didn't let me in. They sent me to another block where people were working in an ammunition factory. I went to work there. It was heavy work. By the end of the day I could barely stand or lift my arms. Still, when I went there, I knew right away I must look for business."

My dad paused to smile. Before the war, his father (my grandfather) had made hats. My father would take the goods to market. In the camps, he always found some way to engage in some kind of forbidden commerce.

"I told a couple of the girls who worked there, 'You walk by the crematorium. Talk to the guys working there. You know the guys that worked with the dead people. Tell them to toss you some scarves over the fence.'"

"Why scarves?" I asked my father.

"The scarves were easy to throw over the walls, easy to hide. They would bring them to me. I would give them a piece of bread. They saw the bread, they opened up their eyes. A piece of bread, it was a treasure." He looked up and tossed his hands in the air. Was he asking God for a comment?

"The ammunition plant was hard, rough work. I wore cotton gloves cutting iron." He looked down. His eyes closed before he continued.

"A neighbor from home worked in the place they sorted clothes. They called it 'Canada.' I asked him, 'Take me to work. Take me to work in Canada.'"

He opened his eyes to look into mine as he continued. "I showed it to you when we were there in 1998, when we visited Auschwitz. I wanted to show you the place we called Canada."

Canada was a sorting area located between the Birkenau death camp and the Auschwitz work camp. I found out later that the inmates called it Canada because they thought it was a land of great riches. All the inmates' possessions were confiscated when they entered the camps, and the warehouses had large piles of clothes, suitcases, handbags. The workers, mostly women, sorted through the sad piles. Anything useful or valuable was to be sent back to Germany, but everyone stole from the loot: the SS, the Polish guards, the inmates working there. For the guards it was corruption; for the inmates it was survival.

"So you could just change jobs?" I asked.

"Listen. Listen. Every day, at the end of the day, when you worked in Canada, you had to take off your clothes and get disinfected. The foreman from the ammunition plant saw me there and he said, 'You ran away from your work at the ammunition plant. What you did is sabotage. This is wartime!'" My father broke the rules. You needed to take chances to stay alive.

Dad told the foreman, "Listen. I am too long in camp. I cannot survive in that job. What you want, you can do to me." Dad stared at the floor in front of him and then looked up. Once again, he shook his head back and forth slowly and continued with his story.

"'What are you going to do?' Whatever the foreman was going to do, he would do. He didn't do anything. I went back to the clothes work. Right away I looked for a partner. One guy had friends working in a magazine of food. It stored provisions like rice, sugar, and macaroni that were used to feed the prisoners and guards."

"Did you get fed macaroni?" I asked.

"No, it was for the guards. We got a thin potato soup." He paused.

"The place I worked was an overflow from the main Canada. I used to take every day something to make a living. I find a few *pengas. Pengas* is Hungarian money. People would hide the money in their clothes, but all their clothes were taken away. Our crew would rip them up. We would find stuff hidden in the clothes, some coins, a piece of jewelry. We would steal stuff we found shredding clothes and trade it for food. I had a little business. I even saved a little money, a few hundred marks. But eventually, the transports slowed down. They were not taking in enough stuff. They closed us.

"After Canada, I needed to find work again. I had a friend who worked at a laundry. He cooked for an SS man, and I asked him to find me some new work. And he got me a job in the laundry. In Auschwitz there were 24 blocks. When you changed jobs, you changed blocks."

"Did the SS come into the block?" I asked.

"No, not much. The Red Cross came every other month, maybe more often. They didn't go to Birkenau, to the death camp. Our camp was clean. In the bathroom there was a sign: 'One louse means death.' I especially remember one guy; he was a giant, seven feet three, a Greek. He used to walk around with a stick with a nail on the end picking up little pieces of garbage, cigarette butts. The camp was very clean. No, the soldier would not come in. The capos ran the blocks. They were sometimes Polish or German, even a few Jews.

"After Canada, I worked in the laundry at two big machines, five, six feet tall. They would gather laundry for all the nearby camps: Buna, Birkenau. In Auschwitz alone there were more than 22,000 people; in Buna, 10,000. With the other camps, maybe 80,000, 100,000. They would drop off bundles from all the camps and at the end of the day pick them up. And every so often a bundle would disappear." Dad smiled. "We would divide it up: every day something, a pair of pants, or a shirt. You had to live. That's not stealing. We called it 'organizing the supplies.' I worked and I worked."

My father sighed. "Listen," he said. "I must tell you this story. When I worked in the tailor shop, one guy, a capo, he was a young man, maybe 22 or 23 years old. He all the time hit the people. He hit them in the head or in the ribs. 'I'll give you a *patch in punim* (a slap in the face).'" Dad waved his hand in front of his face, reminding me of my bad boy scoldings. He continued, "A German capo came over to the Jewish guy and said, 'I don't beat up my people. Why do you do this?' The young man was insecure. He wanted to show he was in charge.

"Maybe there is no justice, but one day they came looking for ten young men for a castration experiment. The Jewish capo wound up on the top of the list. They cut off one or maybe both. The same happened to a couple of my landsmen. I got one guy from my town. They cut him off and he got infected and he was suffering and I brought him all the time a piece of bread, some margarine."

My father's stories sometimes seemed to end midstream. They poured through a faucet that opened and closed capriciously on a reservoir of memories. He told me stories about the camps, about his adventures before and after WWII. He told me about his family, my family, my grandparents, my four aunts and my uncle. I was named after my grandfather. I knew their names, but I never knew them. The Nazis killed them before I was born.

The Chicken Farm

∞

My father did not invest in Manhattan real estate. He bought a chicken farm on 20 acres in central New Jersey.

When we first came to the United States, in 1952, we lived in a cheap flat in the Bronx and my dad worked as a *hittelmacher* making caps for $42 week. It was the trade he had learned from his father. He worked off and on for eight months earning $26 a week from unemployment when he could not find work. All the while he tried to learn the language and get oriented.

In 1953, Felix Messer, his partner from his wholesale watch business in Munich, went down to New Jersey looking to buy a chicken farm, and my father went with him to have a look at life in the countryside and visit with a few people he knew from the old country. Dad called them *landsleit*. They were Jews from his area of Poland who had already bought farms.

Why did he buy a chicken farm? When I grew old enough to question my father about his decision, he tended to be a bit defensive.

"What else was I going to do? I didn't speak the language. I had some money to invest. There was a Jewish community in Lakewood. It seemed like a good place to raise a family."

At the time chicken farming must have seemed attractive. One could own land, be independent and relatively unhindered by any language barriers, and have one's kids grow up in the countryside near a Jewish community. When Dad bought our farm in the early 1950s, a few thousand birds could comfortably support a small family.

Then, too, Dad may have seen Fred MacMurray and Claudette Colbert in *The Egg and I,* the movie based on Betty MacDonald's classic memoir by that name. Both the book and movie celebrated chicken farming as an easy road to a comfortable life. So did a 1951 CBS TV series, likewise called T*he Egg and I,* which earned higher ratings than *Search for Tomorrow* and *Love of Life.* However, I am quite sure we did not own a TV until a year *after* we moved onto the farm.

Lakewood, New Jersey, does have a lake and even a bit of pine forest on the south side of town. When I lived there, it was about the same size as Vishne, the Polish town where my mother had spent her childhood. Lakewood had once been a resort in what had once been a garden state. In the first half of the 20th century, the modest lake provided relief for New York City residents looking for a breath of fresh air. By the 1970s, NYC sprawl had become so extensive that even Lakewood, some 60 miles away, seemed like extended suburbs. Housing developments and shopping malls replaced the farms, and the area lost much of its rural character, although herds of deer still roamed in the woods at the edge of town.

Lakewood also had a *Yeshiva Gavohah,* an exalted place of learning for religious Jews, where I would dance with the holy scrolls on Simchas Torah. *Yeshiva* means "a place to sit" and *gavohah* "raised up," so a *Yeshiva Gavohah* is an exalted place to sit and learn. It was a serious institute for Talmudic study that produced scholars and rabbis with beards and long sideburns called *paiyas.* They sometimes wore *shtreimels,* hats made from a circular piece of velvet surrounded by fur. They always wore *tzitzis.* The knotted fringes of wool hung out under their shirts and flashed about while the young men played basketball, an exercise exported from the inner city. The yeshiva was special because the *Rebbe* traced his lineage from the Vilna Gaon, a great teacher from the Middle Ages. Like a supreme court onto himself, the Vilna Gaon could establish new precedents in Orthodox law for dealing with the modern age.

The New Jersey region deserves another footnote in American Jewish history. It is one of the few places where Jewish farmers took root in the United States. In Farmingdale, Howell, Freehold, Lakewood, and elsewhere in South Jersey, chicken farms owned and operated by Jews supplied eggs to the nearby metropolitan areas. Before WWII, Jews were forbidden land ownership in most of Eastern Europe. Tenant farming, however, was not unknown, and my father's family had rented orchards. The family name, Kirschenbaum, means "cherry tree," and most of the orchards they rented were devoted to that fleshy, red fruit with its stony core.

Looking back, it is difficult for me to reconstruct the appeal that egg farming might have had to my parents' generation. Chickens, especially white leghorns, are among the more insipid creatures to inhabit the earth: stupid, mean, timid, filthy birds that can barely lift themselves off the ground. They are, however, factories of protein and cholesterol. I suppose baby chicks are cute. I certainly thought so as a child. I remember the fuzzy yellow balls with tiny feet, huddled by the hundreds in beds of straw under the warm glow of gas-heated umbrellas, but they grow into monsters. For my parents, and for my brother and me, years of tending to the birds, seven days a week, in manure-filled coops and years of standing on cold concrete cleaning and sorting eggs drained all sense of rustic charm from the occupation. We were all happy when, several years after I left home for college, my father sold the farm and moved into Lakewood to pursue a new occupation in real estate.

∞

My memories of our chicken farm begin when I was four. My brother, Benjamin, was born when I was five. We spoke Yiddish at home, and each morning I took a little undersized school bus to the Lakewood Hebrew Day School. My mother would beam whenever anyone paid attention to me or my brother, and my father would check to make sure we upheld the family honor. I needed to be an obedient son, a good student well versed in Jewish traditions, well-behaved, hardworking, clean, and polite. I knew I was loved, but in the struggle of my parents to control their sometimes rebellious children, their history

Kirschenbaum family circa 1959, my brother in a bow tie

could make terrible intrusions. My father often told us stories about his life in Europe. They were tales that wandered from the small town in Poland where he was raised, to the war years in the ghetto and the terrible years at Auschwitz. Sometimes he would also talk about the postwar years in Munich. The postwar stories often ended with a Yiddish song whose chorus was "I don't know where I'm going, but I know I have no home." As a child I listened raptly. I was fascinated and elated to be his captive audience and center of attention, but the stories often left me terrified and the song left me confused. We did have a home, or at least I thought we did.

Our farm was in Howell Township, a few miles north of Lakewood. Our mail came through Lakewood in what was then called Rural Free Delivery (RFD). The farm's eastern property line was about 100 yards up a gravel road from the highway, where the mailboxes for everyone on our road stood in a little cluster. Some of my earliest memories are of walking down to the highway to get the mail. It was my first job on the farm. The few memories that predate the farm are of dinner smells in apartment buildings and getting dressed up to meet my grandfather for the first time. The old photos creep in as memory, too: the young boy with round cheeks sitting on a pony. My parents and their friends had worked hard to implant memories of my first two years in Munich, like the delight I took in playing *Rook tzook,* a toddler's game of push and pull, or my fascination with the old penny gumball machines. I can still picture my mother, with black wavy hair, in a flower-print smock, pregnant with my brother, hanging laundry behind the house while I played in the backyard. On rainy days, I played cowboys and Indians in the basement, pretending the big wooden crate that came over with us on the boat from Europe was a fort. Then one day my brother appeared. His circumcision party, the *bris* (the covenant), is the first social event I remember. Jewish folklore tells us that Adam was born without a foreskin in the Garden of Eden and that the foreskin grew only after he sinned. Does that imply that circumcision is an attempt to return boys to a state of grace as they are already marked by sin?

From my bedroom window on the farm, past the clothesline and the lush green patch that marked our cesspool, I could see the "brooder house," a three-room coop that held our baby chicks. The long, low wooden building was painted white. The tarpaper roof angled slightly from front to back. There were no hens brooding there, but for my father, it was nerve-racking. The chicks needed to keep warm. They were susceptible to diseases. If they became frightened, they would huddle together in groups so dense the poor little birds in the center might suffocate. A bit like raising his sons, lots of things could go wrong.

Preparations for the next group of baby chicks began almost as soon as the previous group of pullets (young adults) had left. To make a fresh start, we had to get rid of the old shit. I started shoveling shit even before I started kissing girls. Manure trucks came to pick the stuff up for the fertilizer mills. As a kid I wondered why anyone would want chicken shit. But some people considered it a treasure. In the late 1950s

19

a small development had sprung up less than a quarter mile south of our property. Small houses with prices well under $10,000 were built on streets called Shady Lane and Sunset Lane and attracted retired people from North Jersey and New York City. Word spread among some old Italian gardeners who had moved here from New York that we would part with the stuff. In the spring they would come to the farm to buy eggs and pick up some manure. A few months later they would return with tomatoes and cucumbers. They wanted to bring eggplant, but Dad never liked it.

Chickens have a short life cycle. The new flock, like any new crop, lends credence to the belief that life is renewed. Dump trucks show up to cart off the manure. The manure gets shoveled onto the trucks. The cement floors of the brooder house are scraped and washed. I especially liked the scraper, a flat piece of metal on a long pole; it made a satisfying sound on the cement floors. There was something rewarding about scraping off the last vestiges of excrement. When the floors were dry, the wooden walls were sprayed with a creosote-based disinfectant. The aroma of the creosote remains a fresh memory, acrid and pungent. Although years later we would learn that creosote was a carcinogen, in my childhood memories it stands as a harbinger of renewal.

From the ceiling of each room of the brooder house hung three octagonal gas ranges; they were suspended from pulleys, the ropes tied off on cleats affixed to the posts that supported the roof. These metal stoves were the center of the little chicks' lives. Eight feet, one at each corner of the octagon, held the stove just high enough off the ground for a four-inch-tall baby chick to duck underneath in search of warm repose. The chicks arrived like little walking lemons. They came packaged in cardboard boxes with airholes in the top and sides. Like most warm-blooded creatures, baby chicks rely on their mothers' warmth for the first few weeks until their bodies can manage heat regulation. They like to be at 95 degrees. The stoves kept them alive. As the chicks grew, needing more room and less warmth, the stoves would be raised, moving the heat a bit farther away.

When my father complained whimsically about the trials of raising children, he used the Yiddish shorthand *blit fargeist,* from the longer

In front of the brooder house

phrase "You have to spill blood to make children." I was a cesarean section baby cut out of my mother's body, separated from the heat, a head too big for the passageway. Approaching 90, my mother still had the scar across her abdomen and she still smiled when she saw me, even when she could not remember my name or confused me with my brother. She spread warmth through the family, but I do not remember seeing her around the baby chicks. Her commitment to the farm revolved around "making the eggs," grading and packing them for our dealers. Even in the egg room, you could tell where the flock was in its life cycle. Pullets produced pullet-sized eggs, just smaller than medium, a size that was rare among mature birds. These eggs were too small for breakfast omelets, but bakeries would use them for pastries and cakes. My favorites were the smallest eggs, the pewees. They sometimes came in weird shapes but were mostly small, round pebbles, much less fragile than larger eggs. Mom would use them to bake. Since nobody really wanted them, nobody cared if I played catch with them or knew if I threw them at passing tractor-trailers from the hills that overlook Highway 9.

21

We belonged to what Dad always called the farmers' *shul*. *Shul* is the Yiddish word for synagogue, from the German and Latin words for school. It was small synagogue on a country road, a half-mile away from the nearest crossroad. Almost the entire congregation had immigrated after WWII, and the war was heavy upon them. Every holiday brought back memories of a childhood lived across the Atlantic and of relatives and friends who died in the Holocaust. The congregants were almost all chicken farmers now, but most of them had never worked on a farm before they came to America. My father was an exception. My grandfather's main business in Europe had been making caps, but he had also rented orchards, where my father and his brother picked fruit in the fall. My grandmother and my father's sisters had made cherry and apple pies. My mother made the pies for her farm boys, but all my aunts and uncles were killed in the war.

Some of the Jewish farmers, especially those from Farmingdale, were leftists, but not the farmers at our *shul*. They were newcomers, the *greeneh* (greenhorns), the Holocaust survivors, mostly Polish Jews. Their encounters with socialism and communism before and after the war left them skeptical and bitter. The Farmingdale folks called the *greeneh* DPs (displaced persons).

Farmingdale is a collection of houses and a few storefronts on West Farms Road and Yellowbrook/Squankum Road, about ten miles northeast of Lakewood. The two towns are not far apart, but for me they represented separate worlds.

Many in Farmingdale had taken up chicken farming before WWII. Some had come out of the sweatshops of New York City. Some were idealistic white-collar professionals who saw farming as a way to return to the land. There was a contingent with German ancestry and one from Eastern Europe. For them, the farming cooperatives in the egg belt of New Jersey, like the kibbutzim in Israel, manifested the collaboration between working people and intellectuals laboring for the common good. Gertie Dubrovsky, whose daughter Lynn was a high school classmate of mine, wrote a book about them, *The Land Was Theirs*. Discussions at their community center were intense and wide-ranging; participants included everyone from apologists for

Stalinism to advocates for right-wing Zionism. I was jealous of kids like Lynn whose parents were educated. Both of my parents had to give up their education before starting high school.

All the Jewish farmers within a 20-mile radius knew one another, or at least they knew the family names and where the farms were located. They were connected by feed co-ops like the Freehold-Lakewood-Farmingdale (FLF) co-op that brought them chicken feed, and the egg dealers who sold their product, as well as by their synagogues and their community centers. My father disapproved of the socialists, but he let me join a neighbor at pro-Israel celebrations sponsored by *Habonim*, a socialist youth group. The *greeneh* were anticommunist, and they tended to label any leftist movement as communist, to them a curse word. Their neighbors in Poland who became communists often gave up their Jewish identity.

Then, too, my parents remembered that during the war, persecuted by the fascist Nazis, the Jews were too often disappointed when they turned to the communists for help. My mother told a story about her encounter with communists as a member of the Jewish resistance. "We were being chased by Nazis. We were starving. We risked our lives swimming across a wide river to get to territory held by the Russians, but the communists sent us back without food. They gave us a few guns and said 'Go fight in your own country!'"

After the war, the story became murkier. The German fascists had been defeated, but the Poles now lived under a new Soviet occupation. A few of the leaders of the socialist state imposed by the Soviets were Jewish, which only reinforced a lingering anti-Semitism among a population unhappy with the Soviet occupation. But the new regime did little to protect the Jews. For my father, the contrast between the failing economies of the Soviets and the resurging economy of the West was an overwhelming indictment of communism.

In his youth, my father was a follower of Ze'ev Jabotinsky, a Revisionist Zionist in the tradition that went on to form the Herut and then the Likud parties. Dad was happy when I gave up Habonim and became a member of the National Congregation of Synagogue Youth. Centered in the more modern Lakewood synagogue, it was a group that still resists the assimilation of Jews into the wider society, a philosophy suited to the Lakewood immigrant crowd, the Orthodox Jews, and Hassidim, who lately had taken over the town.

For me the politics of the different youth groups became identified with the different towns, Lakewood and Farmingdale. For the Farmingdale Jews, moving out of the cities to farms had a political flavor. They were more progressive, less religious, better educated, and most had arrived before WWII. When they gave up their farms, they became schoolteachers or went into social services instead of moving to other businesses the way my father and his more entrepreneurial greenhorn immigrants did.

Places bind you, and the people near you shape your life. I was tied to my parents and their community of *greeneh,* all survivors of the Holocaust. I was bound to our chicken farm and our farmworkers. I lived in the shadow of people I had never met, people who had died before I was born. My grandparents and aunts and uncles were exterminated in the cold fury of a madness that shook the world. The trouble with modern man is that he knows too much. Swimming in a sea of knowledge, he has figured out that he will never understand it all. Even worse, he has finally come to understand that looking at things changes them, and so he looks away, never seeing the thing itself, only the shadow, the echo, the swirling vortex it creates as it passes through the night. When my parents and other Holocaust survivors gathered in our house to tell the stories of what they had seen and endured, I recoiled. Over time, I came to revere their courage, but when I was eight or nine years old, I would hide in the linen closet to escape facing the horrors. I needed to look away when my parents cried for those who were murdered.

∞

As a child, my sense of neighborhood and community was focused on our Rosh Hashanah walk to the farmers' *shul.* The holiday marks the Jewish New Year and comes during the first days of fall. The four-mile walk to *shul* seemed like an enormous undertaking. Most of the country roads we walked on were gravel or cinder. In the 1950s only a few stretches were paved. Dressed in holiday clothes, we passed the Greenblatt farm and Mr. Estel's house. Mr. Estel was one of our volunteer firemen. When the fire siren sounded, I would rush out to the front of our house and watch him come tearing down the road in his souped-up Ford. I think he drove the fire truck, too. About a half-mile beyond the Estels' house, we passed Max Frisch's farm. I went to grade school with his daughters Gail and Itka. Max was tall with a prominent mustache. His face was angular, like Soviet art. He reminded me a bit of pictures I had seen of Stalin, only taller and darker, a cigarette always dangling from his lips.

Max once saved my life. It was 1966. By then we had started renting nearby farms from folks who had gone out of business. My father was determined to hang on, working longer hours and raising more chickens to make ends meet. I got my farmer's driving license that winter. As a 16-year-old, I could drive farm vehicles in the daytime a year before getting a regular driver's license. Workers collected the eggs from the rented farms and left the eggs in the feed room in metal baskets like the ones used to hold golf balls on driving ranges. We would bring the eggs back to the egg room at our home farm to clean, sort, and pack them. It was springtime and rains had softened the earth. Dad had warned me not to take the shortcut across the field to the feed room when I went to pick up eggs from the Meltzers' farm, a mile up the road. Driving the long way meant passing the house and coming back to the coop on the gravel driveway. The shortcut started just after Max's property. The field looked safe to me. The coops were set back about 30 yards from the road, long, low buildings built parallel to the road, painted white with asphalt roofs sloping gently away from the road. I was quite close to the coops when the pickup truck started losing traction. In a panic, I hit the accelerator. The wheels spun faster and faster, mud flying up behind the pickup. Then all forward progress stopped. After a few minutes of methodically rocking back and forth in an attempt to get unstuck, the 15-year-old Chevy had sunk up to its axles in mud. Panic and despair soon turned into dread as I settled in to await my fate. An hour later Dad arrived in the family sedan. He

Max Frisch

pulled off the road, climbed out of the car, and started toward me across the field with purpose in his stride. When he realized what had happened, his eyes grew wide. He started yelling in Yiddish:

"You *facackte* idiot. What did I tell you?" He had just turned 50. All around him his friends were being forced off their farms by competition from southern egg ranches shipping eggs north in refrigerated trucks.

"I'm sorry. I forgot. I didn't do it on purpose, Dad." I edged away from the truck.

"*Oy gevalt,* I don't have enough *tsuris*. Hitler tried to kill me. Now you want to finish the job. You ..." He was briefly speechless as he surveyed the situation.

By the time he reached the truck, I had moved ten yards away. His anger built steadily as he assessed the situation, calculating the extra work added to an already brutal 12-hour day. He grabbed a broom handle that I had tried to wedge under one of the wheels in a feeble attempt to give the wheel some traction. Waving the stick, he rushed toward me. Dad rarely struck us in anger or, for that matter, at all. Usually the threat of a *patch in punam* got our attention. But this time his self-control was in a shambles and his rage in full repair.

"If I catch you, I'll kill you."

I gave up trying appeasement. What could I say? He was right. I had been an idiot, but I was not ready to get thrashed, so I kept darting away from him. He was five feet six inches, and even at 16, I was nearly six feet tall. The small, round, balding man in gray work pants and short sleeves chased a tall teenager in jeans and a City Lights T-shirt. He tried to force me toward the coops, but I sprinted away in ever-wider arcs, hoping he would calm down. Max saw us from his back porch, and he came trotting over, trying not to laugh.

Like my father, Max had survived the war as a Polish Jew. He had lost his first wife and their two children. I never asked how they had died. I knew only that a Polish farmer had hidden him from the Germans.

"Godel, what are you doing?" All of the conversation still in Yiddish, yet my father would not turn toward him.

"I'm going to break his bones. I need to teach him a lesson. He needs to understand that he has to obey instructions."

"Godel, calm down, relax, take it easy." Max had maneuvered himself between Dad and me, but Dad was still circling trying to get close enough to whack me.

"Godel, don't be silly, let go of the stick. I'll help you with the truck."

Max kept talking calmly, staying in front of Dad and herding him like an animal that had broken out through a hole in the fence. Slowly my father calmed enough to be embarrassed and, still cursing, turned and threw the stick toward the coops.

I made sure to keep five to ten yards away from him, and to keep Max between my father and myself. Max finally got my father to make eye contact, and after a moment of suspended animation, they both started laughing, but I was still careful to stay out of reach. Another neighbor came over with his tractor and pulled the truck out of the mud. We loaded the eggs onto the pickup bed, and I got to drive the truck home. I remember being relieved that I did not have to drive back with my father.

On the walk to synagogue, about two-thirds of the way to the old *shul*, the road turned downhill where a brook gurgled as it ran under the road. A grove of trees hung over the road, forming a cool oasis at the bottom of the ravine. This was as far as I was allowed to take my bicycle, a place where I had gone fishing with the Lloyd boys who lived across the street. We had gone fishing, but we never caught any fish. In 1960 the hill up from the brook to the intersection with Ford Road was the last straw for my five-year-old brother.

"I'm tired and I'm not going any further. Carry me!" He sat down and refused to budge.

My mother smiled, first at him and then at me, and I carried him up the hill, piggyback or on my shoulders. Pleased with himself, he would squirm and pull my hair, seeing what else he could get away with. Once we reached the top of the hill, everyone took turns trying to get him to stop whining and put one foot in front of the other.

On many holidays we drove the car most of the way to the *shul*. We parked in a field at some respectful distance so as not to offend the strictly observant members of the congregation, but Rosh Hashanah and Yom Kippur were special, and every year, rain or shine, we walked the whole way to services.

On one of those walks my father told us a story about a Rosh Hashanah he remembered in his hometown in Poland. Things had been deteriorating before the war and the German occupation. Supplies were tight, Jews were targets for abuse, but once the war started, if one was not in the direct path of the short invasion of Poland and kept his head down, one could get by.

In 1940 the Germans started making sweeps for able-bodied people to go off to work camps, the *arbeitslager*. Word spread fast when a roundup was coming, and my father would hide in the woods. He had connections in the countryside because *his* father had rented orchards, and my father and his brother took fruit to the same market-places as the Polish farmers. The Germans would leave town, and my father would return. The next week could mean another roundup.

The town was still managed by the Judenrat, a Jewish committee set up by the SS in all the towns with Jewish populations. One of the members, a Mr. Krum, spotted my father in between roundups.

"Why are you hiding?"

Mr. Krum and other such Jewish officials still identified with the government, with keeping order and satisfying their superiors, maintaining the hierarchy. They had a strong incentive to keep the labor supply flowing. If there were too few people in a roundup, members of the Judenrat would be pulled in to fill out the quota. They were standing on quicksand unaware that the earth beneath them would open up and swallow them all. Later, in the camps, the Judenrat were often the first to die. They knew too much.

"Why am I hiding?"

Irony and disbelief still rang out in my father's voice when he retold the story. "When *you* send *your* son to go, I'll go, too." Small-town politics soon became the politics of life and death. Later that year both Mr. Krum and his sons were conscripted for labor camp and never seen again.

A cycle of hiding and returning furtively for food and changes of clothes continued through the summer. Dad's farmer friends would tell him when it seemed safe. One friend joined him in hiding. The boy's father was a member of the Judenrat. Rosh Hashanah was approaching, and the boy's uncle sent word that it was OK to come home for the holidays.

As my father and his friend entered the town, they spotted a group of men and boys pushing a wagon through the streets. The Nazis had long since taken all the horses. As Dad walked by, a friend on the crew moving the wagon spoke without turning his head. Speaking into the air, he hissed out a warning.

"Today, you come into town? A fire is burning in this place."

The two young men kept walking without acknowledging the warning, splitting up to go to their homes. As my father scurried through the front door of his house, his mother cried, "Oh my God!

Why did you come today? They are looking for you." He kissed his mother, took a half a challah, and kept going out the back door and back out into the countryside.

∞

Dad took my hand, and we walked side by side holding hands to pray for forgiveness for this year's sins. As the years passed, I marveled not so much that God would forgive us but that these survivors would forgive God.

Making Eggs

∞

"Son, you don't know what *tsuris* is. Nobody knows the trouble I've seen." My mother, Bronia, was singing her version of the blues. The black men who came up from the South to work on our chicken farm in New Jersey taught me about the blues. Some of them sang the blues as they worked. All of them lived the life of the blues. It was hard to argue with her. *Tsuris* is the pain and anxiety associated with a time of troubles. Many Jews see *tsuris* as a test of faith. Perhaps it began when God asked Abraham to sacrifice his son?

"You don't know how good you have it," she said tearfully, recalling her mother. "Grandma would mend other people's linen late into the night. She would sit bent over until her hands shook and her eyelids closed."

My maternal grandfather had fled Poland to escape the draft and find a new life in America. Grandmother was left on her own with my mother, her infant child.

"She did it all for me, to have shoes and clothes for the holidays." My mother spoke in Yiddish.

She wore an apron and, in cold weather, a babushka that kept her hair away from her face. Her shoulder-length hair was still black. She was 43. I was 11. It was 1961. JFK had just become president.

As Mom spoke, she lifted eggs out of a basket and placed them in rubber-lined half-tubes that led to the grading machine. Each yard-long

31

tube angled down, feeding the conveyor. Gravity pulled the eggs down the tube. Gravity worked on us, too, pressing us against the concrete basement floor, flattening our feet and compressing our spines. My mother complained that her children were growing but she was shrinking.

On a chicken farm, there were no true holidays. On Christmas and New Year's Day, the farmworkers had the day off, but this meant only more work for us. On Jewish religious holidays, we would dress up, go to synagogue, come home, and have a nice lunch before returning to work. Even on Yom Kippur, the holiest day of the year, we would work, after nightfall. A full day of prayer at the little farmers' *shul* was followed by a quick meal and work in the egg room, which often lasted until two o'clock in the morning.

The egg room and the feed room were in a barn at the bottom of our driveway. A long, low chicken coop jutted from its side, running parallel to the road. An overhead monorail carried eggs from the chicken coops to the feed room. Every day the men who worked on the farm collected the eggs and placed them in the carrier. Next to the feed room was the egg room, set five feet below ground to help keep the eggs cool. The egg room had a cement floor and a ceiling that stretched up to the full height of the barn. Fly strips blackened by dead flies hung from the rafters. The flies were undeterred. I could sweep my hand forward as if throwing a baseball and always catch one or two.

Naked light bulbs dangled from the ceiling some 18 feet overhead. We cleaned the eggs and packed them into cardboard cases sorted by size: jumbo, extra large, large, medium, pullet. My mother always referred to this sorting and packing activity as "making the eggs," but even when I was a toddler, this seemed silly. I knew that the chickens made the eggs.

When we first bought the farm and our modest flock of chickens, we sorted the eggs by hand. By the time I started helping out in the egg room, we had a machine to do the sorting. A platform for egg cases, 30 dozen eggs to the case, lined one wall. The sorting machine took up the other long wall. We called it an "egg grader," but it simply sorted the eggs by size without regard to quality. The contraption consisted of a metal table divided into five channels, one for each egg size, with aluminum separators an inch-and-a-half tall. The table was tilted at an angle so that the eggs rolled toward the center of the room where the packer stood.

I remember a particular day in 1961, when I was the packer. It was the Sabbath, but as I said, the chickens never took the day off. There were always eggs to process. I stood a few feet away from Mom, who took eggs out of the basket, two or three in each hand, and placed them in the queues. They rolled down the machine like cars approaching a tollgate. A tiny rubber-coated bar lifted to let the eggs roll down to a resting area where they were picked up by a metal arm and brought to the next station. When the eggs reached their tipping point, they rolled down onto the table. The bar moved in a circle making a loud thud at the end of each cycle, the *kachunk, kachunk* like a heartbeat. The machine never stopped.

My father had bought that grader in 1957 when I was seven. It seemed wondrous, a mechanical marvel. I would sneak into the egg room to watch it work. At seven, handling eggs was a privilege I had to earn. Could I be trusted to transfer one egg at a time onto the rollers without breaking them?

By age 11, I had become more useful; I was able to grab two or three eggs in each hand and pack them. I still scrambled to keep up. I was a farm boy in a Fritz Lang microcosm, my own little warren of industrial angst. As Mom worked filling the queues for the grader, her arms in constant motion, I caught glimpses of the scar on her left wrist. She was 23 years old in the second year of the war, holding hands with a girlfriend in the dark as they hid from the Nazis in a damp ditch in the Polish woods. The cold breeze carried whispers from nearby and soldiers' shouts from across the valley. A mortar shell fell with its own killing hiss. It took her friend's life and left my mother marked but still alive.

"I lived through so much so I could stand here in this shit," Mom lamented. It was a bad year, and the price of eggs had dropped. One of the workers had gone off on a drunk, and we were all struggling to pick up the slack. My mother was jealous of women who were better off, who did not have to work on the farm and could get by just doing housework. She envied women who had better clothes and who were spared the aroma of 10,000 chickens wafting into the house. She stood for hours on the cold basement floor of the egg room packing eggs into cardboard boxes, seven days a week, mumbling, "For this I survived Hitler?"

It would be another year or so until I could lift the 30-dozen cases and stack them five high on planks laid out on cinder blocks to keep the cases off the floor. But even then, I would still be too short to reach the fifth tier.

My mother's outburst about *tsuris* came after I had complained about having to work while my favorite Saturday morning TV shows were on. I was jealous of people who lived in town, of kids who spent weekend mornings at Little League practice and whose mothers' only job was taking care of the house and the children.

I never missed a day of school. I always had time for homework. I had enough time to read through the entire junior section of the Lakewood Public Library. I even had enough off-duty weekends to become an expert on Saturday morning TV. I have clear memories of idle time in the woods, playing in the basement, and counting the cars on Highway 9, back when the road was just one lane in each direction. Yet I felt like an indentured servant.

When I complained to my father about having to work on the farm, he would sometimes try to reason with me.

"Some of your friends have to do the same farmwork," he said. But this argument lost steam as other parents gave up farming. My dad held on, buying and leasing some of those farms. It made our workload even heavier. So Dad tried a different approach, pointing out that my classmates, Danny and Irving, now worked at jobs in town. The summer sun warmed us as we spoke. His bald head shone, lambent with sweat, and his short-sleeved shirt exposed the numbers tattooed on his forearm, numbers that were always with us. He had little sympathy for my complaints.

"But, Dad, they get paid for delivering newspapers and working at the ShopRite."

"What do you need money for? I give you whatever you want. You just have to ask."

"Oh, sure." Unlike my younger brother, Benjamin, I would not ask for things. I was afraid that I would make my parents wince or pretend not to hear me. I could not push past the "What do you need that for?" reaction.

In the early 1950s, when Dad had first bought the farm, we were a small enterprise with only 3,000 birds. We collected 120 to 150 dozen eggs a day, just four or five cases. This was before the egg grader, when my parents still sorted the eggs by hand. If they were uncertain about how to classify an egg, a simple scale came in handy. It had markings based on the weight of a dozen eggs of each size: 30-ounce—jumbo; 27-ounce—extra large; 24-ounce—large, all the way down to medium, pullet, and peewee.

As the number of chickens we tended multiplied, egg production increased and the technology we used to wash and sort evolved. During the period I came to view as my indentured servitude, the years starting in my tenth summer, we would wash the eggs in the feed room upstairs by setting a basket in a tub of detergent and hot water. An air bubbler gently jostled the eggs to loosen the dirt. I hated this job most of all, especially when I had to reach into the water to clear debris from the air jets. It was like reaching into a horrid witch's brew. My skin puckered, and even though the soapy water cleaned the dirt out from under my fingernails, I felt filthy for the rest of the day.

We purchased a new egg machine when I was 14. It had its own wash-and-dry unit, a kind of car wash for eggs with whirling brushes and a soapy hot-water spray that was followed by a cool rinse and blow-dry finish. With the new machine, we still had to pack the same way; only the tempo increased. The bar that lifted the eggs and set them down established a rhythm that never stopped. Our old machine, an *adagio*, spit out four cases an hour; the new one, a *presto*, did ten. At our peak, we shipped 490 cases a week. Sixty eggs a minute, a case every six minutes: Could I keep up? I had seen my father do it time and again working in an assured frenzy. Close it, stash it, make a new box, and put it in place.

Whether I was upstairs in the feed room or downstairs in the egg room, I was trapped by making eggs, just as I was trapped at the dinner table, an audience for my mother or father as they tried to shape me into a vessel for their dreams and a rationale for their survival.

When I took up smoking as a teenager, my father scolded me, "What do you need it for?"

"I like it. It helps pass the time." What I did not say was that it made me feel like I was a rebel. I wanted to be one of those tough guys in the old 1950s movies. With my pack of Camels rolled into the sleeve of my T-shirt, I felt like James Dean or Marlon Brando.

"You would have been one of the first to die in the camps. The smokers, they were not to be believed. They would trade food for cigarettes." He looked over my shoulder picturing them in his mind. He spoke with awe in his voice. "They were sticks," he said and held up his index finger to show how thin their limbs were. "Those idiots would die for those *fakakte* cigarettes."

Sometimes when my parents spoke about the war, I discovered I had the power to go where no one could find me, where there were no prisoners in striped uniforms, no shaved heads, no gas chambers or corpses lying in open graves. Mom used to say I had eyes like a golem, the Jewish version of Frankenstein's monster. He was a man made out of clay, a legend made familiar by the early silent movie *Der Golem*. Mostly my parents used the word to suggest that I looked like a zombie. Were they trying to make me a better person or just trying to make me feel guilty? Their tactics failed. I liked the idea of being a golem.

The legends tell of a learned rabbi who in the 16th century created the golem from clay to protect the Jewish community from the blood libels of the Christians, who had claimed that the Jews were murdering their children and using their blood in strange rituals. Sometimes the Christians claimed that the Jews mixed the blood into matzo or drank it as wine. These accusations led to the death of hundreds of Jews. The Catholic Church has at various times repudiated these accusations, but church decorations that memorialize the blood libel with images of Jews draining blood from murdered children still exist in Central Europe, chiseled in stone by medieval artisans.

In college, I finally read about the golem, a creature brought to life using secrets from the Kabbalah. The word *"emet"* (truth) is written on his forehead so that he can catch those who spread the blood libel. In these stories the golem's power grows, and just as Frankenstein grew to fear his monster, the Jews themselves became afraid of the golem and turned him back into dust. They took away the *aleph,* the first letter of *emet,* leaving *met,* which is "death." They killed the one who spoke the truth.

Staring numbly off into the distance seemed fairly common in my high school and college years. Smoking pot in college made it even easier for me to be the golem, the boy with slack posture and gloomy eyes who ignored their entreaties as I sat at my parents' kitchen table.

The golem was huge and had great strength but began life with a placid disposition and a vacant stare. I had those eyes, unfocused, unblinking. And like the golem, I grew in strength. I strengthened the bulwarks, holding at bay the raging storm of my parents' words. Still, the images leaked through.

At night, lying in bed as a child, I would look up and imagine the water stains and crumbling plaster in the single room where my father and his family lived in the Novgorod ghetto. I found myself running and hiding in my dreams. Some people escape in their dreams. Some escape from them. In my dreams I run past the walking dead with the Star of David on their breasts. The Auschwitz guards called the ones near death *Musselman* (Muslims) because they looked like mystics or ascetics with sunken eyes and faraway stares.

I wanted to move beyond my parents' pain and the pain of my Jewish heritage. As a teenager, I was proud of my mother and father as survivors and ashamed that they were uneducated. I was content to be a Jew among Jews, but I did not want to stand out as a Jew in the broader community. My brother, Ben, and I both eventually changed our names. I changed my first name. I never had the temerity to think of changing my last name because I thought it would upset my father. But Ben shortened his to Kirsch. When Dad found out, he just shrugged. Kirschenbaum was not his Hebrew name, his Jewish name; it was a necessity imposed on him by a secular society. Later I realized that my change was more of an insult. Maier had been my grandfather's name, my father's father. I never knew him. He was killed in the camps. Yet my father never held a grudge and soon enough was calling me Mike when I came home from college. Years later I would see my name, my grandfather's name, inscribed on a shiny granite wall at the Miami Holocaust memorial.

I hated being Maier. Maier marked me like the yarmulke I wore on the A train to Yeshiva University High School in Manhattan (also known as MTA, the Manhattan Talmudic Academy). It said "Jew boy." It made me feel like an outsider, someone who belonged in the ghetto. It was unmistakably Yiddish, even though the spelling was from a German surname for stewards of estates or farmers with large leaseholds. In Hebrew the name was pronounced like Golda Meir, with the accent on the second syllable. It meant to "shed light" or "illuminate." I liked the Hebrew pronunciation, yet people invariably pronounced my name "MY`-er." My mother would leave off the "r" and I became "MY-ah." She would stand on the porch stoop, her back holding the screen door open, calling me in for dinner from adventures in the nearby woods or in the field behind the chicken coops. I can still hear her shrill cry, the first syllable like a long train whistle.

I am not sure who first called me Michael, maybe one of the farm-workers who couldn't figure out what my parents were calling me. So I chose Michael. The Talmudic scholars treat the name Michael as a question: "Who is like God?" The Book of Daniel identifies Michael as the angel who will stand for Israel in the tribulations to come. I wanted to be proud of being one of "the chosen people," but I was embarrassed to be marked as a stranger.

I was no angel, in fact, especially in my attempts to escape what seemed like the curse of having been born into the home of tortured Jews. Being a golem suited me better. Manhattan's yeshiva high school became a weekly escape from the farm, even though I went from one type of captivity to another. It was the travel from place to place that gave me some freedom: the Trailways bus and the A train through Harlem. But on the weekends and during the summers, it was back to making the eggs.

We had farmworkers, mostly black men from the South, working for $100 a month and living in one-room shacks with a bare lightbulb and a hot plate. They never complained about their accommodations. It was a warm place to sleep with a roof over their head. Looking back, it seems severe, although in 1950 a minimum wage job paid only $120 a month. The shacks seemed bleak, but sadly, the accommodations on the farm were a step up from some of the flophouses where the guys stayed when not working on the farm.

When I was available, the farmworkers almost never packed the eggs. Dad talked about how the workers were clumsy and not careful, but I think that my mother was afraid to be alone with them. Why was she afraid of them? Why did black women flag down my cab on Market Street in North Philadelphia? Because they were afraid to walk the three blocks from the bus stop to their homes.

Mom hated being stuck on the farm. She liked being out with her friends. She enjoyed dressing up for she was fussy about her appearance. She was a handsome woman who in the 1950s rarely left the farm without makeup and a girdle or corset.

Her welcoming smile made me forgive all the embarrassment she caused me in my youth. She had needed me to translate for her while she bargained with clerks in Macy's, unconcerned when they told her to "take it or leave it." At home, she had called on me to help her hook up her bra or help her dye her hair. On the beach at Point Pleasant she would scream my name at the top of her lungs while I cringed as people turned and scowled.

She always smiled when I walked into the room, even when I was about to get a lecture. When I was younger, she would gather me in a hug that pressed my face into her breasts. Even as she sat in her wheelchair in her eighties, with Alzheimer's and Parkinson's disease wearing away at her brain and nervous system, her face would still light up when she saw me. While her eyelids struggled to stay open, the corners of her mouth still pushed her apple cheeks into a smile.

My mother survived the war as a partisan, a Polish Jew in a band of Jews hiding in the woods. It was a struggle just trying to stay alive, but sometimes she and her group would strike back at the Nazis. I

My mother Bronia in postwar Munich

marveled at a photograph of her after the war, just before she met my father, in 1948. Dressed in knee-high boots, a skirt that ended just above the boots, and a tailored jacket, she wore her hair up and a Tyrolean hat with a fancy hatpin sticking out of it. My mother took pride in the sweater-making business she had set up after the war in her Munich apartment. She took pride in the sewing machines she had purchased and girls who worked for her.

My father almost always made fun of her meager earnings.

"You're alive only because of your cousin Adam," he said, then, turning to me, "They had an easier time in the woods. It wasn't like the camps."

My parents spoke to each other, but looked at me.

"Easy, huh, easy?!" Mom complained. She didn't fare well in these arguments. She would get flustered searching for the right words. "What's so easy about trudging 20 miles in the snow with rags wrapped around our feet? There were days when we had nothing to eat and slept on the frozen ground."

My father invariably had something worse to recount, a more all-consuming hunger, a more terrible suffering, a more horrifying death. She would sometimes strike back by complaining about the farm and how much better off she had been when earning her own living.

"Your business," Dad would snort. "You made *wasser fer kasha.*" Not enough to buy kasha, just barely enough for the water to soak the grain in before cooking it.

"Maybe it wasn't much, but it was better than spending the day in this stinking egg room on this farm covered with chicken shit."

My parents' friends would say I was *podovna* to my mother, that I got my looks from her. The men would pinch the round cheeks her genes gave me, and if they held on too long, it was all I could do to keep myself from kneeing them in the groin. My brother was the *kleine Godele,* the little big man. He looked like Dad, with his brownish hair around a face narrower than that of a child. I may have looked like her, but I wanted to be like my father. He was the one who knew the ways of the world, the one I admired. Few people had survived longer than he at Auschwitz. His low number brought him respect. A guard once caught him stealing. Dad's name did not matter to the guard. He asked for his number, but when he saw it had only five digits, he shook his head and sent my father away, saying, "You lived so long, live a bit longer."

In Hebrew, my father's name, Godel, means "big" or "great." For instance, the rabbi whose greatness allows him to resolve a controversy among the scholars is called *Godel hador,* the greatest of the generation. At five feet six inches, Dad was not a tall man and he was certainly no scholar, but in our house, he was the smart one who could make things happen. He was able to fix things and to add and multiply numbers in his head. And yet he spent 18 years with the chickens before he moved on to building houses for the folks moving south from the city.

Mom often spoke of their courtship while we worked the eggs. "When I met your father in Munich, they said, 'Marry this fellow.' I was looking for someone to change money. They said, 'You can trust him.' Trust him? Trust him to bury me in these shit-stained eggs."

Dad's business in Munich sometimes crossed over into the black market. He had traded contraband at Auschwitz to stay alive. In postwar Germany he bought and sold whatever came his way: sugar, saccharin, cigarettes, and gold. Eventually he and his partner, Felix Messer, focused on watches and jewelry. Dad quickly developed a reputation for being an honest broker, a man of his word.

My mother continued, "I had a few dollars saved, but when we agreed to marry, he said, 'Spend your money,' and my friends said, 'You can trust him.' I bought dresses and china and silverware. When we came on the boat, we had six large wooden boxes." (One came with us to New Jersey and sat in our basement filled with baby stuff, toys, and clothes.) "With so many toys, a rocking horse, and beautiful clothes, you shone like a precious stone or a star from heaven." She smiled at me and turned to stack an empty egg basket.

"We brought crystal and Rosenthal china." The Rosenthal china became our Passover dishes, except for a few pieces that were always displayed in a china cabinet in the living room and never used. There were hand-cut crystal goblets of amber, midnight blue, and purple.

"I was so foolish," my mother sighed. "I wanted to come to America where my father was. He was happy to see me, but his American wife was not. They had their own children who thought I came looking for an inheritance. An inheritance, huh. We wound up lending him money. Now I have to wear last year's dresses to *shul* for the holidays."

In the late afternoon, Dad would come in and take over and my mother would leave, shooing flies as she climbed the stairs out of the egg room. She would trudge up the driveway to the house to get dinner ready or to take the laundry off the line.

Years later, I asked my father why he had held out so long on the farm.

"I got no choice. What else did I know how to do? I had some extra money when we first bought the farm, but I made some bad investments. I had no money to start a new business. All I had was the chickens." After my mother died, I went to visit him in Miami. Drinking coffee with him near the beach, I asked how he could stand making eggs every day on that farm. "I don't know. I got used to it. God forbid what you can get used to."

Simchas Torah

∞

The search for holiness begins with the end of innocence. A veil lifts, and we are naked. Stumbling out of the garden we look down at our dark shadows and turn back to squint at the sun. In my tribe, a 13-year-old boy is bar mitzvahed. Often he has just learned to masturbate, and suddenly he becomes responsible for his actions. The awesome power to create living beings makes true guilt possible.

In 1963, reeling from the onset of puberty, my innocence was about to end. Not satisfied with either the world as it was or myself, I was skeptical about God. If He made me in His image, what a sad clown He must be. I was a youth in search of a spiritual plane, a nobler place. Death, an end to meaning, surrounded me. I yearned to reach past it, to grab on to some faith that could transcend mortal terrors, but something held me back. For some the idea of holiness is a salve that covers wounds. For others the search for holiness itself is salvation. The quest changes how we live in the world.

I was searching, but I was never a true seeker. Unwilling to throw down the gauntlet because of my fear of a bare-knuckled fight, I could not take up the duel in earnest. I stood sideways, making myself a narrow target, to death and the spirit world, never looking either in the face.

In the month of judgment, which begins with Rosh Hashanah and Yom Kippur, a week of celebration marks the harvest season. The Feast

43

of the Tabernacles, Sukkoth, celebrates the tribes' survival in the desert. To mark the event, the descendants of those tribes build temporary huts with roofs made of branches. Ancient laws tell us that we must be able to see the stars through the canopy just like our ancient ancestors did. As they wandered through the wilderness toward the Holy Land, they had stared in wonder at the stars through the dry shimmering heat of the desert night.

My parents had also wandered in the wilderness and lived in camps. In 1963, I was 13 years old. I had lived in the United States for 11 years, most of that time in Lakewood, New Jersey, a town settled at the beginning of the 19th century. In deference to a Mr. Brick, who owned the local ironworks, the town was briefly named Bricksburg. Just before Pennsylvania took over as America's coal and iron capital, the Metedeconk River was dammed to create a lake in the woods on the south side of Bricksburg. When the ironworks closed down, the elders turned to tourism and renamed the town Lakewood.

When I first started swimming at the lake, it was called Lake Carasaljo. The local myth was that it was named after three girls who had drowned there, but many years later I found out it was named after Mr. Brick's daughters, Caroline, Sally, and Josephine, all very much alive at the time.

The 1950s population of Lakewood was 12,000. Set on the border of Monmouth and Ocean counties, Lakewood had 14 numbered streets and broad avenues. An old Rockefeller estate on the lake marked the southern border of the town. A Catholic girls' college, Georgian Court, was nearby. All of that property had once belonged to the "King of the Robber Barons," Jay Gould. His heirs sold part to Rockefeller; part became the college, and another chunk became Ocean County Park.

My grade school, the Bezalel Hebrew Day School, was built into a hillside near the center of town. A "new" extension, built in the late 1950s, stood on the high side of the hill, all cinder block with met-al-framed windows. The old part of the school, a converted guesthouse of wood, plaster, and lead paint, opened onto Fifth Street.

In 1963 social movements, science, and technology seemed like mighty torrents moving us ever forward toward either the perfectibility of mankind or total destruction. Looking back, those forces mostly hurled us about like detritus in the flood. They left debris of all sorts in their wake—sediment, sludge, and rubble that soon enough became part of the landscape. Our science had once seemed built on bedrock but now told us nothing was solid. Not just the buildings, but the building materials—the concrete, the wood, and the steel bars—were mostly empty space. The atoms that were the building blocks of solid material were really electron clouds that circled nuclei in empty arcs. Even the nucleus, the dense core at the center of the atom, was just a mass of subatomic particles whirring and ravening in the dark forces that bound them.

Like the electrons, the Earth circled the sun in an empty orbit marking off the seasons. It was harvest time, and the celebration of Sukkoth was ending as Simchas Torah approached. I wondered: Did I live among people who were like vines that lifted you as they grew? Or, like the strangler fig, did they grow down and around you choking off your life?

Every fall, during Sukkoth, the harvest festival, my grade school built plywood *sukkah,* or hut, on a flat piece of land near the Sixth Street entrance. During the holiday we ate lunch in the *sukkah.* Just down the street, the Hassidim at the Beth Medresh Gevohah, an exalted house of learning, also had a *sukkah,* but theirs was larger and more elaborate. Still it displayed the same outward look of haphazard construction, all the decorative touches reserved for the inside.

When Sputnik shocked the world in 1957, the United States rushed to close the "technology gap." By 1963, the Mercury program was winding down, but the Russians continued to steal headlines when they sent the first woman into space. We had secular studies in the morning. We studied current events in our *Weekly Readers.* The march of science was an ongoing theme. Religious studies were in the afternoon. At lunch, I looked up through the gaps in the *sukkah* roof and dreamed of astronauts and space travel. I felt like the ancients who worshipped men as gods and, looking to the heavens, set their gods among the stars. The heavens seemed like distant wonders, far from the hell that was at the Earth's core, far from the evil that lay deep below us, beneath the soil that held us in our graves, beneath crematoriums that returned us to ashes. Modern man had schemed to hurl debris out across the cosmos striving to touch the heavens. President Kennedy had vowed to leave our mark on the moon, still a holy place to some.

On the Sabbath, a holy day, we scrolled through the Torah reading a different portion each week, paced so that the entire scroll was read over the course of a year. A *simcha* is a joyous event. The day the cycle of Torah readings concludes (and begins again) is called Simchas Torah because we celebrate and rejoice in the Torah.

On Simchas Torah we circle about the synagogue dancing with the holy scrolls. How does something become holy? We tell one another stories from the spiritual world about places or objects, visions or miracles, and somehow the words in the stories themselves become holy. We place the words on parchment scrolls, and the scrolls become sacred. The sacred words of the first five books of the Bible are hand-lettered on the parchment of the Torah scrolls in a tradition that stretches back thousands of years. (When I see the rolled-up scrolls now, I think of my Cuban cigars, those dark, sweet wonders rolled by men.)

In the fall of 1963 I was still struggling to forgive the Dodgers for moving out of Brooklyn when Sandy Koufax and the Dodgers finally beat the Yankees in the World Series. We had survived the Cuban missile crisis. A nuclear test ban treaty seemed possible. Kennedy visited Berlin. Martin Luther King had given his "I have a dream" speech, and I had just started ninth grade at Yeshiva University High School. A weekly commute took me from our chicken farm to the dorms just north of Harlem in Washington Heights. The Trailways bus stopped for me on Highway 9, and a little over an hour later I had traveled the 60 miles to Port Authority in downtown Manhattan. From there, I took the A train through Harlem to the school campus. My father had warned me about pickpockets, and I carried my wallet in my front pocket and reached in to cover it with my hand if anyone suspicious approached. One of Dad's New York City friends had taught me how to read the *New York Times* on the crowded subway, taming the broadsheet by folding it lengthwise so that it took up less space than the *New York Post* or the *New York Daily News*. I sat with my suitcase between my knees, my yarmulke hidden in my front pocket covering my wallet. Classes ran from 8:30 in the morning to 6:00 in the evening. Half the day consisted of religious instruction and the other half secular studies, just like at my religious grade school.

When my Yeshiva rabbis heard that I came from Lakewood, they spoke in awed voices of the Beth Medresh Gevohah there. The basic meaning of *Medresh* or *Midrash* comes from the Hebrew "to search out, to investigate"; it refers to an investigation that aims to discover deeper meanings in the text of the scriptures. A *Midrash* does not view the text as simple communication or normal language. It places the focus on the personal struggle of the reader to interpret the text. Every letter of the Hebrew scriptures is of divine origin, every detail fixed, but the reader can project his or her inner struggle onto the text. This allows for some very powerful and moving interpretations, which can seem to have very little connection with the text. Some would say that it requires the presence of mystical insight not given to all readers.

My teachers explained that the chief rabbi at the Beth Medresh, Rabbi Aaron Kotler, was the *godol hador,* the greatest of his generation. There is no one who can make new law for the Jews in the way the Pope and the Holy Synods can for the Catholics. The last codification of Jewish law that all the sects accepted is the Shulchan Aruch, the set table, written in the 16th century by Yoseif Karo. Even that accepted text is always published with dissents and addenda included, usually in italics, from Rabbi Moses Isserles, another of the *gedolim* (giants) of that century who had himself been compiling a similar code when he heard of Karo's work. They call Rabbi Isserles's addendum the "table-cloth" for the "set table." The *gedolim* are sages, the most learned men of their generation, and the study of Torah transfused them with a holy aura.

Even in the old farmers' *shul* I had always liked Simchas Torah. On Simchas Torah all the legalistic scholarship was put aside. In an old pine chest in the front of the *shul,* the Torah scrolls were rolled up on rods with wooden handles and bound with linen belts. The scrolls bore a covering garment of silk or velour decorated with text in gold and silver threads that named the congregation and attested to all those who had donated funds for the scroll. Each scroll cost thousands of dollars and took months to complete. Experienced scribes had worked under strict rules using a quill or reed to carefully place ink on animal skins. When these skins were taken out of the ark, the lame and the infirm, even the most severe and sour man, would smile and kiss the fabric when accepting the scroll. The scroll was passed from hand to hand as the men in the congregation danced with the Torah. They would sway from side to side or spin in place, sometimes raising the scrolls up to show off the treasure they held.

All through my childhood, on the Sabbath and other holidays, my friends and I had rushed to try to touch the Torah as it was carried from the ark. No one was allowed to touch it directly. To kiss the Torah, we would prod it gently with an edge of our prayer books and then kiss the spot where the book had touched the holy object. When we were old enough to wear a prayer robe, a *tallis,* we used the knotted strings that hung at the corners of the garment to transfer our kisses.

In the Book of Numbers, whose Hebrew title is *Bamidbor* (in the desert), the Lord tells Moses to have his people tie fringes to their garments: "Look at the knots and recall all the commandments of the Lord and observe them, so that you do not follow your heart and eyes in your lustful urge." These fringes are made of four strands, one longer than the others. The four are folded over and knotted together to form a tassel with eight strands. The long one is called the *shamash* (servant), and it is coiled around the others in between the knots; first seven times then eight, 11, and 13. The mystics delight in the fact that Hebrew letters have numerical equivalents. They delight in the convergence of language and numerology: Gematria is the branch of inquiry that looks for the relationship of words and phrases that add up to the same number. The total of the knots and twists of the tassels, the *tsitsis,* is 39, the numerical equivalent of the Hebrew sentence "God is one." Stretching even further, the Hebrew letters for one spelling of *tsitsis* add up to 600; add in the eight strands and five knots to get 613, the number of commandments in the Torah.

The truly Orthodox men, as well as the boys like me who went to religious schools, wore a special undergarment every day so that we could observe the commandment. These *tsitsis* consisted of a rectangular cotton cloth with a hole cut in the center for the head and fringes of string tied at the corners. The garment was worn underneath the shirt, but often the tassels were left to hang out over one's pants. It led to an unkempt look. It was hard to keep your shirttails tucked into your pants. Afraid of being hassled, I would tuck the strings into my pockets or hide them in my pants when I was on the subway. I had never been attacked, but I had been called "Jew boy" more than once and usually with overtones of malice, not humor. In synagogue, we wore the more elaborate *tallis godol*. These prayer shawls, of ivory cloth with blue or black striping, can be as large as blankets. Sometimes they look more like scarves, narrow rectangles shiny blue and white like the Israeli flag. A yellow-gold section along the top holds the prayer to be said on donning the cloth. Orthodox boys usually give up wearing them after their bar mitzvah—until they get married. It makes it easier for the mothers of unmarried daughters to find the single men in a congregation. As kids we were still wrapped in these holy garments. We would struggle from our seats across the bony knees or fat thighs of the men in the narrow rows toward the end of our pews, leaning across those sitting on the aisle stretching toward the word of God. The old men encouraged us: "Do a mitzvah!" "Kiss the Torah!"

I had studied Torah at the day school. Even though the big yeshiva was only one block over on Forest, just around the corner from my grade school, I had never been inside. I had seen Rabbi Kotler on the street, but from a distance he looked like all the other old rabbis with his white beard, long black robe, and a hat with a wide, fur-trimmed brim. My rabbis in New York had spoken with such reverence of "Rav Aaron" that I was determined to visit this holy place to personally hear the rabbi teach.

On this Simchas Torah I got my chance. My grade school friend Gershon Biegeleisen invited me to join him on a visit to the big Lakewood yeshiva. His father was the *shammos*, the caretaker for the Sons of Israel congregation in Lakewood. Mr. Biegeleisen helped manage services; he also decided who was called for *aliyot*, the privilege of ascending to the raised stand to say a blessing before each Torah reading.

He was the one who had recently stood beside me on that platform as I read from the holy scrolls on my bar mitzvah. His son, Gershon, was already 14. Gershon had not begun to shave, but he had just enough hair on his face to look a little scruffy. I was still 13. I had played with my father's razor but could not find any reason to use it. Gershon had been to the Beth Medrash at the yeshiva before, and I followed him in.

The building was a bit run-down. It could have been an abandoned hotel except for some faded Hebrew lettering over the door. The carpets were frayed at the edges. The main *shul* was a large room whose walls were covered with bookcases holding copies of the Talmud and other religious texts. Prayer books were scattered about with other books; the books lay in disheveled piles reminding me of study hall during finals week. The texts were in Hebrew and Yiddish and Aramaic and other languages I did not recognize. Some of the books lay open, and here and there a stray word of English stood out. The chairs and tables were all mismatched and worn. Yeshiva *bochurs* (boys) filled the room. *Bochur* once had a pejorative connotation of someone who was indigent and living on other people's money. The more polite phrase was yeshiva *leit,* or yeshiva folks. Nowadays *bochur* is usually used as a fond term. I had seen them on the streets in their uniform of black suits and white shirts. I had played basketball with them when they came to our play-ground after school, their *tsitsis* flying on top of their T-shirts, bouncing in all directions as we ran up and down the court wearing canvas sneakers and black pants. Rosy cheeks on skin that was pale from spending the day indoors studying looked even redder in the flush of exercise. Their coats and white shirts hung on the playground's monkey bars like a used-clothing sale on Delancey Street.

At the Lakewood yeshiva, a few rabbis, the teachers, were mixed in with the yeshiva *bochurs.* But mostly it was a room full of pale young men with long sideburns or scruffy beards. They prayed with their whole bodies, swaying back and forth, some shaking in a tight rhythm as they bent from the waist. The prayers went by quickly, and then a reverential awe settled on the room as Rabbi Kotler rose to speak. I cannot remember what he said, but I can still see the look on the faces around me. They were transformed. For me the feeling in the room

Carrying the Torah

still underpins what I understand as awe or reverence. Rabbi Kotler told us how we should live and what we should strive for. When he spoke, it was not as a prophet, because the time of prophets had ended with the destruction of the second temple; it was as an old man who had studied fervently his whole life. The community believed that, because of his great intellect and because the Holy Spirit lived within him, he was the man in his generation who was closest to understanding God's plan for us.

After prayers the chairs were pushed to the sides of the room to make space for the dancing. Studying the wisdom of the Torah scrolls is a mitzvah, and men who have more learning and a deeper understanding fulfill the commandment at a higher level. An ancient sage explains that when you dance with the scrolls rolled up and covered on Simchas Torah, you worship with your body, not your mind, and all are equal in the quest for righteousness.

I was already infected by the excitement in the air when the rabbis started taking the scrolls out of the ark and passing them around. I looked around wide-eyed, my ears pulled back and the skin on the back of my head tight and trembling. The whole place started moving. Arms and legs flew about, and voices rose up in song. Some dancers were like whirling dervishes taking energy from a spinning core deep within them. Others were swaying and jerking like tripping flower children at a Grateful Dead concert, mouths agape, lost in the mystery of it all. Eventually, I was handed a Torah, and I danced about in its glow before handing it off to another celebrant. When a scroll passed into someone's hands, it was like a child returning to a father's embrace and new energy would enter the dancer. I was transported, carried along by the throng. They say that when you dance with the Torah, you become one with it. It becomes your body and you become its legs. I continued to float in suspended animation until my classmate Gershon pulled on my sleeve and said it was time to go.

On the ride home, the radio in Mr. Biegeleisen's car played the top 20 countdown. "Do You Love Me," by the Tremeloes, topped the charts with "She Loves You," by the Beatles, close behind. "You'll Never Walk Alone," by Gerry and the Pacemakers, was just showing up on the charts. The tires crunched in the gravel driveway. I was a little surprised when I opened our porch door and looked into the house. Nothing had changed. Mom was cooking at the stove. Dad was sitting at the kitchen table reading the Jewish newspaper. It was October 11. The screen door slammed shut behind me, and suddenly, I was home.

Bar Mitzvah

∞

Our heart is the altar. In all you do, let a spark
of holy fire burn within, so that you may fan it into a flame.

Baal Shem Tov

My bar mitzvah was approaching. It was a performance in front of the community, and I was preparing to uphold the family honor, to do a good job and earn Dad's respect. Some kids had it easy because they just had an aliyah: They were called up during the Torah reading and said a Hebrew blessing. At my Hebrew day school, we were expected to work a little harder, so we read the haftarah. More arduous still was reading the entire week's chapter from the Torah scrolls. On top of that, for extra credit we could make a speech to the congregation about one of the themes in the day's readings. Encouraged by my rabbis and my father, I signed up for all of it.

The haftarah is a section from the Prophets read on the Sabbath after the Torah reading. This tradition began when the Romans banned reading from the Torah scrolls. The ancient rabbis chose texts from the Prophets that dealt with a similar theme to replace that week's Torah reading. While the rationale for reading the haftarah has disappeared, the tradition persists.

In addition to reading the haftarah, I was to become the *baal koreh,* the Torah reader who sings out a chapter from the holy scrolls in front of the congregation. What is so hard about reading out loud from the Bible? It is more like chanting than reading. For me the preparations focused on quieting my nerves, staying focused on my place in the text, and learning how to interpret the symbols, *Ta'amim,* that tell the reader how to sing the phrases. My tutors had emphasized how the phrasing of the song helped to preserve its meaning.

Studying the haftarah was easier. My passage was from Isaiah 27 and 28. I would read it from a book that was printed in the same type as the Hebrew books we had studied from in school. The Torah scrolls, on the other hand, are written by hand in Hebrew without the *nekudot,* the Morse code of vowel dots and dashes that attend the consonants. The same consonants could yield different words, so you need to memorize pronunciation. For example, דָּבָר "da-var" (a word) and דֶּבֶר "de-ver" (a plague) look just the same: דבר without the *nekudot.* The names of people and places were a special challenge. In addition, those *Ta'amim* are not on the scrolls and need to be memorized.

My Torah chapter was the first in the Book of Exodus. In it the new pharaoh decides that the Jews have been too fruitful and that their multitudes need to be oppressed. God comes to Moses and instructs him to prepare for an exodus and to go to Pharaoh and tell him, "Let my people go." But Pharaoh will have none of it. Moses goes back to God and complains that he has been sent on a hopeless errand, but God reassures Moses with these words: "Have faith; before this is over, Pharaoh will be eager to see you go." And thus the chapter ends.

I studied with Cantor Aaron Lieber, who also taught at the Hebrew day school. He had tried to recruit me for the boys' choir, and I sang with them for a while, but I lived so far out of town that I needed a ride to get to the practices. My father often placed a higher priority on my help on the farm than on driving me to choir practice.

I was a chubby kid who loved his mother's honey cake with a glass of milk. Like a Pillsbury doughboy wearing husky-size pants, I had a round face and apple cheeks that adults pinched mercilessly. I would squirm and try to tuck my face into my neck wishing I had the courage to kick them in the shins as they tormented me. But I was still trying to be a good boy, watching *Lassie, Fury,* and *Sergeant Preston of the Yukon* on weekend mornings or *Queen for a Day* and *Lawrence Welk* with Mom and Walter Cronkite and the news with Dad.

Even so, my life was changing. We lived just a few hundred yards from Highway 9 on Lloyd Road, a dirt and gravel strip that was named after our neighbors. The Lloyds lived across the street. The Lloyds were not Jewish. Jeff, the closest of my Hebrew day school classmates, lived almost two miles down the highway toward town. His father made hats. I remember Jeff because he explained the wonders of masturbation to me. I was 12 when the lingerie section of the Sears catalog took on a new significance in my life.

Mr. Lloyd was a Navy flier, clean-cut and upright. His wife was thin and almost always wore a loose skirt over narrow hips, her dark hair pulled back in a ponytail. I always thought of Mrs. Lloyd as Popeye's Olive Oil, all legs and arms, with a southern accent. They had five kids. The youngest boy, Danny, was just a year older than me. He was a little taller than me with freckles. The rites for coming of age vary from tribe to tribe. When Danny turned 13, his dad bought him a BB gun and that fall took him hunting. I doubt my father ever fired a gun. I know we never had one in the house or on the farm. I have never owned one or wanted one, but that summer, every time Danny took out his BB gun, I followed him into the woods until he finally let me shoot it at tin cans. We were at the gravel pit, a large gash in a nearby hillside where the road crews harvested loose rocks. Maybe it was the cowboys and Indians on TV or perhaps the war movies, but when I shot that little gun, I felt a little closer to becoming an American.

I was only four years old when I started kindergarten. My parents had pushed me into school early. Were they trying to give me a head start in the race to get an education? Maybe it was to give Mom more time to breathe or to free her day for more work on the farm, or perhaps it was to give them some time alone together. I never got a clear answer from them, but I do know that my brother was born the following summer. Eight years later, at age 12, I started studying for my bar mitzvah. I was still shorter and younger than all the girls in my class.

Cantor Aaron Lieber was the biggest man I knew, even bigger than our butcher, though not quite as solid in the chest and arms. He was still young enough to carry his 300 pounds with agility. When I sat studying for my bar mitzvah with him, beads of perspiration decorated his huge forehead. His eyebrows moved a tremendous distance when he raised them. Just keeping his engine going required a bit of sweat to cool things off. He sat in a large armchair, sweat soaking through his shirt, balancing the book we studied from on his huge thighs. Unlike most of my religious teachers, he had a sense of humor and cracked us up with his collection of the less scatological borscht belt jokes.

I studied and I practiced. I watched my parents make plans for a small party at the synagogue and a big party in New York City. I hated being the center of attention, but I got ready to try to make my father proud. On the Sabbath of my bar mitzvah, after the morning prayer, it was time for me to take center stage. I carried the Torah up to the *bimah,* the raised platform, in the center of the congregation. The lambskin scrolls were laid on a table, and I held the *yad,* a pointer. A tiny silver hand with an outstretched index finger emerged from a silver ball at the end of the pointer. Custom forbids touching the parchment, and the pointer helps the reader keep his place in the Hebrew text. The *shammos* stood to one side calling men for *aliyot (Aliyah*—"to go up.") My father was called for the first *aliyah* and stood beside me on the *bimah.* As I held the *yad,* my hand trembled and the little silver hand amplified the tremor as I sang the first few paragraphs. The rabbi was the tallest of the men who loomed over me as I read. To my right, Mr. Biegeleisen read along from the text, ready to correct me if I made a mistake with pronunciation or intonation. After getting through the seven *aliyot* of the Torah reading, the haftarah reading seemed easier, with all the *nekudot* and *Ta'amim* included.

The speech I made in synagogue on a religious theme from the day's reading was in English and seemed effortless after the Hebrew tasks. I looked out over the congregation as I spoke, but I'm not sure I saw a single face. I kept my eyes focused on the gallery railing. I feared that if I looked directly into someone's eyes, I might falter. Perhaps the glimpse into their soul would overwhelm me. It was years before I

Bar Mitzvah speech as Bronia looks on

could make eye contact in ordinary conversation. As I made my bar mitzvah speech, I occasionally turned from side to side to address different parts of the crowd as I had been coached. Fortunately the balcony formed a full semicircle, and the railing, the safe haven for my eyes, ran all the way around it. When I came out of my trance, I could see my dad was beaming, but when I asked him how I did, he answered with his usual restraint and said in Yiddish, "Maybe, not bad." I took it as high praise.

In a few years, the boy who had stood in front of the congregation would be over six feet tall. The day of my bar mitzvah, however, I stood only five feet, almost as tall as my mother if she wasn't wearing heels and a bit shorter than my father. I could just see over the lectern at the men below me. I am not sure I ever looked up at the women sitting in the balcony. We were in the Lakewood synagogue, not the farmers' *shul,* but like in any Orthodox congregation, the men and women sat separately. The farmers' *shul* had just a *mekhitsa* (a curtain) dividing men from women. For the shorter women this meant an obstructed view of the proceedings. Many women found the gallery a better solution. We were in the Lakewood synagogue for a number of reasons. First, it was bigger and nicer. In addition, I went to school in Lakewood, and it was the congregation of the rabbi and cantor who had coached me for the event.

I had to make a second speech that night, at my bar mitzvah party at the Burnside Manor Hotel in the Bronx. My parents had friends and relatives in New York, so the Lakewood folks got to travel to a fancy place in the big city. A chartered Trailways bus transported those who did not want to drive the 60 miles. My party speech was meant to be a witty thank-you to every adult who had shaped my life. There was a five-piece band and there was a smorgasbord, but I don't remember if there was a chopped liver sculpture. I sat on a dais at the front of the hall with a dozen kids my age. The bandleader introduced the *chazzan* (the cantor), not my teacher but a famous New York singer who specialized in traditional Jewish songs. The lights dimmed, and the candles on the tables lit the cantor's procession to the dais. He sang his blessings and then introduced me as they turned up the lights. He was six feet tall and wore a tall headdress. I stood beside him, a foot shorter, in front of hundreds of guests, looking out at the crowd without seeing anyone. I was a boy pretending to be a man. It seemed like an eternity before I could get enough air into my lungs to make a sound.

When my parents had planned the affair, it had seemed to them a reasonable expense for an important celebration. By the time the event actually happened, the egg business had collapsed and my father had to borrow money to pay for the party. Still, that night he was aglow, his bald head shining. My mother sparkled in a white dress covered with elaborate beadwork. Her blond hair that I had helped bleach was piled high on her head. The party was three days after my birthday, and my parents were also celebrating their 14th wedding anniversary.

Years later I asked my father about his bar mitzvah party in Poland. He laughed. "Who could afford these things in those days? I was already finished with school for two years and was working. They called my father and me up for an aliyah, to say the blessing, and then later my

The Kirschenbaums

father had brought a bottle of schnapps so everyone could have a drink after services."

My bar mitzvah had been a big test, but I had studied for yet another big test that year. I had studied to become an American citizen.

Years later my father gave me the citizenship document he had stashed in his desk drawer. It looks a little like old money, with the same typefaces. In the body of the document, my photograph, an eighth-grade snapshot, has a U.S. government seal embossed over it. The document says my country of birth is Germany, that I am a male with fair complexion, brown eyes, and dark brown hair, five feet, 110 pounds, 13 years old, single, with no distinguishing marks. Earlier, my parents had been so proud when they became American citizens. I had helped them prepare for their citizenship test, but that day in 1963, it was my turn and I remember standing proudly in front of the judge as he asked me questions about the government of the United States and its history.

Mercifully, the questions about American history and government were easier than the tests at school. Taking my citizenship oath in the U.S. courthouse in Red Bank, New Jersey, I stood before the black-robed judge and swore allegiance to the Constitution of the United States. I looked up to the judge as I had looked up to the cantor in the Bronx in his sacred robes. The courthouse seemed a kind of holy place where people became quiet after entering and kids were not supposed to run around playing. And like the *shul,* some adults wore ceremonial garb and dispensed justice from on high.

The next few years would change my attitude toward our government. Reading the history of the labor movement, watching, and in small ways participating, in the civil rights movement made it clear that opportunity, equality, and liberty were not shared by all. Greed and racism were rampant in our best of all possible worlds. In the idealism of youth, utopian visions called out to me: socialism, communism, and anarcho-syndicalism. I searched out and found a counterculture that was never seen on the Saturday morning TV that had shaped my child's view of America. But that day, standing before the judge, my own version of the American dream was still intact.

I felt like I had climbed a mountain. High school was just around the corner. I was an American citizen. I had taken on the bar mitzvah and made my parents proud. Yet somehow it would take other rites to make me an adult. A Jewish Haiku that captures it pretty well: "Today, I am a man. Tomorrow, I go back to the eighth grade."

Farmworkers

∞

When my earthly trials are over
Cast my body out to the sea
Save the undertaker's bills
Let the mermaids flirt with me

Mississippi John Hurt

As the years wore on, the endless grind of chicken farming wore down all of us. Unlike my mother, my father rarely complained. He became upset only when he was having trouble with the farmworkers. He hated finding their quarters abandoned, forcing him to go into town to look for them. He would check the "drunk tank" to see if the cops held them and cruise Fourth Street to see if they were still in one of the bars. He would usually give them a couple of days to show up, taking over their work himself and enlisting my brother or me to help before seeking a replacement.

Our farmworkers came and went, working for a few days or weeks or months. Too often, they would go into town on payday and vanish. When that happened, Dad would take off his black work shoes, mottled with chicken shit, and put on his newer, clean work shoes and drive to the employment office. Sometimes I would ride into town with him when he went to hire a new farmworker. Lakewood's employment office was flanked by the bars and pawnshops on Fourth Street. This forlorn establishment provided human fodder for the farms and hotels. If you needed a busboy or a dishwasher or a farmhand, you came to this long narrow room with benches lining the walls and a waist-high counter at the back. The place was straight out of the 1930s: hungry or hungover people, mostly people of color, sat on the benches. As a child I seldom questioned my parents' attitude toward blacks: To my young eyes, they seemed like desperate people beyond despair, worn out from carrying the white man's burden and their own. I was in high school, and the civil rights movement was a staple on the evening news before I pushed back.

Were these men victims of an unjust society? How much responsibility did they bear for their situation in life? It is hard to say, but they were sloshing around at the bottom of the barrel. In Munich, my father had worked around the "smart set," people trading currency or selling jewelry. In New Jersey, he worked with men who were on the lowest rung of the social ladder. They were drunk or had "learning disabilities" or "behavioral problems." (In the 1950s we would have said they were retarded or crazy.) Being dependent on them to keep the farm running was a crushing blow.

Jimmy, our farm's first employee, had given Dad the wrong impression. My father always said that Jimmy was a mensch, a decent person you could deal with. Yes, he got drunk on his day off, but he went to church twice a year and was in general a hardworking man who stayed out of trouble and showed up for work every day. Only later, after Jimmy had left and was replaced by a series of new men, did my father start to get calls from the police asking if so-and-so really worked for him. Dad would usually go into town and bail them out because they had gotten into a fight or had been taken in for being drunk and disorderly. Some of the guys headed into town and just disappeared.

So that day in the late 1950s, we were headed for the employment office in Lakewood. A sad-looking collection of men in crumpled clothes sat outside the office on a long flat bench, and my father talked to them in his broken English trying to find a new farmworker. They all smoked cigarettes. Sometimes you could see the long neck of a beer bottle poking through a brown paper bag. The street was Lakewood's black slum and had a couple of rooming houses, some run-down bars and pool halls, and a few merchants servicing this itinerant crowd.

"Dad, where do these men come from?"

"Ich weis nicht. Von ahin un aheir?"

"What do you mean from here and there?"

"Why you ask so many questions?"

"How do you decide who to choose?"

"I'm searching for someone who won't kill me and who will work the whole week before getting drunk."

Dad may have been thinking of Crazy Joe, who talked to himself as he shuffled around the farm, often generating both sides of an argument. I'm not sure what my father did to upset him, but one day Joe came up behind my father with a shovel and clobbered him on the side of the head, drawing blood. Dad wrestled the shovel away from him and went after him. He never caught up with him, but someone called the cops, who showed up and hauled off Joe.

∞

Jimmy, our first worker, lived for a few months in a room made out of a corner of our basement. Unpainted cinder blocks served as two sides of the room, and some unpainted drywall made up the other two walls. It was 1954, and he had come north from Alabama. Whether he was running from something or just looking for work, I never knew.

Jimmy's face was dark brown, and most of the time he had reddish bags under his eyes. I was four years old when I met him. Jimmy was somewhere between 35 and 50 with hard lines etched in his face. He was the first black man I ever spoke to, the first employee to come work with our chickens. Dad used the German word *Arbeiter* (worker) to refer to the guys until they had been around for a few weeks and their first names had taken hold. In the 15 years I lived on the farm, I never knew any of their last names. Do the Mexicans that cross the border to find odd jobs on farms in the Southwest suffer the same fate? Our workers had no bank accounts. They were paid in cash. In all those years, not a single piece of mail arrived for them.

On warm days we ate on the porch, and at dinnertime my mother would sometimes make a plate of food up for Jimmy. She put it together from whatever she had cooked up for dinner: brisket, meatloaf, breaded veal cutlets, chicken on Friday night with potatoes and kasha or kishkes (sausages), and peas and carrots with raisins. Round and soft, just over five feet tall, Mom cooked the same stuff her mother had cooked in their small town in Poland, except that in postwar America we had more meat. The square porch on the western side of the house had big six-pane glass windows in wooden frames. In the summer, wooden screens replaced the windows. From the porch, one door led into the kitchen and the other into the basement. Dad or I would take the plate down to Jimmy. My father loved telling the story.

"Your mother would make a nice plate and Jimmy would say, 'Thank you, Mrs. Kirschenbaum,' and the next day she would ask, 'Did you like it?' and he would say, 'It was wonderful, delicious.' So your mother kept cooking for him. Later on, I find the food in his garbage. 'Delicious, Mrs. Kirschenbaum, delicious.' Meanwhile, he threw it all away."

I think Mom never trusted the workers after that. Throwing away food was a sin, especially if it came from her kitchen. It did not help that my father teased her about it at every opportunity. Jimmy came home from the market with cans of pork and beans, collard greens, lard, and other items that had no place in a Jewish family's kitchen. I thought Mom's cooking was fairly bland, except for the liver and onions, but maybe kreplach and flanken didn't suit Jimmy's palate.

Jimmy fed the chickens and collected eggs from galvanized metal nests that hung from the coop walls. The nests had straw in them. Well, almost straw. It was this stuff called Stayz-Dry, which was chopped-up straw treated with chemicals that came compressed in 60-pound square bundles. Our little two-bedroom house stood near a yellow gravel road. Behind it were two long wooden chicken coops with tar paper roofs and a three-room brooder coop. A larger coop, eight rooms with an attached feed room and egg room, was farther down the road. A large horseshoe driveway made of yellow gravel ran by the house and spread out at the bottom of the U to let trucks get to the feed and egg rooms. A big iron barrel that we used to burn garbage sat midway between the two coops. For the first few years a single-seat outhouse sat farther back near a chicken-wire fence that marked off the "range" where the chickens spent the summer under the New Jersey sky.

The feed room was a barn with a cement floor. A huge metal bin holding more than a ton of feed dominated the space. The main feed was a ground meal we called "mash," which was delivered to the feeding troughs by an automatic feeder. The mechanism consisted of a chain hundreds of feet long that ran through the coop in one continuous loop. A chute ran down from the feed bin and hung over the feed hopper that fed the troughs. As a child I loved opening a sliding door and watching the mash pour down into the hopper. I stood there in awe, a four-year-old kid with big round cheeks wearing striped pullovers.

Jimmy's day started in the feed room loading feed buckets onto what we called a "carrier," a two-tiered trolley that hung from a monorail. He pushed the carrier from room to room down the length of the eight-room coop spreading supplemental feed, a mixture of whole grains and dried corn "scratch." On the way back he collected the eggs from the nests hanging on the wall. He came out with loaded egg baskets.

I would tag along with Jimmy while he did his work, riding on the carrier, along with the feed. It was my own amusement park ride. I had a chicken coop trolley cruising above the manure.

I became Jimmy's helper, mostly writing down the count of eggs, room by room. Our work helped Dad monitor how many eggs the chickens produced. Any major drop in production brought the vet out for a look at the birds. Our counts went into old black-and-white composition books from the school-supplies section of the drugstore. My other "job" was checking the floats in the automatic water dispensers. I delighted in pushing the floats down into the water bowls and making the water fill right up to the edge of the bowl.

I was Jimmy's pal, and he was my protector. He would scold my father when I got disciplined, telling him, "Don't touch that boy. He an angel."

The coops were slanted. The high side of the coop might have been nine or ten feet tall and the low side more like six feet high. The configuration was strangely trapezoidal, like a painting with overstated perspective lines. The coop's low side, holding the roosts where the chickens slept at night, seemed compressed. These roosts were set on a low stage, barely two feet high, with wooden rails with wire mesh nailed to them so that the birds' droppings could pass through. Large windows lined the south side of the coops and smaller ones on the north. The large windows were tall rectangles divided into nine panes. They slid down to open. A large rusty iron counterweight hung on a pulley for each window, and I would amuse myself raising and lowering the windows while Jimmy was busy with the eggs. Mechanical advantage helped my chubby four-year-old arms as I pulled on the counterweight to raise the window and then, easing the counterweight up, watched gravity do its work. An occasional audience of skeptical chickens wondered what all the noise was about. Chicken-wire screens kept the birds from escaping. As a four-year-old I did not have the strength to lift the feed pails onto the carrier, and I was not trusted to carry baskets of eggs. However, my ability to push the carrier on its track and to open the windows made me feel like a sorcerer able to achieve magic feats.

We would open the door between rooms carefully, trying not to spook the chickens. Hundreds of white Leghorns with their red combs and beady eyes would turn and look at us, swiveling their heads from side to side to give each eye a view of the visitors. They were mean birds, and they would peck welts in your hands or scratch at you with their claws if you tried to pick them up or gather their eggs while they sat in their nests. Over the years I learned the technique required to emerge unscathed: I used a smooth looping motion that pushed the head out of the way with the wrist while the hand reached underneath for the eggs.

Perhaps Dad's friends whispered in Dad's ear that having Jimmy live in the basement was weird, or perhaps it made Mom uneasy when Jimmy tromped in and out of the house to use the outhouse in the middle of the night. In any event, having Jimmy in the basement was not working out. Dad brought in some folks to build a room for Jimmy attached to the coops. I think by the end of the year it had indoor plumbing and eventually a gas range and a shower.

Jimmy stayed with us for a couple of years. When Jimmy left us, I had already started school, and for a few years I did not really get to know any of the other men. Many who came to work on the farm were illiterate, but there was only one who did not know how to count. As a nine-year-old I taught a 20-year-old young man named John how to count so that he could tally the eggs during collection. I could not believe he didn't know how. My dad had me adding and subtracting before I started school, and by the time I was ten, I could multiply two-digit numbers in my head. Maybe John had learning disabilities or was from so far back in the woods he never got any schooling. He could count to ten, but he had trouble with the next step. We started by marking an "X" in our egg count book every time he put ten eggs in the basket and then started on the names for each X. He had heard all the words for numbers—20, 30, 40—but they didn't mean much to him. I got him counting pretty well, but he missed home too much and on payday he took a bus heading south.

Our farmworkers were paid once a month, and many only stayed until payday, but over the years a couple of guys settled in with us for longer stretches. Neal stayed with us for years. He was a little taller than my father, thin with bony shoulders and a laconic drawl. He was strong for such a scrawny fellow, easily tossing the 100-pound sacks of feed around with a Pall Mall cigarette dangling from the corner of his mouth. He had a long, flat face and bloodshot, rheumy eyes. Every day he drank Italian Swiss Colony sherry. My father bought cartons of Pall Malls and cases of the sherry. Two packs of cigarettes and two pints of sherry each day kept Neal going. He wore suspenders, because his hips were too narrow to keep his pants up. On payday he would go into town. Every so often he would bring a woman back to the farm. You would see Neil walking down the road with some woman four times his size, thighs bigger than his waist. I was about 11 when I asked him why he always hooked up with fat women, and he smiled. "I likes a 'Big Mama.' I likes a soft ride." I still hadn't figured out about such things. I thought he might like sitting in her lap. Perhaps I wasn't that far off.

Over the years, we had taken on more chickens and needed two workers, so we built an additional room beside the original worker's flat, and the two guys lived side by side. One night we heard loud yelling out in front of the living quarters. It was Christmastime and there was snow on the ground and on the roofs of the coop. In the moonlight we could see that smoke was pouring out of the place. Here and there you could see flames reflected in the windows.

"You trying to kill me, you bastard! You trying to burn me up in my bed, roast me like a pig. What I ever do to you, you try to kill me...!" The new man was yelling at Neal, moving toward him menacingly as Neal skittered about doing his best to stay out of reach.

I ran over to the egg room to call the fire department while my father tried to act as a barrier between the two taller men. Neal kept dancing away from his assailant, one loop of his suspenders flopping around behind him as he turned. My brother climbed on the roof trying to push snow on the fire—until my father realized what he was up to and yelled for him to come down. It took a little while, but the fire siren sounded and we could hear Mr. Estelle's Ford zooming down the street. He and the other volunteer firemen showed up in their trucks soon afterward and got the fire out before it spread to the coops. Neal had fallen asleep half-drunk. The lit cigarette had spilled from his lips and started the fire, but he emerged unscathed. The new guy left, but Neal stayed on for years.

Carl was another farmworker who is etched in my memory. He was darker than Neal, shorter and thickly muscled in the chest and arms. He might have been 30 years old or 50. As a child, all the farmworkers seemed like old black men, brown dust on their boots. Carl always wore a plaid shirt bought at Woolworth's. I can still see him setting down the feed sack he had been carrying and shaking his head. Was he ruminating about his fate or just shaking some of the sweat out from behind his ears? He was thickset, but when he started with us, his upper body overshadowed his belly. Of all the people who worked for us, he had the most dignity, the most respect for himself—not that he didn't drink. As near as I could tell, they all drank. Mom was a little afraid of Carl, though I am quite sure he had never threatened her. If she was not planted squarely in front of him, Carl sometimes chose to ignore her when she was trying to get his attention. My father had the same ability. Mom found being ignored extremely unsettling. I never acquired that skill. She had a special voice for calling my brother or me. To us, she seemed hard to ignore.

Whenever we talked of Carl after he left us, everyone remembered the gun he had made. I do not know if he learned metalwork in the army or in prison. He could have become a metalworker, except that he liked his whiskey and did not really like being around people much. He was one of the smartest farmworkers we ever had. He was one of the few who ever brought back a newspaper or a magazine from his trips to town. Carl had a wide face, broad shoulders, not tall, less a fireplug than a radiator. I was with him at the end of one day as he rolled a cigarette, his pink tongue as thick as the rest of him.

"You don't know the trouble I seen." He stood beside me conjuring his own take on *tsuris*.

"A piece of land, a kind woman, a good suit for Sunday, bacon already fryin' when you step into the kitchen in the morning; it was a good life." It started to fall apart when he was 19, just beginning to shoulder the burden of manhood.

Carl's neighbor Jones had a cousin visiting from St. Louis. Jones and his cousin were at Willy's tavern playing cards with a few other gents and Carl joined them. At first Carl sat amicably with them playing poker and drinking cheap cherry wine (the taste for whiskey came later in his life). As the night crept along, he was losing money and he began to distrust the stranger from St. Louis.

"The dude made the cards jump in his hands. I know he must be cheatin'. Now he's got my money and he laugh at me. Maybe if I had the words to cut him down. Maybe if Jones had gotten to me sooner, but I already had him by the neck when I kicked Jones away. I had his throat in my hands so he couldn't laugh. I had his eyes buggin' out and his tongue flapping. When I threw him through the window, I didn't really mean to kill him. Though when he first laughed at me and curl his lip, I thought, 'You son of a bitch, I'm gonna bust your head in.'" Carl shook his head wearily as he paused. I was beside him, but he looked through me into his past.

"Still, when I held his feet off the ground, arms flapping useless and harmless, I didn't want to kill him no more. I threw him away like a child throw down a toy when he tired of it. I just stood there, blood boiling like a young man's will. The two women in the joint were screeching. Old Willy, whose place had just been busted up, went over to calm things down giving me a wide berth and looking at me sideways saying, 'Boy, what you go and do that for?'

"The judge, just a few days later, told me that since I hadn't been much trouble before and I probably just killed a useless nigger anyway, he give me ten years to think about what I done.

"That first year I thought I'd been better off dead. Every day last forever, and thousands more just like it stretched out in front of me. But I guess some fellas get used to anything."

Carl would talk with my father. He liked my father. "Just wanted a day's work for the going wage," Carl said. He always called Dad "boss." After I left home, I started calling him boss, too. When I spoke with my dad on the phone, I usually began the conversation by saying, "Hey, boss. How you doing?" One day Carl and my dad were riding in the old 1951 Chevy pickup, and he turned to my father and asked, "Boss, why you do the farming?" He recognized that my father was not a farmer at heart. My father looked at Carl a little surprised by the question, and he thought for a bit before saying, "God gave me this work to do." The answer surprised me when he told me the story. At an early age I had become upset with God. I questioned his wisdom when it first occurred to me that I might die someday. I often wondered how my father believed in God at all given what had happened to him and his family. I never had the heart to ask him how he could believe in a God who would kill off his whole family.

Religion sometimes seemed like masochism to me. God, my master, hurts me, but he loves me. Is the pain proof that I am getting attention from someone I worship? The notion that God is good but allows terrible things to happen is the kind of paradox that fights with intuition, something illogical, impossible. Years later, one of my college professors explained that a paradox is a contradiction within a frame of reference, like the quiet in the eye of a hurricane. Paradoxes often appear in parables, tales with a moral that prepare you for some of life's vagaries. Such a parable might talk about the all-powerful, omniscient God who gives us free will. Often paradoxes are a refuge for the powerless, telling tales about their lives. The Jewish woman comes to the gates of a city whose king declares that all Jews who enter will be killed. If they admit they are Jews, they will be hanged, but if they lie, they will be decapitated. When asked if she is Jewish, she answers, "You will cut off my head." Is she lying? More to the point, why do we tell this story? I think again about the folks who sing the blues, songs whose parables and paradoxes are layered like harmonies that counterbalance the melody. You sing a sad song and then smile.

Like my father, I clung to the western idea that intelligence properly applied could control destiny, that the world was somehow perfectible. This attitude came into play in my eventual career as a computer programmer. The computer was a machine with well-defined rules, and if you were clever enough, you could make it do what you wanted. My father and I both learned that the world we live in is a machine beyond our comprehension, a place whose rules might dissolve before our eyes. In some ways we both moved toward a more Eastern philosophy embracing the Eastern commitment to accept one's own karma. A raging river had swept my father away from his home and family, but he had resisted the currents with all his energy and will. He often felt that the men who worked on his farm had not struggled hard enough to reach a better life. Yet, he had a certain sympathy for people resigned to their fate. I was amazed when he and the men who worked on our farm could find a way to smile and take some warmth from the world that punished them.

My father readily conceded that he was not well suited to farming. "I didn't speak the language. I didn't have a profession. What else was I going to do?" was his standard refrain. While Dad had always been guarded about family and financial information, at his core he was an extroverted schmoozer happy to trade gossip with friends. Being alone on the farm with just his workers and his family and thousands of chickens grated against his desire to be out and about and in touch with what was going on in the community.

The first few years on the farm were not bad. Egg prices were high, the flock was healthy, and in one period that first year, Dad made $10,000 in three months, which, in 1953, was about what it cost for a new house in the suburbs. A bit of good luck roped him into what became a long difficult siege.

But by the late 1950s, refrigerated trucks made it possible to ship eggs north from places like Alabama and Mississippi, and the price of eggs dropped. Many chicken farmers in New Jersey gave up, but my father used his strategic reserves to expand. When our neighbors the Greenblatts gave up he rented their farm. When the 1960s got into full swing, with Kennedy, Selma, Cape Canaveral, and the Beatles, Dad had chickens at three other farms. My father had been renting these farms, but when the price was right, he bought some of the farms from Chaim Meltzer, another Holocaust survivor.

By the time Vietnam became a daily news item, I had my farmer's driving license and I was ferrying eggs from these farms back to our main farm where "making the eggs" became a more automated but even more time-consuming operation. I did not complain much, but I envied the kids who lived in town, whose free time was not sucked up by farmwork.

At our peak we employed four farmworkers and tended some 50,000 birds spread out over four farms. Every so often, we hired a married couple; the one I remember best was a white couple from Arkansas. They were the only people to live on the farm who ever had a car—a 12-year-old Mercury, big and wide with touched-up paint that competed for attention with rust and chrome. Glen was a little redneck fellow with Popeye forearms. He had a crew cut and sported either a two-day beard or razor burns. His wife looked even more like Olive Oil than our neighbor Mrs. Lloyd. She was a head taller than Glen and shaped like a string bean with a round head and expressive arms. She had a high-pitched hillbilly twang so surreal, it took me a few days before I stopped giggling every time I heard her speak. Mom was happy when we had a couple because the woman took over some of the egg-packing duties.

Before a Shop-Rite supermarket opened on Route 9, we would take the workers down to the general store in what was marked on the map as Southard, an intersection on Highway 9 with a firehouse, a gas station, and the general store. The workers would buy food that Mom would never have brought into the house: lard, bacon, collard greens, pig's knuckles, Spam. Sometimes the purchases would gross me out, and my father would remind me that he had learned to eat pretty much whatever he could find during his 30 months at Auschwitz. The only one whose taste in food bothered him was a white man name Steve. He was blond and Slavic. He looked a little like one of those squat fishermen on frozen fish packages. He cooked cabbage almost every day, and my father hated the smell. Cabbage had been a staple at Auschwitz. Dad had never liked it as a kid, and by the time the war was over, he despised it.

If a man put in a couple of weeks of honest work, Dad could be very tolerant of an occasional mistake. Most of the workers considered my father fair and honest, and for the most part, Dad's enjoyed peaceful relations with the ragtag group that passed through the farm.

But, as Dad would be the first to admit, *tsuris* came in different guises. One morning in the early 1960s we found Neal standing outside the feed room. It was 7:00 a.m. Neal had been living and working some two-and-a-half miles away, at Cream's farm, which we had been renting. My father approached him.

"What are you doing here?"

"Nuthin."

"What you mean nothing?"

"I couldn't sleep."

"Didn't you get your wine last night?"

"No, it wasn't that."

"So what was it?"

"I had a bit of bad luck"

"Bad luck?"

"Yeah, I had a problem."

"What happened?"

"We had a little fire."

My father's shoulders fell and his fists tightened. I thought he was going to explode, but he caught part of his lower lip in his false teeth, exhaled fiercely through his nose, and motioned for Neal to join him in the pickup. They drove off to assess the damage. Neal had once again fallen asleep smoking a cigarette, starting his second fire. In high school I had learned how to smoke nonfiltered cigarettes sneaking packs of Pall Malls that we kept around for Neal. Mercifully, Neal had managed to put out this fire, or rather, this one put itself out after burning a hole through his mattress and part of the floor. So this fire didn't require a major construction project like the one Neal had started when he was living on our home farm.

As a child, the only black person I interacted with who was not a farmhand was Mrs. Bloom, an administrator at my grade school, the Bezalel Hebrew Day School. I did not think much about my parents' attitude toward black people until years later when they could no longer afford to send me to yeshiva and I was forced to transfer to Southern Freehold Regional High School back in New Jersey. As a 15-year-old junior, my worldview was so skewed that when I got a crush on one of the smart, preppy girls in my honors English class, I was aghast when I found out she wasn't Jewish. I was also stunned to find a black student in my honors math class and to discover that my best teacher was a black Korean War veteran who taught chemistry.

It should not have been so shocking. My two years at yeshiva high school in Manhattan had exposed me to blacks who were very different from our farmworkers. I had played against black kids when the chess team competed against teams from the public schools, and once or twice on my Sunday commute to yeshiva from New Jersey, I had gotten off the A train at 125th Street, taking off my yarmulke and tucking in my *tsitsis,* to take a peek at Harlem. There were well-groomed black men wearing clean, well-pressed suits in the daytime and stores run by blacks. And mine was not the only white face in the crowd.

By the time I returned to New Jersey for high school, Martin Luther King had received the Nobel Prize, Dick Gregory had appeared on the

Jack Parr show, and Bill Cosby had been winning awards on *I Spy*. I had just revisited the Civil War in American history, and in my mind there were strong parallels between the African-American journey from slavery to civil rights and the liberation from slavery of the Jews in Egypt. I was surprised that my father's attitudes were not changing with the times. Back then he was a Democrat; the Republicans still had an anti-Semitic reputation while the Democrats were the party that supported immigrants and ordinary people. Most of Dad's politics revolved around Jewish issues and how strongly politicians supported Israel and other Jewish concerns. Sadly, like most of his immigrant friends, my father had little good to say about the *swartzes*, literally "the black ones."

I gave up discussing political philosophy with Dad, but I would argue with him about his racist attitudes.

"How can you have seen such discriminations against Jews and still think things like that?"

"Like what? That the *swartzes* are dirty and lazy, that they are drunks and criminals?"

"But that's just what Hitler said about the Jews!"

His cheeks would flush, color creeping as far as his balding head.

"But it wasn't true about the Jews," he insisted.

"Don't you think if you asked a black person, he would say the same thing?" I asked him.

"Maybe there are a few *latische* (decent people), but most are *gemein- iste* (the lowest sort). They move into a neighborhood, and it becomes a slum."

"But they never had a chance. They were discriminated against from birth. In everything they do, society puts barriers in their way."

"In this country, if you want to work, you can find a way."

It was hard to sway him. The Germans had killed his entire family. He had been underweight, dead broke, and alone in the world with his sixth-grade education. He barely spoke the language and had worked ten hours a day, every day of the year, to keep the farm going. He had no sympathy for people who gave up when society put obstacles in their path.

High School

∞

I had heard it so often: "You live in my house, you follow my rules." "You spend my money, you do what I say." "How can you go out in the street like that? You look like a bum." My parents wanted my clothes to say: "I am successful. I respect the values of the community." I desperately wanted to find some way to hang out with the hip kids. I wanted my clothes to say: "I am cool. I am a rebel. "

My father needled me about what he saw as my lack of ambition, undercutting my accomplishments. He was frustrated and angry at the seeming indolence of his teenage son.

"You don't know what it takes to make a living. You're lazy. Everything comes too easy for you. You would have been one of the first to die in the camps. You don't know what it means to struggle, to work hard. You think you're smart. You fool your teachers, but you don't fool me. I survived for this? So you could lie around and watch TV and bum around with your hippie friends?"

Was he being fair? I was a good student, or at least my grades were good. But I was still a growing boy, a teenager who could sleep 12 to 14 hours at a stretch without any chemical assistance.

"You are just hiding in bed because you don't want to work."

I did work on the farm, grudgingly. While other kids played baseball after school, I was doing my homework, working through the SAT prep book, reading almost anything I could get my hands on. One part of me understood that my father was just trying to prepare me for the world, like any parent, just trying to get me to fulfill my potential. Another part rebelled, withdrew, shut my ears, and stared blankly into space as he dug up yet another story of poverty in Poland or terror in the camps. When we talked about politics or the news of the day, he used his experience like a sledgehammer, smashing away at my Marxist arguments for social justice.

For my first two years of high school I attended Yeshiva University High School in Manhattan.. I marveled at the subways and skyscrapers: The city was a throbbing kaleidoscope, after my isolation on the farm. I was miserable in high school, but these two years in New York City left me with few opportunities to indulge my anguish. I was absorbed by the demands of the yeshiva regimen and by the city itself.

Then, for financial reasons—the price of eggs was dropping, but my yeshiva tuition was not—in September 1965 I transferred to the local public high school back in New Jersey. Now living at home, I had more time to focus on my miseries. I was a 15-year-old, starting his junior year. My hormones were raging, an endocrine system in disarray. Born in January, I was pushed into school early and was usually the youngest in my class. My social skills were minimal after two years in an all-boys religious school. At Southern Freehold Regional High School, I was suddenly in the company of girls, girls who wore push-up bras and knee-length skirts that crept up just above the knee when they sat down in class. Dropping a pencil led to a dizzying view of knees and calves and a hint of fleshy thighs and cotton panties. Not only were the girls in my class a year older than I, I was still suffering with braces and acne. Any chance for romance seemed hopeless.

My world was in disarray. Highway 9, where our farm mailbox once perched on a fencepost, was changing from a country highway to a relentless strip mall with Dunkin Donuts stores, Dairy Queens, real estate agencies, plumbing supply houses, and other merchants and services. Bad signage loomed over single-story storefronts with parking in front, dumpsters and wasteland behind. Developers had just built "Candlewood" featuring two- and three-bedroom houses costing $20,000 for people willing to commute 40 to 60 miles to jobs in North

Jersey and New York City. *My Fair Lady* won an Oscar, and Stan Getz had a hit with "The Girl from Ipanema." The first U.S. combat troops arrived in Vietnam, and Martin Luther King was arrested in Selma.

At first, public school was frightening and exciting, but very soon it became deadly boring. Classes helped me understand the word "tedium." At yeshiva, we were compared with students at Bronx Science and Stuyvesant, the best of New York City's public high schools for gifted students. There was a bit of competition among the schools for the highest scores on the Regents, standardized achievement tests, a longtime fixture of the New York State school system. Academic standards were high. Some of my science teachers at yeshiva were professors at the college and taught "the boys" out of a sense of nostalgia or civic duty. They were enthusiastic and brilliant. By contrast, the local New Jersey high school seemed surreal as I sat there in class trying to resist the urge to correct my math teacher's mistakes on the blackboard. His body language and tone of voice showed murderous intent the first time I offered advice. The students were likewise mostly clueless. The one place where I lagged behind was in my physical education classes. I began a two-year struggle to do push-ups convincingly and get my chin up over the chin-up bar. Paul Simon lyrics come to mind: "Why am I so soft in the middle when my life is so hard?"

I think it was my friend Pearl who pointed out that there were honors classes in English and math. I gathered my courage and stormed in to see Miss Crumbling, my guidance counselor at the high school.

"Oh no, I'm sorry, that won't be possible. These students have been groomed since they were in grade school. They were specially selected; you couldn't possibly join them now."

She wore a calf-length skirt and opaque hose. She looked through horn-rimmed glasses with an earnest, if somewhat vacant, stare. She would have been described as mousy, but I was so full of hormones, I still took note of her button-down sweater hiding smallish breasts and of her hips and buttocks flexing under her skirt when I saw her walking in the hall.

"Look, give me any test, use any fair standard. Let me talk to the principal. I'm trying to prepare for college."

Yearbook photographer

She was adamant at first, but letters that I wrote and had my parents sign and a whining persistence on my part got me into an empty room with some test booklets. The school relented when the test scores came back. I was good on standardized tests. I had a perfect score on the geometry Regent, and I was in the top percentile on the tests they gave me. So four weeks into the term, I joined the honors group.

I was not surprised that half the kids in the honors classes were Jewish even though Jews comprised only 15 percent of the student body. I am now embarrassed to admit, however, that I was surprised to find one of the six black students in our 250-member junior class sitting next to me in honors math. It took me a long time to get over the impression that our farmworkers had left on me and the training my father and others had instilled in me to not make eye contact on the New York subway and to cross the street when a group of black teenagers came walking toward me.

Another minority lived in our area along with Jewish refugees from the Nazi Holocaust: the Kalmyks, or *Khalmag*. Originally from

Mongolia and once known as the Oryats, the Kalmyks had settled on the lower Volga in Russia. The Kalmyks were accused of collaborating with the Nazis and banished to Siberia by Stalin during WWII. In 1951 part of the group immigrated to the United States and settled between Lakewood and Farmingdale. They had been Buddhists originally, and some preserved the tradition, but many were now members of an eastern Orthodox church whose Kremlin-like golden onion globes stood out as the only foreign architecture in Howell.

Judy Gugajew sat next to me in English. Her flat face, round nose, and slightly darker skin reminded me of pictures I had seen of the young Chairman Mao. We became friends working together on the school yearbook. I had volunteered for the yearbook hoping that extracurricular activities might help get me into college. In my senior year I became editor in chief. The yearbook gave me an excuse to get hall passes so that I could wander the school as the yearbook photographer and stay late at school and not have to go home to work on the farm. My brief stint on the track team as a feeble discus thrower had also kept me out of the egg room.

Ken Nappa took me under his wing; he was yearbook editor and a senior when I was a junior. I had met his older brother, Mike, when he came to the farm working with Albee Stuhl, our chicken culler. At the time, I was too young to help herd the chickens and hand them one at a time to Albee. When I was in high school, I took over the job. I would reach into the crate to grab both legs of a chicken and hold the bird upside down and hand it up to Albee. He poked a finger into the bird in a brief gynecological exam and on good days made sure to point the bird's butt away from me for the discharge that popping his finger out provoked. The work was gross, but I enjoyed playing chess with Albee when we stopped for lunch. I have never known anyone to wash his hands more meticulously before eating.

The kids in the honors classes were reluctant to admit new members to their exalted group. Through high school, and in many ways through college, I perched warily on the outside of the inner circle, an electron in the ether, held by the nucleus, but not bound by the strong force that held the protons at the core. Being the yearbook photographer suited my role as an observer wandering about on the periphery of school life.

Dad did not read books, but I did. I gurgled up semidigested ideas from Erich Fromm and Herbert Marcuse. I tried to gain some traction with my father by quoting from writers who were Jewish and had studied Talmud, but he would dismiss them. Anything that came from the left was communism, and no one he knew who had a choice went back behind the Iron Curtain. He insisted that the few who did were fools, especially the Jews. He used himself as an example of the wonders of American capitalism. "A few people may be unlucky, but most people in this country are poor because they are lazy: They don't want to be educated. If you want to work in this country, you can make a living." He was working seven days a week on the chicken farm so that his family could have a better life and to realize his version of the American dream.

Cashmere

∞

I set off for the University of Pennsylvania determined to break away, to find a separate identity, to find someone to love. I wanted to live my own vision of the American dream and climb out of my parents' nightmares. College was my escape. It wrapped me in a sweet swamp of free time and freethinking, new ideas, drugs, strange people, strange bedfellows. In 1967, as a freshman at Penn, I had a scholarship and a job doing a few hours of administrivia in the college office, but my dad still gave me a monthly stipend to make ends meet.

There was turbulence in the air. The civil rights movement, the student demonstrations, the hippies, the antiwar movement, the beginnings of women's liberation all funneled though my college years in the late 1960s and early 1970s. I dived into "the revolution." Can you make a revolution on an Ivy League campus where the graduates become the establishment? Too often, I felt like a fake. I believed in "the movement," but I was a young radical taking cash from his conservative father.

I found myself studying European social history at first because it had a lighter workload than my science classes. Those science classes with weekly labs and problem sets seemed an unreasonable burden in my marijuana haze. History was easier. I guess Dad was right. I did take the easy path. I could drop into the occasional history lectures and catch up on reading and assignments at the end of the semester. The history classes were also an attempt to put in perspective the turmoil and tragedy my parents had endured. I was also struggling to come to grips with the world I lived in, a world dominated by the Cold War and the threat of nuclear obliteration. I was climbing out of the linen closet where I had hidden when my parents and other survivors talked about ghettos and camps. I was standing up from the fetal crouch of the "duck and cover drills" of the 1950s.

When my parents sent me to college, they were hoping for a doctor or lawyer, professions that implied a standing in the community and a secure income. When I told them my degree would be in history, my father said I still had *feohlkes in koph* (butterflies in my head). "Bats in the belfry" would be another translation, but I liked the butterflies better: a flurry of color, a psychedelic mangling of the visual field as objects melted into one another, wings beating, one against the other, calling for attention from a disordered consciousness. For my father, it meant I had no idea of what it took to earn a living, to survive. When my mother heard about my history major, she imagined me as a professor, another honored profession, not leading to substantial wealth, but still a title that commanded respect.

I studied history to understand how, after the lessons of two world wars, after the millions who had died in combat, the millions who had died from wartime starvation and sickness, the millions who were killed by the cold calculations of an evolved society intent on genocide, after "the good guys" had used "the bomb" to level not one but two cities in Japan, after all these horrors, we seemed ready to push that button again. We had hidden under our desks in grade school waiting for the nuclear blast but with no plan for coping with the fallout. Barry McGuire captured the madness in his popular recording of the P. F. Sloan song. I did believe we were on the "Eve of Destruction." "Can't you feel the fears that I am feeling today? When the button is pushed, there's no running away."

I had given up the search for holiness, unwilling to search for a God who let us kill, a God who let us die just to make life more precious. Or had I really given up? I was still a seeker looking for salvation, a seeker but not a true believer, still ready to deaden the nerves and the senses, to rebel and reject, but somehow also ready to reach out for redemption, for salvation. I was alone, but also part of a generation; I was among the children of survivors, with parents who had survived the Holocaust, the war, and the Great Depression.

The history courses seemed to confirm my anomie. Mankind seemed hopeless, but perhaps it was just a few who were corrupt. I turned to the working classes looking for salvation in those who were poor but honest. I studied European social history and Eastern religions seeking answers.

Then, too, I frittered away hours playing pinball at Cy's Luncheonette, on the corner of Philadelphia's 34th and Walnut streets. Everyone called it "The Dirty Drug" or, more simply, "The Drug," a name the luncheonette inherited from a pharmacy that had been across the street decades before I arrived at Penn. It was about as clean or dirty as any other inner-city luncheonette, but it had a great jukebox and a great pinball machine. Cy Braverman was usually behind the counter serving up grilled cheese or tuna fish sandwiches with Cokes or malted milk shakes, but he loved pinball machines. He would sometimes step out to watch when the better players were on a run. We were on a first-name basis.

One of the other serious players, Peter Rothman, dragged me off to the Tau Epsilon Phi fraternity to play their pinball machine, The North Star. I had never been in a fraternity house. It had never occurred to me to consider joining one. Fraternities conjured images of smug guys in letterman sweaters carrying spanking paddles. This place was more like *Animal House* a decade before the movie. The North Star is a Gottlieb machine circa 1964 by Roy Parker complete with his signature "Parker Blonde." Gottlieb was my favorite manufacturer; the artwork on his machines was far more subtle and detailed than the artwork on the Williams or Bally competition. The North Star's back glass featured a host of characters on ice floes. A young blond woman in a fur coat mini holds a fish on a spike in one hand and a polar bear on a leash in the other. A shark-tooth belt gathers her coat just beneath her breasts. A man sitting cross-legged sings to her as he strums his guitar; a walrus on a separate floe sings backup. Mom is in the background standing outside her igloo holding an alarm clock set to 2:00 a.m. In the distance, a captain is speaking on a walkie-talkie from the deck of his submarine.

Behind him stands a barbershop pole with a North Pole sign on it. All of this is set against a wild display of the Northern Lights.

We were playing in the days before inflation, when 800 points would win you a free game. It was a "rollover" game where you scored points for rolling through gates and rolling over dime-sized rubber protrusions on the playing surface. You could also score by bouncing around in an array of five bumpers at the points of a star in the center of the machine. If you were skilled enough to get your balls to pass through all 13 rollovers, the machine went into an orgasmic state in which "kickout holes" on the sides and a red rollover in the middle of the bumpers produced free games.

A "tilt" mechanism protects pinball machines from abuse. Bang a machine too hard, or lift it so that the ball won't drop, and the "tilt" sign goes on and you lose. This North Star had a forgiving tilt, which gave the player more room for displaying skills in nudging the machine about. It also had a devoted following among fraternity members, and when I demonstrated my skills, with or without the aid of the pot smoke that seemed to fill the air whenever I visited, I became an unofficial, honorary fraternity member. I later learned that Dwight Eisenhower had accepted honorary membership to this same fraternity, as well. I don't think it was the marijuana. He joined in 1958. The fraternity was started by some Jewish boys who were barred from older frat houses; notable alumni included Jonas Salk and Larry King.

Charlie Chan movies were shown weekly on Philadelphia TV. On "Chan Night," the frat boys sat on couches in a meeting room smoking pot until the haze made identifying people on the neighboring couch difficult. As movie time approached, they made a Chan Train, each brother holding the hips of the young man in front of him as they stumbled down to the TV set in the basement. A year earlier, in 1967, the Museum of Modern Art in New York had hosted a Chan-a-thon showing all 33 movies. The 21st century has not been kind to Charlie. Criticism of implicit and explicit racism has made the movies hard to find on cable TV. The critics complained about the "Caucasian in yellow face paint, slant-eyed and buck-toothed speaking bad English" who played the title role and the "bug-eyed black chauffeur" who provided comic relief. Ellery Queen thought Charlie was "a service to humanity and to interracial relations." We thought the movies were hysterical. "Chanisms" would pop up weeks afterward: "Bad alibi like dead fish cannot stand the test of time…. Person who ask riddle should know answer…. Very difficult to estimate depth of well by size of bucket…."

None of this served to further my academic career.

College was an escape from the farm and greenhorn immigrant culture. I was in the Ivy League, a proletarian masquerading among the bourgeoisie, a scholarship student with a $20-per-week allowance. Almost as soon as I got to college, the counterculture beckoned. It was a chance to remake myself, a cleansing immersion, a new age baptism erasing the past.

The Vietnam War, Woodstock, the draft lottery, Kent State, and a host of other events created a counterculture that made the antiwar movement a vital part of student life. As a sophomore I shared an off-campus, two-bedroom warren in West Philadelphia with Thomas Francis Patrick Burke III. It was 1968. He was seven years older than me, touring the Ivy League on the GI Bill, a Vietnam veteran with dark hair combed like that of Beaver's older brother, Wally Cleaver. Burke and I smoked furiously watching Kirk Douglas give hell to the enemy. Burke, thin but not small, sat throbbing on the edge of the sofa, raging during combat scenes about how different the outcome might have been with modern weapons.

Burke drove an Austin Healy whose gear stick would rattle about in neutral. He had been to Vietnam but acted more like he had been to prison. No one ever got behind him in a room. Sometimes when he talked about combat, he became manic. He would briefly stare at you as he described some encounter—jumping from a chopper, machine guns blaring—"gooks" everywhere. He would stare at you, through you. Then he would turn away, and his face would twitch. His stories were surreal. Was he pumping himself up, telling others' stories as his own? He had seen things in Vietnam that I was glad I had not seen, but I had the sense that mostly he drove a jeep and got stoned.

When I first met Burke, I had trouble deciding which of us was more hopeless. We were in the student housing office. He had just arrived on campus, and I had come back from summer vacation expecting a dorm assignment. Somehow I missed the news that dorm assignments were only guaranteed to freshmen and that returning sophomores were expected to have made arrangements the previous June. We stood side by side staring at three-by-five-inch cards with information on available rentals. His car was in the shop for repairs, and I offered to take us to look for places in my Volvo.

The Volvo came to me through Mr. Kalig. He would come to the farm looking for the freshest eggs, eggs still warm if we could find them. He sucked raw egg yolks through holes he poked into the shells. The first time, I had no idea what he was doing and watched fascinated. Later, I would need to turn away. He went to Sweden every few years and bought a Volvo, used it while he visited his homeland, and then shipped it back to the States. It was a time before every Volvo you saw was a station wagon with moms transporting kids to soccer practice. Mr. Kalig was getting ready for his next trip to Sweden, and my father bought the Volvo 122S from his last trip. The 122s was blue and sturdy with round bulges that seemed a bit anachronistic compared with American cars that featured a boxier look. I was embarrassed by my Volvo's automatic transmission. My teenage friends thought automatics were something old ladies drove because they could not figure out how to work a stick shift. I was leaving home, and Thomas Francis was coming back home. Neither one of us was in a happy place.

Tom seemed like a truck driver's son or perhaps an orphan from Pittsburgh. Perhaps the tattoo on his forearm had misled me. On Thanksgiving, Thomas Francis Patrick and I drove to his parents' home. The two of us pulled into a sweeping driveway. We stood before a baronial manor north of New York City. From the size of the house and the manicured half-dozen acres that we passed between the road and the front door, I had expected a butler to greet us. Columns framed a magnificent oak front door. It was my first contact with the landed gentry. The Burkes had impeccable manners, especially Mrs. Burke. She shook hands with me first and then with Thomas. I think it was the only time they touched each other the whole weekend. Tom's father, TPF II, stood more than six feet tall; he was heavy but erect, with just a bit of thickness settling in under the chin. These people were restrained. They never touched one another. A reunion after three months in college and no hugs, pats, kisses?

Thomas's sports car had no backseat, and later that day I folded my six-feet two-inch frame into the passenger seat and his girlfriend sat in my lap as we drove off to a nearby state park to drink expensive scotch and smoke low-grade reefer. She was not wearing a bra. I had heard about her from Thomas. His stories were rooted in a long tradition of talking about the "girls back home," that soft-focus collection of smiling eyes and heaving bosoms. Being Tom's roommate seemed to combine college with the military and summer camp, complete with tales of getting drunk and high and mischievous. An army veteran, Tom somehow remained an adolescent. In those late-night conversations it seemed that if you loved anyone, if you believed in love, it was the girl back home. "Relationship" was a word just crossing the plane from objects in geometry to social and sexual behavior. "Meaningful relationships" were just around the corner. "Love affair" and "affair" by itself had very different connotations. Thomas spoke of her as the closest he had ever come to being in love. Tom's girl back home wore pink lipstick. Her long blond hair was gathered in a ponytail. When we set out, she squirmed in my lap. Was it just the awkwardness of the cramped cockpit or something more provocative? We drank so much that on the way home, we had to stop so I could puke leaning against a tree on the side of the road. I rinsed my mouth with scotch and got back in the car. She sat down on my lap and put her arm around my shoulder to comfort me. A few miles later she had her hand in my crotch and we were necking. I tried to look over to Thomas, who was driving, but my eyes wouldn't focus. Did he know what was going on? Had she done this to him before, or was I somehow special, a treat she needed to sample? I would never find out. He gripped the wheel fiercely, staring resolutely at the road, cornering at 40 miles per hour and doing 80 on the straightaway. Alcohol, fear, and lust surged through my blood, and for a few miles I was in love with someone I did not know, someone with loose breasts under cashmere.

Charas

$$\infty$$

A year later, in 1970, Israel was the end of the line. I was 20, a nihilist mired in an existential malaise. I was searching, but I was also hiding, pulling a curtain between myself and the world, but peeking out, eyes open wide, shining out into the darkness. I was a college kid who believed that we were on the eve of destruction, but my parents were proof that faith could supersede the horrors of a tortured history.

Steeped in Judaism, I had rebelled against the confines of religion and tribalism and yet traveled to the Holy Land. I cherished and despised my Jewish identity. I had long curly hair, a Jewish Afro, and a dark tan. As I had traveled east across Europe toward the Holy Land, I had been pleased when people mistook me for a visitor from a neigh-boring country. I had the same problem identifying myself as an American as I had labeling myself a Jew. I was happy when the Germans thought I was French and when the Italians thought I was Spanish. My journey was a coming-of-age ritual that mixed cultural awakening with a hunger for "experience." I was one of thousands of college-age kids carrying backpacks and a copy of *Europe on $5 a Day*, traveling between landmarks and youth hostels. We wanted to break out of the safe middle-class enclaves and look beyond *Lassie* and *Father Knows Best* toward a darker world; we were searching for roles in some film noir movie where danger and lust mingle to create suspense and excitement.

I had been one of the hundreds of students who had stormed Penn's College Hall in the student protests of the late 1960s. I put epoxy in the locks in an attempt to keep Rizzo's Philly cops out of the building. I was more familiar than most with the building because my work-study job had been in the dean's office. I stood close to the establishment and took potshots at it when its back was turned. I had been a campaign worker for Eugene McCarthy in the Democratic presidential primaries canvassing door-to-door in Anderson, Indiana, and other forlorn bastions of patriotism and social conservatism. I had been "Clean for Gene," knocking on doors in my white shirt and blue sports jacket. I had marveled at how polite the Hoosiers were to strangers in their midst and how invulnerable they were to arguments against the Vietnam War.

I had harbored romantic ideas about life on a kibbutz; I had expected a new way of life not tied to a system that measures success with dollar signs. We *mitnadvim* (volunteers) lived in simple wooden huts with cement floors. Mornings, the huts were pleasantly cool, but all day long the sun beat down on them, and by nightfall the huts were torpid and malevolent. After breakfast, we rode in a cart out to the orchards; it was pulled by a tractor driven by a Swedish girl. Our first day on the kibbutz, we had ridden horses down this same path exploring the kibbutz. Riding horses had been a pleasant idyll, but now it was time to work. The survival of the orchards depended on irrigation: avocado, orange, and grapefruit trees spread out across the valley and up the hillsides.

We were dropped off at one of the irrigation centers. A six-inch hose ran for a quarter mile through the trees. Every five yards a smaller hose, 20 feet long and attached to a sprinkler, branched out at right angles. We volunteers scurried through the orchard hauling sprinklers to their new locations; we would cross the central hose, moving a sprinkler 20 feet into the trees from one side to the other. The outside rows held carefully pruned trees, widely spaced with lush foliage and pendant fruit. As we moved deeper into the grove, the trees were crowded closer and closer together as though afraid to be alone, and the orchard became a forest. The undergrowth too began to flourish, scratching at our arms and legs. The terrain, which had been smooth fields in the valley, became choppy and convoluted as the orchard spread out on the hillsides. Low-hanging grapefruits and avocados slapped me on the side of the head as I ran the gauntlet, lugging the sprinklers into their midst.

In the distance soldiers patrolled with submachine guns. The soldiers and guns were always present, no matter how bucolic, how seemingly pastoral the scene. Military service is mandatory for Israelis, both men and women. They serve in the reserves until their early forties, ready to resume active duty in times of crisis. Soldiers in uniform are everywhere, in the cities, in and around the kibbutzim. Their presence is a constant reminder of the conflict embedded in the region, of the vigilance needed to protect a way of life.

The first weekend I called some relatives, distant cousins who lived near Tel Aviv. They jabbered excitedly into the phone. I could not understand their Hebrew, and they had trouble with my English. We were at an impasse until we settled on Yiddish as a common language. They were excited, happy about my visit, but they scolded me. My parents had been calling for weeks worried because they had not heard from me. My relatives called my parents immediately to let them know I was still alive and that I would call when I came to visit. I was stunned. I thought I had sent them a postcard recently, but when I counted backward in time—Turkey, Greece, Italy—it had been six weeks. When I finally called, my parents took turns berating me: I was heartless, the lowest form of life, a callous idiot. They explained in detail how they had feared for my safety, worried that some calamity had struck down their son. They were working like slaves trying to get me through college while I was trying to bring back their nightmares, to torture them, to shorten their lives. I made no defense. I had none. I listened until they had spent their fury and devolved to tears. Eventually they calmed down and asked me about my trip. They made me promise to call them again in a week.

The next weekend I made excuses to my relatives and went exploring with Sarah. She was also a volunteer on the kibbutz. An English schoolgirl with an upper-class accent, she had a ponytail that reached down the middle of her back. We would go for walks after dinner, but we had barely moved past kissing and holding hands. I had shared my sleeping bag with a couple of girls in my travels on the continent, but Sarah was somehow different. She seemed shy when I met her, though she was clearly looking for adventure. The dating algorithm seemed complex and mysterious. Appraisals began at first contact. I had decided that Sarah was someone I could fall in love with, and that acted as a brake on my libido. It was a different time. Could I love someone who would sleep with me on a first date? I did not want to find out just yet.

We headed for the city. The bright little suburbs crowded around Tel Aviv reminded me of the chaotic interior of the orchards. New houses had already begun to gray, and the smell of decay hung faintly in the nostrils. Murmuring like a muffled jackhammer, the city ground forward in some never-ending cycle turning concrete to rubble and rubble to dust and dust to concrete. In some of the office windows young women, with plump thighs and alabaster mounds in Playtex bras, worked with manicured fingers on business machines. A shop-keeper nervously eyed a German shepherd that guarded his enterprise. High school kids on their way to terminal acne were laughing, eating greasy burgers. Where am I exactly, I am not sure. There were signs, but there were always signs and who wanted to look anyway.

Jaffo (also known as Jaffa or Yafo), nestled next to Tel Aviv, is an ancient city, a port in the days of Solomon. It had been conquered by the Egyptians, the Greeks, the Romans, and in 636 AD by the Arabs. Arabs still live there. We toured the flea market and wandered through the Artists' Quarter. The artists were mostly Israelis, but they seemed comfortable with their Arab neighbors.

I had visited Jerusalem before I reported to the kibbutz. The temple wall, the Wailing Wall, was the first concrete visage to rise up from my Torah studies. I first understood the word "antiquity" there. I had lived in Philadelphia, an old city for the United States, and I had traveled across Europe with its medieval castles and churches scattered across the landscape. I had marveled at the ancient monuments in Rome and at the Greek Acropolis, but here I was in a place whose civilization and religion stretched back beyond the Greeks and Romans, perhaps beyond the Egyptians. Jerusalem was a place whose history seemed to grow more complex with each millennium, a place where Christians, Muslims, and Jews had yet to find peace at the holy of holies.

In the Wailing Wall, scraps of paper, folded prayers, were tucked in among the stones. Years later, after he sold the farm, my father would come here to pray. He would put on his *tallis,* his yarmulke not quite covering all of his balding head. He would say prayers for the dead. Was he honoring a contract his ancestors made? Had he forgiven God, or did he fear Him? It was years later that I heard the story of another visit to the Wall. A religious Jew whose nephew had died a horrible death from brain cancer as a seven-year-old stood at the wall and wept. He tried to pray, but anger and outrage overcame him. He kicked the wall and screamed, "Fuck you, God!"

As I wandered about with Sarah, I was still getting used to being in the Holy Land. Wimpy, an English take on McDonald's, had amused me in London, but finding one in Tel Aviv seemed wrong. It set off a round of free association—Wimpy, Popeye, William Randolph Hearst—the capitalist conspiracy, the Protocols of the Elders of Zion... The Israelis in Tel Aviv seemed so smooth, oily. They were dressed in the latest fashions for their walk down Dizengoff, past the cafés, the almost-European shopping. Tel Aviv felt like a parody of a European capital. In Paris there were promenades past cafés, but you rode the Metro with first-class and second-class cars. Here there were buses that looked like they had been in use during the War for Independence. Hard seats if you could find one. The passengers bouncing around as the drivers hurled the buses through traffic. I am not sure what irked me, not the hard seats, perhaps just the Israelis' wardrobe, their flashy shirts and shiny shoes. I still wore a T-shirt, hiking boots, and torn jeans. The Israelis seemed a bit like the Parisians, but the French made the style. This was an awkward imitation. My mother would have liked the way the Israelis dressed. She never understood the appeal of hippy costumes, the torn clothes and tie-dyed T-shirts. Like the Parisians, the locals seemed to think they were quite smart, spending most of their time sitting around watching other people walk by. But perhaps there was a difference between them and the Parisians; the Israelis didn't seem bored.

In Jaffo, we had found relief. Yes, we were still walking dollar signs, but in Jaffo, they tried to rob you on a more personal level.

"Welcome, welcome." The Arab shopkeepers would do business with the Israelis if they had to, but they found the tourists a far less cynical bunch when it came to buying trinkets.

Sarah stood at a counter in a shop; well, it was more like a stall. A corrugated metal panel leaned on one of the outside walls. It became the door when the shop was locked. I reached in and toyed with rings while Sarah nodded her head or grimaced as my hand went from one to the next. I laughed when she made faces wrinkling her nose, making the freckles on her cheeks dance. She finally decided on a silver ring with three turquoise stones, one larger than the others. There was a bit of intricate work in the silver, and it looked old, though it might have been made last week.

I bargained with the man, a skill I had learned as a young boy translating for my mother as she shopped in New York City. I was uncertain about the exchange rate for the lira, the Israeli currency at the time, but the item's true value was less important than getting him to a lower price. The vendor began cursing in Arabic, a controlled show of outrage. Sarah started to giggle.

"Eight lira and not less, and you will get no blessing from Allah for your larceny here today."

He did settle for less.

We walked for a bit and wandered into an artist's studio and found ourselves drinking and smoking with two Israelis. Jeremiah and Reuben were old friends. They had an admirable command of English, but speaking or perhaps just thinking had become more difficult after a fifth of vodka and two grams of hashish.

Jeremiah was the older of the two, almost 40; his hair was dark brown streaked with lighter highlights, bleached from sitting out in the sun painting. He never wore a hat, preferring to squint in the bright light. Jeremiah sat beckoning for Sarah to hand him the ring.

"I used to sell junk like this, but now I'm respectable. I spread some paint on canvas, put a fancy price on it, and they come. And sometimes they buy.

"Today I finished a piece your mothers would love: a rabbi, glazed eyes, yellow-white beard—the works. Bless those rich Americans. A few days' work and they pay me hundreds of dollars. Not everything I do is trash, but things have become too easy for me, and most of my work has less quality than that ring."

"Some of your work is really beautiful." Sarah, small, lithe, and earnest, reached for the ring.

"Bootiful. Smootiful. There are days when I think I'm the one, the seventh son of the seventh son, born to work miracles. And the next morning I am hungover." Jeremiah pauses to shake his head, hunch his shoulders, and finally shrug it off.

"Your mothers come and look and ask, 'How much for the rabbi?' Americans are better than the Israelis. At least they give you some respect. To them I am an artist. The Israelis, especially the women, cactus fruit with suntanned legs, they think you owe them something because they walk into your shop.

"Listen, the world is *charas* (shit, also slang for hashish). Smoke it, eat it, or throw it away."

"Ah, you're full of shit and you can't hold your liquor," Reuben said. They laughed lest we mistake the harsh words for true venom.

Reuben was just past 30. Called up for reserve duty, five days a week he slept under a bridge with his submachine gun. The tourists who stumbled across the bridge pausing to marvel at the view sometimes caught him in the corner of their eyes. They would lean over the railing and he would be there at the bottom of the gorge, propped up against the concrete bridge support. If he was awake, he would smile at them, occasionally wriggling his mustache to chase off the flies.

"Reuben, what do you think of our young American friends who sit here so quietly?"

"Jeremiah," Sarah spoke. "Not that it really matters, but I'm not an American." The words seemed an effort for the girl from England. It was so much easier to lie back and listen in the warm haze.

"An old line imperialist, eh! I knew an English woman once. All she understood was this." Jeremiah grabbed at the crotch of his pants. "She wanted an artist for a lover. She gave me this broken piece of shit."

He pointed to a tape recorder. "I could have milked her good." Jeremiah leaned back in his chair, rubbing his belly, pursing his lips, and shaking his head.

"So, Reuben, what do you think of our little English girl? The young ones are so tender, so ripe." Sarah peered out through half-closed eyes, somehow both fierce and innocent, her face seemed about to burst as she smiled. It was a Stan Laurel smile, impish, and it made her look very much like a schoolgirl who had just gotten a kitten for Christmas.

"She's very pretty. Yes. She's fetching, eh, fetching? Yes, that how you say it, no?"

"But she's too young for us. Better to leave her for our young American friend."

"Leave her, Reuben, you peasant. So you think the American has no balls. Do you think we'd have to leave her? He'd take her away from two old *mamzayrim* (bastards) like us even if he were the one-eyed son of a rabbi and didn't know a cunt from a hole in the wall. Eh, Meir. I use your Hebrew name. I hope you don't mind."

The last of the mud that had been our Moroccan coffee lay in our cups. Sarah stretched like a cat waking from a nap. She had been curled up on the low couch, and as she raised herself, her small breasts pressed against her blouse. Jeremiah scowled, then smiled and took her hand.

"Listen, American, perhaps she loves you. She has wild eyes, but a warm heart. She is probably a virgin. Look at how her face turns red, Reuben. She's so ripe. And if it turns out the American has no balls, you can come back anytime. You don't even have to bring a tape recorder!"

We had been smoking some hashish that one of the Dutch volunteers on the kibbutz had given me. I got up to dig out what was left of the hash from my jeans. The buzz was wearing off and it was getting dark and the buses would stop running soon. I playfully squeezed Sarah's ass as we moved toward the door.

"Here, Jeremiah, keep this. I don't need to carry it around." I handed him the hash and took Sarah's hand.

"OK, I guess it's a fair trade. You keep the girl, and I get some shit."

A few days later Sarah and I made our good-byes. The summer was ending, and I had to get to Paris for my charter flight back to the States.

I had $13 and a sleeping bag when I arrived in Paris and a week to get through before my plane left. I did a quick bit of financial planning on the plane. I figured I could afford $2 for a youth hostel every other night for a safe bed and a shower, which left me with three nights to find a park to sleep in and about $7 for food and expenses. An American in Paris… I was reduced to stealing leftover croissants from empty tables after the patrons got up from their summer breakfasts. A six-feet two-inch urchin with curly hair and a backpack bumming cigarettes from fellow travelers, I was too stupid or too proud to ask my parents for a bridge loan, still embarrassed about being a missing person with parents frantic about my safety.

Coming home I was the skinniest I would ever be, barring some wasting disease, since growing to my full height.

∞

A couple of years later I got a letter from Sarah:

Dear Kirsch,

Did your mum tell you that I phoned you last summer? Actually it was rather a strange phone call as I was feeling a bit nervous—we had broken into an office and the night watchman was walking down the corridor.…
Anyway I was ready to go to the States where I was promised a job, but then I went to Paris for the weekend to say goodbye to my old friend V and instead we went to Afghanistan only we couldn't stay because there was a revolution so we went to India and it was quite a relief getting there as our Afghan friends had plans for smuggling and some of them wanted to keep me for a hostage. I wound up in this tiny village in the Himalayas where the dope grows to amazing heights. A carpenter worked next door to our cottage and he called me "sister" and we would sit together for hours smoking chillums and having long conversations even though he speaks no English except for "sister" and I hardly speak Hindi.

It was very peaceful up there—in fact a lot of sadhus go there to find peace in the mountains. We were near a little town where there was quite a large population of Tibetan refugees and a few Tibetan monasteries have just been started there. There was a beautiful little Tibetan temple with fantastic pictures all over the walls.

V and I were getting very pissed off with each other by then so he used to storm off in the mornings and a little 14-year-old sadhu would come and give me apples and smoke with me. But he had been stealing the apples and in the end the children drove him out of the village.

By the end of my stay there I was very strong and used to think nothing of sprinting up the mountain to where we lived. I was very sad to leave especially as Delhi is such a dump. Although there was a nice milk shop there where I could buy yoghurt in an earthenware pot— he kept his cow inside the shop, in the back.

The rest of the time was a pretty bad trip and I had almost married the idiot! I now look back with absolute amazement when I see how perilously close it was. Imagine me married. Anyway I managed to escape that and I am now happily single again.

When I got back I had hepatitis and so had to spend a month in the hospital for tropical diseases. At first I was too ill to realise what was going on but now I feel much stronger and apparently I should be completely better in another 6 months to a year. That means that I'm taking a year off college, which really depresses me in some ways, but I think I've learned to accept things much better than I used to.

I've got to look for some kind of work to keep me going in the meantime. Maybe I can teach English to foreigners or something. It's a pity I can't do street trading but I'm not strong enough and anyway the police aren't as lenient as they used to be. Sometimes I think I'll go to Paris as I know a man there who is very fond of me, but I don't really think I want to be kept for long. I might stay with a friend who lives on a houseboat in Amsterdam. But probably I'll stay in London as I'm happy here and I have friends. I might try to do some more philosophy at the same time.

How are things with you? Have you got a house, car, wife, job and prospects or are you the same old bum?

Lots of love,
Sarah XXX

College Jobs

∞

My father, like so many Jews from small towns in Europe, had a great deal of respect for educated people, for *kopf arbeit* (working with your head). Working with your hands was what you did when you had no choice. Talking about one of his block mates in Auschwitz, he said, "He was *intallaged* (an intellectual), a professor, a famous musician. A violinist, the Nazis made him play in the camp orchestra, the ones who played at the gate when we walked out to work in the morning." Other times my father pointed out that very few of the intellectuals survived in the camps. Yet he still spoke of them with respect—even when a rueful smile sneaked in and he remembered them coming off the train in fine clothes with leather suitcases only to find themselves waking up the next day with shaved heads wearing striped prisoners' uniforms.

He saw college as a way for my brother and me to become professionals or businessmen while I, like so many of my generation, was desperate to live guilt-free as a member of the working class. Some of the romance of the working poor was left over from the Great Depression, the New Deal, and Hollywood films, which celebrated the dignity of the working poor, people whose hard work and sweat made them the salt of the earth. Campus politics of the 1960s added another layer to this vision: We were a "student movement" that fought against the "establishment," that sought a new order. In "movement" discourse, many of the conversations we had, the speeches we listened to, whether from stolid labor union guys or flaming radicals, were, in the end, aimed at improving the life of the "worker," the one least likely to be tainted by privilege or the corruption inherent in living off the labor of others.

In the early 1970s I had most of a college education, but in the workplace, I was definitely unskilled labor. Somehow I found that state ennobling. Casting about for work, my height and broad back seemed like assets when one day I answered an ad for temporary work with Allied Van Lines.

Luther, my crew chief, walked into the Andersons' house. Boxes were piled in corners, major pieces strewn about here and there. I followed behind. This was my second day at the Andersons'. I was the kid who could go 20 minutes without spitting or scratching his privates. I was clean enough and white enough so as not to scare Mrs. Anderson or her husband. So they sent me in to help the Andersons pack the dishes and the books. I was part of the crew that had come to load the Andersons' worldly possessions for the trip from Philadelphia out to Seattle.

Luther had Mrs. Anderson well in tow. He surveyed the house, stopping in the living room, den, each of the three bedrooms, and the family room in the basement to note the condition of the furniture: Was it scratched, marred, scuffed, torn, battered, bruised? Luther took everything down on his clipboard. He might have spent 20 minutes in the house. Then he walked back to the moving van, put the clipboard in the cab, and grabbed his thermos. Wilbur and Carl had been airing out the pads we used to protect the furniture. The three of us would carry the Anderson stuff out to the van for the rest of the day. Wilbur was big, my height, but thicker around the chest and waist. He moved slowly and purposefully and he never walked back from the house empty-handed. Carl was thin and wiry, a man who drank more than he ate but still managed to keep his strength. Luther was an older version of Carl, wiser and softer around the edges. He drank only beer these days and saved the whiskey for special occasions. Luther and Wilbur were black, while Carl was white with the red-faced flush of a working alcoholic.

As the chief, Luther was responsible for packing the truck. For all of us the goal was to make sure that none of the possessions were damaged while in the company's custody. I had been out on jobs with Luther before, but I still could not believe the way he worked. He started calling for pieces at 9:00 a.m. and by 3:00 p.m., we had carried out every stick of furniture in the place by special request. Luther had called for each piece. He had a gift. He not only remembered every piece of furniture in the house, but he could picture its size and shape and fit each into the van so that no space was wasted. He was like the child savant who was able to effortlessly place puzzle pieces into place. I mean he was not absolutely perfect. Every so often he would put something aside and ask us to bring out some other piece that might fit better, but he was right so often, it was uncanny.

"Go get me the dresser with the claw-feet in the master bedroom." I walked into the house to the master bedroom and searched high and low for the dresser with the claw-feet. I walked out sheepishly.

"OK. I give up. Where is it?"

He replied without rancor or sarcasm, "When you walk in the door, it's in a closet with sliding doors on your right, behind the box springs. You find it in there."

When I came to understand this parlor trick that Luther could play with all the rooms at once, I assumed, naturally, that Luther was close to God and would soon take time to tell me the meaning of life and why some of us are born to suffer and die in the suburbs of our great cities.

The Andersons were moving from Philadelphia to the Pacific Northwest, but they were taking everything with them. I learned to differentiate between moves paid for by employers and those in which the householder foots the bill. When Joe Homeowner paid, we used old newspapers to wrap the dishes. When the company paid, we used Van Lines' wrapping paper for the dishes and the old newspapers were packed separately.

The one physics class I took in college helped me to understand that everything boils down to your frame of reference. Things stayed fairly simple until people started being able to imagine traveling at the speed of light. Relativity brought new conundrums. Here I am experiencing an event while people traveling away from me at the speed of light will never know it happened. Of course, if they are not moving that fast, they may find out about it eventually, but when they tell you about it through their frame of reference, you still might not recognize their description as the same event. Neither the Andersons nor their furniture would move anywhere near the speed of light on their trip across the country, but except for the very few things that would be thrown out or left behind, from the point of view of their possessions, the Andersons will hardly have moved at all.

Everyone knows so much about what is likely to happen that we go through life filling in the endings in advance. When you hear the screech of tires in a long, wailing complaint, your mind is waiting for the sharp thud of a collision and the sound of breaking glass. You often understand what people want even before their words and actions make it explicit. In part, this is because you share enough of a frame of reference that you assume you will understand them. As you cross over into a different culture, some of these assumptions drop away. Unless one is truly fluent, a Westerner in Japan may find it hard to convince a Japanese stranger that the sounds he is mouthing are Japanese. The Japanese person, approached by a foreigner, will assume he is speaking a language that is not Japanese.

Working with a new crew is a little like being in a foreign land. It takes a few days before they think you understand them. I had to put up with a couple of days of "hey, college kid, if you're so smart, how come you're cutting your hands on the bottom of that refrigerator?" But if you don't hide when it comes time to lifting the heavy stuff and you don't hurt the furniture or your coworkers, you eventually reach what might be called a comfortable working relationship.

Wilbur and I would walk up to a dresser, bend our knees, grab hold, and lift. It did not even require eye contact. Of course, going down the stairs with the more cumbersome pieces might require a bit of conversation.

"You're all right. Still OK. Watch the lamp! Lift up over the rail. OK, set it down."

Occasionally, Luther would be called in for a brief strategy session on how to maneuver a piece through tight turns. And then there were pianos. There was a group in Boston called Deathwish Piano Movers. The name really captured the experience, especially that of hanging out of a sixth-story window in a stiff breeze trying to maneuver a ton of ebony and ivory, a beautiful instrument that would like nothing more than to have you give up your life for music.

When you watch professionals move furniture, sofa beds seem to rise on their own and float through the halls and down the stairs. Watch some college kids with the same items and the event takes on much more drama, a Nietzschean struggle against implacable forces. There is a paradox hidden in the strength it takes to make something look effortless.

I took pride in being among the working people. This pride was in part a reaction to my parents and their recurring message that I was spoiled and had no idea what it took to survive in the world. My father wanted me to find *kopf arbeit* and not rely on the strength in my *plaitzes* (my shoulders and back). Still, I think he had some grudging respect for my work as a laborer.

Moving furniture paid pretty well for unskilled work, but it did not fit in very well with my college schedule. My roommate, Donny McGee, and I found work at the airport with more flexible hours. In my senior year, I found myself working Mondays and Fridays and some weekends for Hertz, shuttling rental cars from place to place. We also drove cabs some nights to supplement our income.

Don and I were like brothers from different tribes: stoners, both over six feet tall, both born in the winter of 1950. I had a Jewish Afro, black and dense. He had shaggy light brown hair and a wide, open face with blue eyes that were curious and mischievous. Don's parents were Evangelical Christians (Church of God) from Louisiana. When he was an infant, his family had moved to San Diego, just after the outbreak of Korean hostilities. The family settled in Mission Beach, where in 1950 a poor enlisted man could afford the rent. Today, the bungalows on Mission Beach rent for $2,000 to $3,000 a week! His father was a marine, and his duties sometimes took him away from the family.

"Mom and I studied morality together on the TV," Donny said as we walked through the back lot at Hertz. I had the same teachers: Donna Reed, the Beaver, even Mr. Ed, who taught us how to behave, and the laugh track, which told us which parts were supposed to be funny. Later on we figured out the more subtle cues in movies made for grownups. We learned in the 1950s that even if you were in love, if you didn't marry, the woman's life would end in tragedy, even if she were as pretty as Ingrid Bergman. Divorced women and other "fallen" women had little hope of marrying the hero. It was different for men: As long as the leading man was up front about his intentions, he could expect to live a happy life, even if he had sinned, as long as he made some act of contrition.

Don's parents took him to church on Wednesday evenings and twice on Sundays. They went to every revival meeting and similar events, "sometimes driving some modestly tedious distances" to attend them.

A sense of rueful disbelief festered in Don's memories of his parents. "My mother always participated extensively and diligently. She taught Sunday school classes, played a central role in the Women's Missionary Society, and helped organize various social and volunteer projects for the church. She lived explicitly for Jesus, subordinating all else and all others [to] her duty to the God and its Bible. Images of Jesus and Bible verses adorned the walls in every room of every house we lived in.

"My parents and I basically had a simmering hostile relationship. As severe Fundamentalists, and as Marine Corps parents, they often declared, 'We believe in being strict with our children.' Their authoritarian rule valued nothing higher than obedience, first to the Bible and then to lesser authorities. My dad insisted that as a parent, nothing mattered as much as forcing his children's obedience. Everything else was subordinated, well below second place, so far below that he literally asked, 'What else matters?' I was smothered by the crush of their meticulous micromanagement until I left home.

"Years after I had left home, my mother said she found peace giving her rage to Jesus. From the context, I thought she was referring to matters related to her father: perhaps his behavior in her childhood, or perhaps she referred to the man's behavior during her courtship with my father. Her father disliked my father, and my parents ultimately eloped. He met them with a shotgun when they next visited. He said he would kill them if they took one step forward, and he would have, too. In any case, my mother had reasons for seeking solace in Jesus."

Don's mother, Lucinda, had been part of the New Orleans aristocracy. Andrew, his father, was not, but Andrew was tall and handsome and always spoke softly, even when he was cursing. Lucinda had red hair and green eyes, and sometimes when she sat at the kitchen table with the candles lit and the tarot cards spread out before her, she would become a dragon, eyes burning, teeth gleaming. When she laughed, the women who had come to have their cards read would wince. You could see they had their thighs pressed close together under their cotton dresses.

People in the South complained that Donny spoke too fast like some Northerner, and people in the North marveled at his slow southern drawl. He was driving a cab one day when a gentleman he was taking from the airport to Center City remarked on what an interesting voice he had. In a high-class English accent he proceeded to recount Don's history, beginning with his origins in Louisiana, his move to California, and key details about his parents' origins. Don's paranoia peaked. He was sure some FBI agent had been tracking him and was about to take him off the streets, for either his politics or his drug habits, when the man revealed that he was a linguist and that deconstructing people's accents was a special hobby. Tall and loose-limbed with a broad forehead and tousled hair, Don looked like an innocent but had a devilish laugh. He was bemused by the Eastern elitists in the Ivy League and aghast at the military-industrial complex. He also gave me a new view of my parents.

Being a shuttle driver for Hertz was fun at first. We zoomed around the airport in fairly new cars. Driving a car was, and probably still is, a youthful elixir. It implied independence; it was part of the mating ritual, a sign of manhood. It was how you escaped home into a space where you controlled your own destiny. Groups of young men drove around in search of adventure. No destination was necessary. The trip was its own reward. Four or five of us would pile into the shuttle car, usually one of the older models, to pick up cars when the demand for rentals heated up (Monday). When the returns were hot and heavy (Friday), we would make the trip in the other direction and the shuttle car would take us back to the drop-off zone.

After a while, driving the stodgy rental sedans seemed boring and we would get excited only when luck brought us a sports car. We occasionally got a Mustang, but even an Oldsmobile Cutlass seemed like a hot car after maneuvering through the airport in Ford Fairlanes or some of the other monster-sized family cars, the gas guzzlers that predated the SUVs of the new millennium. If none of the supervisors were nearby, we would burn rubber and try to control fishtailing turns as though the airport causeways were a Formula One racecourse. In idle moments we would get high and stand around at the end of the runways while planes took off over us. We jumped up and down like water dots on a greased skillet, as the tremendous noise and vibrations tried to decompose our body tissues and explode our brains. The thrill brought to mind crystal meth; I am not sure which was more destructive.

We would occasionally be asked to move cars between the airport and nearby Hertz locations. We were getting paid ten cents a mile and usually pocketed two or three times the minimum wage, which in 1971 was still under $1.50 an hour. I remember one trip in particular. We drove up to New York City in a slightly beat-up 1969 Ford Fairlane station wagon. Six of us, all between ages 19 and 21, all in torn jeans driving up the New Jersey Turnpike, not sure what was waiting for us at the other end. Our T-shirts featured the Rolling Stones, Pabst beer, Jack Daniel's whiskey, Che Guevara, and exhortations to "Make Love, Not War." There were more than a dozen of us working in overlapping shifts at Hertz. A few like me and Don were college kids from Penn; most of the crew were from West Philadelphia, neighborhood kids, townies, guys with names like Puddy (poo-dee), PJ, and Brutus, kids whose fathers were bus drivers and mechanics living in little white pockets of a neighborhood that was predominantly black. It was a time when most whites who could fled the city.

One of the guys on the crew, Craig, was an upstairs neighbor. Don had met him before I moved in. Don had been tripping one day and heard some music he liked coming from the apartment upstairs. He walked up the stairs and knocked on the door in a pleasantly dazed and confused realm. He smiled at the bearded youth who greeted him and said, "Hi. I'm tripping. Can I come in?" Craig let him in. A nice guy with a demonic sense of humor, Craig was trying to figure out how far-gone Don was. He spoke to him in a homespun pig Latin (some Philly jive, I could never understand it, even when quite sober). It was somewhere between a taunt and an adolescent test of intoxication. Donny just smiled and nodded and moved past him toward the music.

We showed up at the Hertz lot in New York City fairly stoned and became ecstatic when we found five brand-new Cadillacs waiting for transport to Philadelphia. Trying to maintain decorum, we signed out the cars and carefully made our way to I-95 headed for the George Washington Bridge. We knew we were quite a sight, a parade of Cadillacs gleaming in the afternoon sun rolling through the Bronx. Once we got onto the New Jersey Turnpike, we started making formations across the three lanes of traffic: wedges, squares, diamonds, and L-shaped phalanxes. Then someone discovered the electronic seat adjustments. I had never seen them before, those buttons or levers you push to raise and lower the seats to lean forward and back. Suddenly, we were like kids on a merry-go-round: rising up and sinking down, sliding forward and back on our plush leather seats. Everyone had a cigarette dangling out of his mouth, and the townies had tattoos on their arms sticking out the windows under rolled-up T-shirt sleeves. I had a pack of Camels rolled up in my sleeve, something I'd learned from one of the men who worked on our farm, or was it James Dean?

Donny and I often worked different shifts. One afternoon, I was working at the airport when my mother knocked on our apartment door. Years later, he still vividly remembered meeting Mom for the first time. My parents had given me an old Volvo when I set off for my sophomore year. Part of my newfound financial independence meant not driving home to New Jersey for regular visits, not asking for cash, and not calling home on a fixed schedule. I had a history of going incommunicado.

My parents had made contact with Interpol the previous summer trying to track me down in Europe. I had been surprised by their concern, happily careening about the continent with a young blond woman from eastern Washington, until I arrived in the Holy Land and my Israeli relatives rushed me to a phone to call home and prove I was still alive.

Years later in Florida, my father, almost 90, still talked about how much trouble I had staying in touch. I still didn't call as often as he would like, and I would get delightful messages from him on my answering machine. "Mike! Daddy's calling. I not hear from you for so long."

My parents worried about me again that senior year at Penn. They had tried to call, found the phone had been disconnected. Donny and I were too dysfunctional, too far-gone to pay the phone bill on time. We didn't use the phone much and didn't really miss it.

∞

When the doorbell rang, Don had to struggle out of bed to answer the door. A small woman wearing a hat with little bits of lace pinned to it looked up at him and asked: "Have you seen my Maier?"

Once Don woke up enough to figure out it was my mother, he invited her to come in. At six feet two inches, he towered over her. When Mom became convinced that she had found the right place, she wanted to call my father. She asked Don where she could find a phone. Ours was still disconnected. While Mom was solidly built, he decided that leaving her alone to wade through the wilds of West Philadelphia looking for a phone booth was a bad idea. With the air of a southern gentleman, he settled in to babysit my mother. They had a cup of tea and chatted about her history, and by the end of the day he was convinced that she was probably better at taking care of herself than he was.

Most days Don wore an old army surplus jacket in a khaki that dated back to WWII. But Don had had little exposure to the Holocaust or even a European view of the war. Over tea, Mom told him her story:

"In the war, I was in the Jewish resistance. We lived in the woods. Mostly running and hiding from the Nazis in eastern Poland. You would not believe what we went through.... One night a big company of soldiers was searching for us, and the leaders of our group of partisans said we must swim to Russia. I had to throw away what little I had and jump into the Bug River to try to escape the Nazis. One boy died in the water. It was miracle we came to the other side, but the Russians sent us back. They told us 'You must go back to Poland. You must fight on your own soil.'

"We had a few rifles and whatever ammunition we could steal. We tried to make some sabotage against the trains or small outposts, but mostly we tried to stay alive. When I talk to you, it is like it happened yesterday. I can still feel the cold, the snow, the mud. When they thought they knew where we were, they would throw bombs at us." She struggled for the English word. "Mortars. They shoot mortars.

"One night I am hiding in a ditch with my girlfriend. Winter is coming, and there is ice with mud, but we must lie down to hide from the bombs. We were holding hands. The noise was terrible. Dirt and broken branches flying in the air would fall on top of us as we lay there. Then suddenly it was black, a bomb landed almost on top of me. I thought I was dead. After I don't know how long, I open my eyes and think 'I am still alive.' I look for my girlfriend and I am still holding her hand, but when I look, she is not there. I just have the hand."

The poor girl had been blown to pieces.

"I was lucky. We had some smart boys in the troop. Once, the Germans captured us. They put us in cattle cars, maybe to take us to interrogation, probably to take us to the camps. But the boys kept looking for a way to escape. They started scraping at the boards on the bottom of the train car. The train was already moving. They managed to pull the boards up from the bottom of the car, and one by one they dropped down to the tracks. I looked at the ground moving below, and I was afraid. My cousin held my hand and told me, 'Bronia, we must go. If we die, we die, but we must take a chance, we must try to live.'"

Mom told him stories about Dad, too, and, when my father came to town for graduation a few months later, Don was reverential. He was eager to have the same type of conversation he had with my mother but afraid to ask direct questions.

Thirty-five years later, I stood next to Don's hospital bed in his house in Mukelteo, Washington. My mother had chatted with him for much of the afternoon three decades earlier, and he remembered almost all her stories. Don was now a survivor, too, as he had taken a fall on an offshore oil rig and broken his back. He still had a quick wit and a sharp intellect and just about enough use of his hands to send email and work the remote for the DVD jukebox and the flat-screen TV that hung suspended from the ceiling next to the oversized screen that was connected to his computer. He had a great place perched on a cliff overlooking Possession Sound. A wooden deck ran the length of the house with a gazebo in the far corner. On a couple of visits when the weather was good in that mysterious northwestern climate, I had helped one of the stream of young women who helped care for him to roll his bed out onto the deck, and we had shared a joint in the afternoon sun. When I asked him about our days in Philly, he said he regretted only two things: not graduating from the university and not asking my father about his life.

He had had an accident in our college days, too, not nearly as tragic. That winter Donny's days at Hertz ended when he crashed a car on the Pennsylvania Turnpike. He laughed when he talked about it. "The accident was like a slow waltz. I hit the brakes and the car started spinning, an unhurried majestic turn on black ice, bouncing off the guardrail and touching other cars as if they were dance partners, sending them twirling about to some unheard music." The Hertz folks were not amused. He started spending more time in his cab, and so did I.

In Philadelphia, Yellow Cab's lot was at Grays Ferry off 37th Street. For some reason they had us dress like busboys with white shirts and black trousers. I always thought that cabs were for rich people. I got the idea from going to school in Manhattan where poor people took the bus or the subway. At 20, a college junior, I had never flagged down a cab and only rarely rode in one as someone's guest. Driving cabs taught both of us a lot about inner-city life. Time after time we would come home with stories of some old black women taking a cab home from Bingo or shopping, who looked at us almost in tears, grateful that we had stopped for them, but still terrified, pleading with us to stay until they crossed the street and got into their houses.

I did not understand what it meant to be poor in America until I drove a cab in Philadelphia.

Many of the drivers, both black and white, would not take fares into the worst neighborhoods. If they found themselves in a troubled part of town, they would drive by folks looking for a cab, not wanting to take a fare that would keep them in the ghetto. Don and I were too idealistic or too sure we would live forever to concern ourselves with safety. Many nights I would wind up with a fare that took me into the depths of North Philadelphia and spend the rest of the night ferrying people back and forth from Market Street to their homes. Market Street was the main drag and major public transit route. It was fairly well lit and occasionally patrolled by Frank Rizzo's Philly cops, but many people were afraid to walk even a few blocks from Market Street to their homes. People were afraid of getting robbed, beat up, or raped. They were almost all black. Old and young women, old men, and anyone who felt they had something to lose. They felt unsafe in their own neighborhoods. Even gang members would try to take cabs to get through other folks' turf.

Those were the days before inner-city cabs put in bulletproof plexiglass to separate drivers from their armed passengers, but I had few concerns about safety. I was a dumb kid who looked at driving the cab as adventure travel. I got beat on fares a couple of times a week. The passenger, usually a young man, would simply open the door and run when I stopped at his destination. After a while, even I would pass by some of the young black men trying to flag a cab on Market Street. One day a fellow in his thirties had been entertaining me with jive talk about the problems he had with his women. "I knock on her door and she say, 'Boy, you don't live here no more' and I say, 'Woman why you wanna talk like dat?' and she say ...."

He was chatting away while I focused on the road, and then he tapped me on the shoulder and I looked back to find a gun in his hand. My eyes grew wide. My knuckles were white as my hands gripped the wheel. I had a brief conversation with my bladder, which mercifully did not let loose. My college buddies who drove cabs imagined different strategies for being robbed: crashing the car into a fire hydrant, coming to a screeching halt, and running from the cab. Some of the older men carried guns for protection. I had a speech prepared:

> *If you want my money, you can have it. If you want the cab, just drop me off near a bus stop, or if you are looking for some excitement or a story, you can tell your friends. We can siphon some gas out of the tank and burn the cab right here on Market Street!*

I looked at the gun and the man holding it. I was trying to get some saliva into my mouth so that it would open and I could start my pleadings when he started bragging about how cool the gun was, how he won it in a poker game, and how he had not had the time to get bullets for it yet. I grimaced and nodded and was still waiting for my throat to unlock when we reached his destination. He opened his wallet, paid for the fare, and gave me a tip.

Duprass

∞

I dreamed of a tree last night whose roots were in the air
and whose branches were very fine. The tree so large, the earth
a mere twig dangled among the roots, our lives a gentle breeze
that ruffled a single leaf. The tree was awesome.
Swirling leaves dancing in the light played tricks with our vision.
Every death was a season and the tree grew slowly in time.

1974 entry in my journal

Events pop up in life's stream, like driftwood floating along and crashing into rocks until they find some resting place along the river's banks or the ocean's shore. Looking back we build the events into a story, pile them up in the campfire, and watch as the kindling sets the larger pieces aglow.

In the spring of 1972, after graduating a semester late with a degree in history, I packed up my Volvo and headed for Boston. I scrounged around for work and lived out of my car, sometimes crashing with friends. The leaves were in full bloom, the days getting longer, and I was returning from the work that my liberal arts education had prepared me for—as a day laborer sanding the rust off pipes in a lard factory in Quincy. Even after washing up, my arms were still coated with rust, my gray work pants streaked with red stains, and my work boots slippery from the congealed fat that coated the plant floors. That day, I had been thrashing about with my goggles and my sander amidst the residue of swine. We never had any pork products in our kosher home, but I was not the first person in my family to work with pig fat. Just after WWII, my mother spent some time lying atop boxcars on Polish trains with bacon strapped around her belly, trying to make a few zlotys smuggling pig fat into cities still caught in deprivations of postwar rationing.

One afternoon, after work, I set off to visit Pearl, a high school friend from New Jersey, with some vague notion of renewing romance. She had gone to Boston University and lived on Magazine Street in Cambridge with two roommates, Frances and Rhonda.

Pearl was late, but Rhonda was home, and when I asked if it was OK to smoke, she ushered me out onto the porch. Frances did not allow smoking in the apartment, which, in 1972, seemed prissy and arbitrary. I smoked Camels or sometimes Lucky Strikes. Rhonda smoked Old Gold Filters. Years of cigarette advertising had left a web of images associated with each brand. The brand implied something about a person, some affinities, some hint at character or sensibility. Old Gold, not a top brand at the time, tended to feature ads with sophisticated women or smart-looking couples. One I remember had a man's hand reaching for a woman's snow-covered mitten holding a pack of cigarettes with the tag line: "Old Gold offers you the warm friendliness of fine tobaccos." Its longtime slogan was "Not a cough in a carload." Camels got a lot of "placements" in WWII movies and had a more masculine cast with the "I'd walk a mile for a Camel" slogan. I am not sure that Rhonda noticed which brand I smoked. Cigarettes brought us together, and later they took her away from me.

When I met Rhonda, she had long, curly hair, which she worked hard to straighten but often wore in a wavy ponytail or braids. Her aura, her intense blue eyes, cast a spotlight on me, and for a moment I was on center stage at the heart of the universe. She was warm and kind, shy yet engaging, and at times fiercely stubborn. Do I remember falling in love? Can I remember not being in love with her?

Ronnie and Pearl

Rhonda was pleased with me, at first, because I took an immediate dislike to Frances, whose large bosom and long dark hair usually made her popular with boys. I was drawn to Rhonda because she laughed at my jokes. Most people didn't even notice I was being funny. At 21, I thought I had an arcane wit, the result of years of Saturday morning TV and a shorter exposure to the existentialists. The Rocky and Bullwinkle cartoon captured it pretty well: After an outrageous pun, a scowling Rocky would look up and in his high-pitched flying squirrel voice murmur, "I get it," while Bullwinkle, the tall moose leaning on a signpost, would turn to the audience and say, "Thousands won't." Rhonda was not among those thousands, and when she laughed or smiled, the world glowed and sparkled.

Rhonda and I smoked and drank coffee, traded personal histories, and bemoaned the state of the world. Nixon was president. White

House burglars had been caught at the Democratic National Committee headquarters at Watergate. We were pulling out of Vietnam but still mired in the conflict. George Wallace was running for president until he got shot in Maryland. Hopes had faded for the promise of a better America that JFK seemed to carry into the White House; the "Great Society" of Lyndon Baines Johnson had generated skepticism and derision among many of us, not just the radical students. There were those who still held on to the idea of an alliance between students and workers to push a leftist agenda, but "come the revolution," once an uplifting phrase, now seemed ironic if not comic.

Rhonda's family name was Lebensbaum. In German, the *lebensbaum* is the tree of life. My mother's maiden name is Winderbaum, which in Yiddish is the miracle tree. The name I inherited from my father, Kirschenbaum, means cherry tree, so much more mundane. Rhonda's father always called her Rhonda, as did our friend Pearl. I held out for a while, but like many of our friends, I wound up calling her Ronnie or just Ron. My nickname was Kirsch, and early in our relationship, most people spoke of us in the same breath as Kirsch and Ronnie and then over the years as just K&R.

K&R became a brand name, a chemically bonded item. Some of our old friends had individual relationships with one or the other of us, but most thought of us only as a couple. We were bound together, but I might never have known her if I had not stopped in to visit Pearl in her Cambridge apartment that afternoon.

Rhonda was a generation further along on the immigrant axis. Her grandparents had come over from Eastern Europe and settled in what was then a thriving coal town, Scranton, Pennsylvania. Her parents were born there. Her father, Sam, and both of his brothers had served in the U.S. Army during WWII. Sam went to college on the GI Bill and wound up selling used cars in Scranton.

Until I met Rhonda, I had despaired of finding a "true" love, although I had fallen in love with every pretty girl who smiled at me, at least until a conversation started. A raging sex drive helped me suspend judgment if there were any hope that lust might find refuge, even when broader interest waned.

Smoking with Rhonda on the porch that day, I was still of a "whores and mothers" mind-set: Some women were targets for lust and some for a kinder, gentler love. Perhaps the division was not quite so extreme, more like that in the movies with the sultry woman who stirs men's lust and the earnest one with the pure heart; the "complex" woman with a past and the virgin with perky breasts, bright eyes, just a bit playful. At the time, only the rare film showed the hero winding up with the sexy lady. Sex was something that men pursued and women resisted. Ronnie was the nice Jewish girl you could bring home to your parents, someone who might end up a mother to your children. Yet, in her torn jeans and worn-out T-shirts, she was not my mother's ideal "catch."

My mom was always careful about her dress and her makeup when she left the farm to go into town. For my mother, looking your best when you went out in public was a social inheritance and a personal mantra. Mom was dismayed that Ronnie was a young woman for whom putting on makeup was reserved mostly for Halloween and high heels a form of torture she eschewed. I was delighted. I wasn't drawn to the girly girls with long fingernails, fancy purses, and shiny jewelry. They were part of some other species. Over time Ronnie and I both moved a bit from being fashion apostates, particularly when we started ballroom dancing more than a decade later. On the dance floor, Ronnie's wardrobe changed dramatically: skirts, heels, pantyhose. It was, to borrow my father's expression, "not to believe."

Part of my mother's obsession with clothes was simply European. Even during the hippie era, careful attention to style prevailed on the continent. Did Mom's intensity about cleanliness and style in public also come from being a fatherless girl growing up in a household just scraping by?

I married a motherless girl. They say that young men are looking to marry their mother. Did Oedipus visit me on those early days on the farm? I had to wait until I grew to be taller than Mom before I stopped finding myself crushed against her breasts, in hugs at first welcome and then embarrassing. My mother was kind, warmhearted, emotional, but she seemed less in touch with the world than my father and not as smart. In our family, my mother was not truly my father's peer. He loved her, but any intimacy they shared was private. I can barely remember seeing them touch except when dancing at weddings and bar mitzvahs. He respected her, but when she offered opinions on business or politics, his reply was often *"Mach sech nisht narrish"* (don't make yourself foolish). She pushed back, giving him a hard time for getting them stuck on the farm and pointing out the better choices she had in postwar Germany.

I wanted a different kind of relationship. I wanted someone I could treat as an equal. Like myself and many of my closest friends, Ronnie was the firstborn. Her mother died giving birth to Ronnie's sister when Ronnie was just two years old. Following in the Jewish tradition, Ronnie's sister was given the name of the most recently deceased relative, her mother, Marion. I had been named after my grandfather. I struggled with my name and was happy when "Kirsch" settled in as my nickname. For Ronnie's sister, the name Marion was a curse. None of the family could say the name out loud without crying. She was called "Little Sister" at first and then "Sissy." Her grandparents on her mother's side took in the girls. Sissy bonded with her grandmother, but Ronnie stayed Daddy's girl.

I met Ronnie through Pearl, and I met Pearl because she, too, had grown up on a chicken farm, about six or seven miles away from our farm. I think I first met Pearl through Habonim, the left-leaning, socialist Zionist youth group.

Almost all the kids I knew in New Jersey attended religious schools, all except Pearl. She belonged to this mysterious set of families whose kids went to public schools, even though the parents still spoke Yiddish at home. I joined them in the fall of 1965, when, as a junior, I transferred to Southern Freehold Regional High School. That fall Bruce Springsteen was playing with the Castiles and doing concerts at the Freehold Shop-Rite.

Pearl was one of the few faces I recognized at the public high school, but she was one year behind me, so we had no classes together. Like me, Pearl was shy. She remembers me as a kid who was tall and thin. I had grown almost a foot since my bar mitzvah, but I had not outgrown my self-image as a short, chubby boy; even in college at six feet one and 180 pounds, I still saw a belly looking back at me in the bathroom mirror. In high school, Pearl and I had a few furtive movie dates, walks on the boardwalk, and an awkward good-night kiss. We were both shy and quiet, and any notion of entanglement quietly faded away.

At the new high school, I made another friend, Nathan Fox, who is probably the main reason I now live in New England. Ken Napa, my yearbook colleague, introduced us. A stocky version of Woody Allen, Nathan wound up at Williams College in Western Massachusetts. During the winter of my senior year, I went up to visit him. I was trying to sort out colleges, and it was my first trip to New England. The snow was piled high. A succession of snowstorms had piled fluffy white blankets, one after another, on the countryside. Squinting in the noon sunshine, I marveled at the cloudless, blue sky and Arctic air sweeping down from Canada, which gave the campus an oxygen-rich sparkle. Deep channels cut through chest-high snow and connected the buildings. I moved to New England in search of the romance of a snowbound countryside, a pristine dream that stood in contrast to the suppurating grime of inner-city life in Philadelphia.

Back in Boston now, I had found some work and I was tired of living out of my car. Judy, an acquaintance of Ronnie's, mentioned some MIT folks who were looking for a summer roommate. Ronnie warned me against it. Judy had latched on to Ronnie's circle of friends; some thought she had a crush on one of the women, but whatever drew her to the group, she soon got the nickname "Judy the Menace" because she squirmed her way into any activity she got wind of and was hard to deal with and hard to ignore. Small, mousy, with a bad complexion, she had a whiny high-pitched voice and a vocabulary full of clichés. I was very much following the path of least resistance and called the guys she mentioned. I met with a few and promptly moved in.

In Kurt Vonnegut's novel *Cat's Cradle,* he creates a self-deprecating religion, Bokononism, that freely admits it is mostly lies invented to make us feel better about a hopeless world. In Bokononist mythology Judy was my *kankan,* the instrument that brought me into my MIT *karass* (a team of people who do God's will without ever discovering

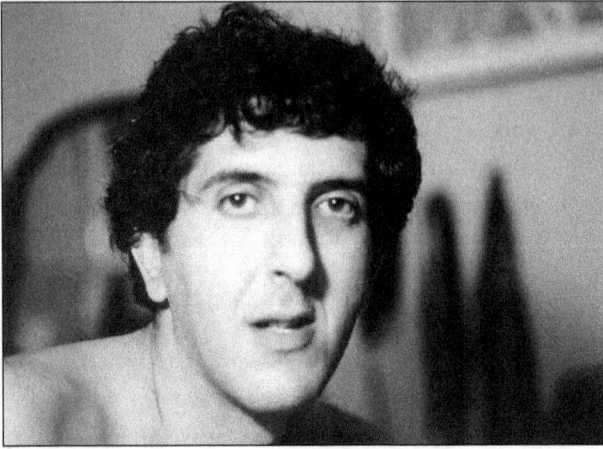

Kirsch

what they are doing), or perhaps Pearl was the *kankan* who brought me to Ronnie and then Judy. Within that *karass*, Ronnie and I were a *duprass* (a *karass* composed of only two people).

The casual conversation with Judy the Menace led not only to a place to live but also to a new career and a set of lifelong friends. I moved into a house in Watertown on the corner of Waverly, Waverly, South Waverly, and Duval. The haphazard city plans that are common in New England left Waverly and Waverly at right angles. The folks who lived there called the place ALF. It was an acronym for "America Loves Filth," an epigram on the back of a painting they found in the attic when they moved in. At times, more than a dozen college-age youths lived in this huge house on top of a hill. A widow's walk sat at its apex, a crown that provided awesome views of Boston and the western suburbs.

Some of the folks who lived there had helped to create and run a food co-op. Back then people would have called us hippies. Mescaline, marijuana, and LSD circulated freely. The house had a huge mattress room dominated by a giant water bed with irregular mattresses covering the remainder of the floor. For some this room served as a regular bedroom; for others, it was a place to crash or party. I wound up with

Ronnie

one of the two bedrooms in the attic and mostly remember the sweat on our bodies when Ronnie and I made love in the afternoon heat.

I remember lying naked with her in our bed after making love; we were still in our twenties, chest to chest, her head pressed into my neck, her pubic bone pressed into my hip, her thighs straddling one of mine. It was a warm night, and the sweat was drying slowly on our skin. Our breathing, ragged at first, settled into the same rhythm; even our heart-beats seemed set to the same metronome, as though we shared the same blood, a single soul spread over two bodies.

We were in love, but that phrase is so overripe, so burdened with passion and pain, with fickle smiles and longing. Our hearts were open to each other. I could tell her anything and not be judged. It was a strange time, the 1960s that dragged into the 1970s when "love affairs" became "relationships." Other words entered the vocabulary, words from the world of academics. "Unlimited positive regard" suited us. Not that we could do no wrong, but neither would believe that the other could start with bad intentions.

There is a quote I like attributed to the Baal Shem Tov, a Jewish mystic and founder of the Hassidic movement. "From every human being there rises a flame that reaches straight to heaven. And when two souls that are destined to be together find each other, their flames flow together, and a single brighter light goes forth from their united being."

Our love was ebullient, not blind to failings, but ready to forgive, eager to touch, to bask in the warmth of tender regard. For some of my friends we were the archetype of couples in love. We made love throughout our marriage, and my male friends viewed that as an indicator and a metaphor for a blissful union. We had issues. I was grumpy in the morning, before coffee. I was a bit more eager to move into the middle class. She was content with student furniture and clothes from Goodwill, still cultivating a "poor, but honest" image. There was a romance associated with being part of the working classes that may seem strange in these post-yuppie days. If you were not part of the elite, the ruling class, you were not responsible for its sins, its greed. We haggled over housework, struggled with feminism, but friends still talk of us as a couple that had a fairy-tale love.

In college, Ronnie had been part of a troika, a female version of the Three Musketeers. Three young women, Rhonda, Pearl, and Colleen, who were roommates, best friends storming through college at Boston University in the late 1960s. Colleen was the wildest and Ronnie the smartest and the most restrained, the least likely to get drunk or disappear with a new lover. Pearl, my New Jersey friend, was somewhere in between: willing to take chances but looking over her shoulder at that little bit of guilt chasing after her, a guilt that Colleen never seemed to acknowledge but sometimes saddened Pearl.

Ronnie was a very private person but still gave the illusion of being very open. She hid from cameras. She almost never wore makeup, and when she did, it made her feel like a clown. It took a while to be admitted to her inner sanctum, but for those who took the trouble to get to know her, her compassion, her honesty, her dry wit, her intelligence and loving kindness made knowing her sublime. Ronnie was a night owl; we both were, in those years right after college. We talked for hours into the night. She was soft-spoken but sometimes would wear wild clothing—and when she danced, she became electric, lighthearted, exultant. Flares went off around the room. We were truly soul mates, one completed the other—like currents that come together and flow as a larger river. But we both had a kind of complacency; she did not have great expectations from life, for a career or a family. Perhaps it was her mother's early death that had left her a fatalist.

In our *karass,* our New Year's Day brunch became an institution. In my youth, I had always hated New Year's Eve. As a child, it was one of the few nights my parents abandoned me to go off and celebrate. Later, I hated the forced ebullience, the drunken mobs. I was a quiet drunk standing by the wall like someone who was not offered a chair, circling on the periphery, a voyeur and not a participant. What was it that made the New Year so worthy of celebrating? Was it that we survived? A cold, dark December night that lifted spirits. It is set on the feast of the circumcision, seven days after Christmas, when the child became viable, marked as a Jew. I did not really look forward to the New Year until I found Ronnie and then we found a great excuse not to go to New Year's Eve parties. Ronnie and I began having a New Year's Day brunch. We could turn down party invitations and tell our friends that we had to get ready for our brunch.

The first was in 1973 in a loft that a friend had remodeled in a slum near Central Square. An enormous rubber tree that we inherited with the place stood in a large bay window that faced south. Tendrils crept out of the huge pot that housed the tree like the arms of a buried octopus. The leaves that slept plastered against the western exposure lifted up and turned east to meet the rising sun. The giant leaves traced an arc through the room as they followed the sun.

The doorbell started ringing around noon, and people would drift in like popcorn, one or two at a time and then a crescendo 90 minutes later. Finally, the last few kernels popped, latecomers drifting in after dark while the unpopped kernels made excuses for not making it to the brunch. In 1973, Ronnie was working part-time behind the counter at King Bagel in Brookline, and bagels and lox with sliced tomatoes and onions became a party staple. Ronnie had baked a couple of quiches, and we had gallons of orange juice and half a case of champagne. I would float about the loft, pour champagne, greet people, and have short interchanges while Ronnie sat on the coach having longer conversations with our guests, but a small part of her tracked me, amused,

a little proud of her guy. It took me a while to realize we had run out
of plastic forks, and as I went scrambling to get out our mismatched
silverware, a rhyme my father taught me jangled about in my head.

If der gibst mich nicht a gupel, al ich essen me dem hand.
If der gibt mich nicht a benkel, al ich shteying bye dem wand.
If you don't give me a fork, then I'll eat with my hands.
If you don't give me a chair, then I'll stand by the wall.

After the last guest had left, sometime near midnight, we lay back
exhausted and Ronnie grabbed her journal to make a list of who had
attended. I lay back in our bed, a foam mattress we had on the floor,
the wall serving as a headboard. Ronnie lay between my legs, her head
resting on my chest trying to remember all those popped kernels. Some
were easy, the inner circle, but others came slowly, the outer bands and
the few newcomers, friends of friends, who had been dragged along
to our party. It became a ritual, and each year we made a list of our
guests.

Ronnie was closer to me than anyone I have ever known, than anyone I could have imagined. I was sometimes more honest with her than
I ever dared to be with myself.

A journal entry from October 1977:

I am not much used to sleeping alone. Ronnie is away at her
grandmother's funeral. The news, while not totally unexpected given
her age and troubled health, is unsettling and sad. It was a disori-
enting day as Ronnie scrambled to get back to Scranton. Only the
next day can I think about R & I, of our togetherness. I showed
her so much of myself that I forgot the self that was private, or
rather, separate. Our friends have been settling in around our
marriage as we show them more of our love. The sudden separation
and the pain it creates makes me realize how unified we are. We
... I am suddenly afraid even to write of it lest we excite the gods
or their hubris ... how can the truth bring evil ... we have so much
... such a rare thing our love that denies neither the intellect nor

the body. We are bound closely, yet free with each other. We have made a small paradise for ourselves, letting our love overflow its bounds and wash all around us as though we suddenly realized that the fountain replenishes itself. If R had left at another time or for another reason I could have thought of our separation, of our separateness, differently. Tonight, mostly I miss her.

One issue did divide us for a while. Ronnie loved animals. She rode horses in high school, and the beagle she left behind to go to college in Boston was still alive when I first visited her family in Scranton. I held out for years, but we eventually got a dog. She found a black mutt at a shelter, a six-week-old puppy, part lab and part German shepherd. I rejected a couple of early choices for names. I wanted a name I could feel comfortable yelling in public. Dorothy, our downstairs neighbor, had a dog named Yoyo, a sheep-herding dog with a long snout and clever eyes. We would baby-sit for Yoyo. Every so often she got to go off leash to run on the lawn of the Harvard Divinity School. I hated having to yell "Yoyo!" to get her attention, my small-town roots showing in my concern that someone walking nearby might look askance at the bozo yelling for Yoyo. For our new puppy we settled on Roxanne, which soon became Roxie, our own moving theater, an endless source of entertainment.

We had had dogs on the farm. The first was a half-breed collie a little bigger than the standard. I had watched *Lassie* on TV and was delighted to wander around the farm, an eight-year-old with a steady companion. My father was hesitant at first. His family had never had pets in Poland. The first dogs he knew were the guard dogs of the SS that had patrolled the concentration camp. But my father came to see the usefulness of a watchdog that would bark when people came onto the farm. He had watched *Sergeant Preston of the Yukon* on TV with me, and all our dogs were named King. The dogs were never allowed into the house. I had no idea how to train a dog, but King's shepherd instincts kept him nearby when we went exploring in the woods, and King would come when I called him. He was also happy to wrestle and lick my face and play tug-of-war with a stick.

That first King was hit by a car while I was at school, and my father buried him before I came home. I never bonded with a farm dog again. The next dog we got was more of a German shepherd mutt, and he had entirely too much interest in chickens. I wanted the dogs to run free, but my father disagreed and the next Kings settled into a life in which most of the time they were chained to their doghouses at the bottom of our circular driveway.

Ronnie set out to house-train Roxie, to get her to heel on and off the leash, and to sit and "sit pretty," her weight on her haunches as she lifted her paws waiting for a treat. Somehow she taught Roxie to "GI Joe," and the big black dog would crawl on her belly across the floor like a soldier in combat trying to stay under a hail of bullets. Ronnie eventually put her training talents to good use at a place called Red Acre Farm training dogs to assist deaf people, alerting them when someone rang the doorbell or when the phone rang. They would run over to their masters and touch them with a paw and then lead them to the sound of the noise, that is, except for fire alarms, when they were taught to touch them and then lie down and let their master decide what to do. They were almost all small dogs. Many of the people they served were old and frail, and big dogs tended to frighten them or knock them off balance.

It was hard for Ronnie to visit my parents, something she endured, work she did on my behalf. She lacked the skills or temerity to train *them.* They wanted to change *us:* how we dressed and how we lived. Almost from our first visit together, they pushed for us marry. Ronnie's father was more reserved. Five years later, when we finally set a date and drove to Scranton to tell her father that we were getting married, he said, "That's great. I've been meaning to talk to you about that."

We usually visited New Jersey for Jewish holidays, and most of the time I would go to synagogue with my father. Ronnie would accompany us at first but soon stopped going to services at my father's Orthodox synagogue. A bit of vitriol stayed in her voice over the years as she described "sitting behind the chicken wire" in the women's section. Orthodox synagogues have a *mechitzah* (a partition to separate the men from the women). Ronnie might have preferred the old *shul* where the women sat in a balcony with arguably a better view of the proceedings, but in the new *shul* a three-foot-tall ironwork rose up behind the last rows of men's seats forming a semitransparent fence offering only the tallest women a clear view.

As I tried to break away from my parents, from their history, from the small-town sensibilities, Ronnie gave me sanctuary. But I had not really broken free. They wanted us to have children, but Ronnie was not eager to become a mother. My mom's greatest joy was her children. "Where are the grandchildren?" She was bereft. Both my parents pressed me at first, but I put them off. Eventually my mother focused on Ronnie. My mom saw a poor, motherless girl and persisted in hoping she could make Ronnie see the light.

"It is so beautiful having a baby. Such sweetness, such *nachas,* such beauty. You will make your father so happy." Ronnie would smile at first, whispering a few "oohs" and "ahhs" as Bronia showed her my baby pictures and then my brother's. The years slipped away, and the exhortations became more desperate: "You have a home, your husband has a good job. It is time." Ronnie was well practiced by then at ignoring the demands, the smile more thin-lipped, eyes that did not make contact.

I was ambivalent about becoming a father. It was something I had expected to happen. It was the natural order of things. You married and the woman had these biological imperatives, built in forces and desires for motherhood. A good man stepped up to the challenge and helped raise a family. Men wanted to spread their seed, and women wanted to conceive. For me, making Ronnie happy, especially making her happy with me, was the prime directive. When we talked about having kids, she was open to the idea. It was clear that it was a sacrifice she would make for me if I had an overwhelming desire for children. I did not think that was a great starting point for making babies. Part of our magic as a *duprass* was that we so often moved in the same direction naturally based on common needs and desires. I did not want to push her anywhere she did not want to go.

When Ronnie hit 40 and my folks gave up on getting us to start a family, the visits home became a bit easier. Still, my mom wanted

Ronnie to wear fancier clothes and some jewelry, to enjoy the things my mom had lusted for all through her youth and in the early days on the farm. Ronnie loved her torn jeans, her flannel shirts; she wanted to be ordinary folk, not the ruling class and especially not a Jewish American Princess, the worst of the nouveau riche. We were veterans of the civil rights movement, antiwar protesters. Many of our friends still viewed history through the lens of dialectical materialism and class warfare. In this war the good guys were the working class.

∞

Ronnie was fascinated by my parents' stories from the war, but she hated having to compromise her principles to accommodate others, especially my parents. From Ronnie's point of view my parents had bought into the wrong side of the American dream. They were striving to reach toward wealth and power instead of cultivating egalitarian values. They viewed the Jews as persecuted. She grew up seeing them as the privileged class in her hometown. They were not the ones who worked in the coal mines.

The phrase "affirmative action" was just taking hold, and on one New Jersey visit, Ronnie revived a conversation I had had several times with my father, an argument that continues in American households today. Ronnie argued that the government needed to support black people climbing out of poverty. My father pushed back, arguing that some were lazy, that they did not value education, that in this country hard work could lift you from poverty. He used himself and the other survivors as a counterexample. He had a sixth-grade education, began working at 11, his family had been wiped out. When he was "liberated," he stood looking over the brink, dry skin stretched over a sack of bones, near death in an abandoned train. He had been shuttled through the Austrian mountains toward Italy as the Germans left the death camps taking prisoners with them. Liberated, he had made his way in the world, working feverishly, taking chances, doing what it took to make a living. He said he had little sympathy for those who complained of not getting a fair deal.

We both argued with my father that he could not judge black people by the folks that he hired for farmwork. He conceded that there were a few "upright" blacks, people who were hardworking, sober, honest, educated, but he claimed that was not the norm.

I had heard it all before, but Ronnie called him a racist and stormed out of the house.

After Ronnie stormed out, I went out to look for her. It was a time before cellphones. She had taken our car and disappeared. My father could not understand what *he* had said that would drive her out of the house, and somehow I could not explain that it was what *she* said that made her leave. I borrowed my father's car and drove around for an hour looking for her until I thought it would be better to be at home in case she called or came back. She had found a bookstore to hide in. Books remained a refuge for her throughout her life and reading a passion we shared. Five hours later she walked sheepishly into the house, just in time for dinner.

My attitudes were similar to Ronnie's. Much of what my parents said made me grimace. I often ignored their requests and advice, and yet I respected them because of what they had survived and what they had accomplished. I loved them. I was returning a love that was implicit in my father's behavior and explicit in my mother's. Perhaps it was my mother's "unlimited positive regard" that had prepared me for Ronnie. In my youth I ran away from the burdens my parents put on me. I was the reason they had survived, the reward for all the torment they had endured. I could not bear it. I was a good student. I worked on the farm. And yet somehow I was never good enough. I was lazy, conceited. School came too easily. They wanted me to be perfect, but I was determined to be just another American boy in my "lost generation." My link to my parents evolved from an umbilical cord to my car's Bluetooth connection to my cellphone. My father would tease me when I called. "So, you're in the car again. Where you going today?"

Later, as he and my mother grew older, I started to do things just to please them, doing a mitzvah (a good deed). I shaved off my beard to please my mom, my beard inspired by Jerry Garcia and other hippy icons. Before that, every time we visited, she would ask me when I was going to shave. Did it remind her of postwar refugees or the scruffy men who begged on the streets in her hometown in Poland? Finally, I told her if it was really important to her, I would do it. I was visiting them in New Jersey, staying at my brother's house. My nephews looked on in a kind of awed and amused curiosity as the whiskers came off and the face transformed into something a mother could love.

More recently my father asked me if I had a new suit for Rosh Hashanah. I went shopping with my brother, who has always been better at supporting the GNP than I was. He took me to Barneys in Manhattan, where I spent more for one suit than the combined cost of all the suits I had bought in the previous 20 years. The black suit was made of wool that felt more like satin or silk. That suit served me well in a variety of formal settings from synagogue on the high holy days to meetings with IBM executives and dancing with my wife at weddings.

Getting a new suit is another symptom of my father's need to live up to standards set by his community. He is from a small town in Poland with a large Jewish community and now lives in a small town in New Jersey that is mostly Jewish. I identify the different Jewish subcommunities by their places of worship. These groups have limited interactions: the Hasidim, the Americanized Orthodox, and the rest. Layered into these divisions is the divide between immigrants and native-born Americans. In my father's group of immigrant Orthodox, mostly Holocaust survivors from the old world, keeping up appearances has a surprising importance. Dressing up for Yom Tov, for the holiday, is in part a depression-era holdover, an attempt to look decent in your one set of good clothes. It reaffirms one's respect for the holidays. And it marks an effort to get past the age-old images of the dirty Jew and the 20th-century images of refugees in rags. It also signifies the universal pressure to keep up with the Joneses, which seems amplified in small towns.

When I was younger, I pushed back at what I saw as small-town pettiness, but as my parents aged, I would do what it took to bring a smile to my father's face. The battle between generations had long since moved to another set of generations.

My parents' histories and the turbulent 1960s had left me skeptical of humanity's potential. Ronnie restored my faith. Most relationships go through a honeymoon, smiles, hugs, libido, long conversations about childhood dreams, confessions of trauma and sins, forgiveness. The lust may have softened over the years, but the rest bubbled and gurgled, a wellspring. She was my wife, my lover, and my best friend.

Farm Boys

∞

We humans have a long history with farm animals and a tangled language for describing their behavior. Birds and sheep flock while cattle and horses form herds and geese gaggle. Moving them from place to place and rounding them up when they stray are skills every farm boy learns. The truth is they do not want to leave home, and it is mostly just Brownian motion or gravity, or some temptation like greener fields or plumper insects, that leads them astray. Getting them back is usually just reminding them that returning to the barn is the most attractive alternative. It is true for chickens, and it is true for cattle.

I learned about herding cattle from Jude, one of my MIT roommates when I first moved to Boston. He was born in France while I was born in Germany, and we both came to the United States as infants. We both grew up on farms, born to parents who were not really farmers at heart.

My initial experience with herding was with baby chicks. In the first few days of a chick's life, heat is more important than food. A circular cardboard fence, 18 inches high, surrounded each heating stove. The little chicks, making little cheeping sounds, wandered about in their cardboard enclaves, never far from the heat. They grew quickly, moving from cute little fuzz balls to awkward toddlers with nascent wings. Soon the cardboard would come down and the chicks would be on their own, surviving on the heat *they* produced and shared with the rest of the flock. At some point the birds got big enough to hop onto the roosts, and each evening it was my job to herd them up onto those roosts for their nighttime rest.

∞

Jude would never refer to his family's 100 acres as rangeland, but somehow my family called the 15 acres that our chickens roamed in the summer "the range." In May or June, once the baby chicks began to show feathers, we put them out on the range. The range was surrounded by chicken wire about five feet tall, about as high as chickens will ever lift off the ground unless they are in an absolute panic or hurled into the air by some monstrous wind. At the end of the summer we had a big chicken roundup, moving them into the coops for the cold seasons.

During the early years on the farm, our practice of sexing chicks en masse was not an exact science, and some of the male yellow fluff balls got a free ride. The impostors would never lay an egg. When we moved the flock out to the range, their bigger combs and wattles made it harder for them to hide among the hens. The farmworkers would hunt them down; a young rooster makes a nice meal. When you are making a $100 a month, almost any free meal is a nice meal.

Learning about sexing chickens left me burdened with some vocabulary. One word that still has double meaning for me is "venting." It made me smirk when I heard it in high school, and I still get a slight scalp twinge when I hear it in conversation. The word became popular as built-up angers exploded across the end of the 20th century. Venting steam releases built-up pressure. Venting a chicken is prying apart its vent, or anal cavity, to see if you can find any evidence of male genitalia. I do not vent much anymore.

Jude's father had a small herd of Charolais cattle in Pennsylvania some 30 miles northwest of Philadelphia. Jude sometimes called his dad a hobby farmer. He inherited the farm from Jude's grandfather, who had tried to make a go of it as a truck farm. Jude's father was a teacher and school administrator, which made profits from farming a secondary issue.

While my parents were refugees from Europe who had escaped genocide, Jude's parents had escaped to France for a time in their youth. They were bohemians, escaping the doldrums of postwar America by living overseas. Jude's father had studied French literature at the Sorbonne while his mother got a job at a Bic pen factory. They eventually had six children, five boys and a girl. Like most of my friends, Jude was the oldest in the litter. There is something that seems to tie firstborns together. Trailblazers, they are the first to fight out into the light and, until the next child is born, the focus of all their parents' attention, all their hopes and inexperience. Twenty-one of the first 23 astronauts were firstborns. Firstborns are held to higher standards by their parents, given more responsibility. Then, too, something draws firstborns together, one to another, when they leave the heat of the nest. All my roommates in college were the first out of the womb.

Jude's parents' cattle were brood stock originally from the old French commune of Charolles and neighboring Nièvre in the Burgundy region of Eastern France. Big white brutes, the Charolais were a well-established breed in the 16th century; legends date their ancestry back to sometime in the ninth century. They are described as "white in color, horned, long-bodied, and good milkers with a general coarseness to the animal not being uncommon."

On a warm day in early fall 1973, Ronnie, Jude, and I visited Jude's family on their Pennsylvania farm. Themes from the 1960s were still lurking, and the fan base for the Grateful Dead was still growing. At the time, I lived with Jude and Richard, a young man who would profoundly affect my life and career. Jude and Richard had just graduated from MIT. The three of us lived in a railroad flat in Allston, just across the river from Cambridge. A long corridor ran the length of the flat with rooms hanging off the side like cabins in a passenger train. Ronnie lived in the same building with a couple of other women, in a railroad flat just above us.

We had taken LSD that morning. In between moments of enlightenment and fits of euphoric laughter, I was trying to discourage Jude from starting up the chain saw to cut firewood, one of the cyclic chores he enjoyed. Jude liked anything that moved fast. I think he still has a couple of Lotus sports cars in his garage in Hingham. The chain saw's teeth, a speeding blur, filled me with psychedelic terror, currying images of blood spurting from severed arteries and limbs. For all my youthful wantonness, drug-induced dissolution, rebellion, and attempts at non-conformity, I had often assumed the shepherd role when in a group of tripping people. I asked Jude to take us on a tour of the farm—anything to keep him away from the chain saw. Somehow we had missed breakfast that morning, but even without coffee, walking under a bright blue sky through a field of ripe corn with a warm breeze rustling the corn silk was sublime, especially for city kids living in desolate apartments wedged between a discount gas station, railroad tracks, and the Massachusetts Turnpike.

On LSD all the senses intensify: The edges somehow sharpen and disintegrate at the same time. The sunlight screamed. The breeze tantalized. The earth became a marvelous carpet whose textures became manifest with each step, the horizon an unsteady guide. Mostly I remember Ronnie's blue eyes and blinding smile. She was beaming. I felt like an angel had descended from the heavens to walk beside me. A childlike innocence marked each gasp of wonder as the LSD made every leaf and every cloud magical. She picked up some clover, and we passed it back and forth. Her smile would widen when our eyes met. My heart soaring, I tried to hold her gaze. I adored her. I felt like I was falling into her eyes and, dizzy, I had to look away. We were free spirits soaring, but even in our reverie, we tried to be careful to keep contact with the others, to not let our love isolate us from our friends.

Even as we slowly wandered from the woodpile, Jude would persistently return to his theme of sawing wood. He had a solid grip on the chain saw. I was relieved when a more urgent errand overtook us. One of the neighbors, a real estate developer, not a favorite among the locals, drove up in his Oldsmobile. The old-timers wanted to maintain the place's rural character. This man was an agent from the dark side, converting farmland into housing developments. The idling car hissed like a serpent. The electric window slid down smoothly, and the man's head, like a serpent's tongue, slithered out to speak. We were loath to approach him, and fortunately, just as his nose and lips peeked into the light, one of Jude's brothers walked over to deliver the news that the cattle were out.

Earlier, Jude, in preparing us for our wanderings, had warned us about the electric fence that surrounded the herd's pastures. The brutes had broken through the electric barricade and were on the neighbor's land.

Mercifully, Jude put down the chain saw. He gathered us together and gave us a short lecture on herding cattle.

"They don't really respond much to motion. You need to pretend you're a fence closing in around them, and their natural tendency will be to move away from the fence."

I thought of the cows I had seen scratching their hides on fence posts, but I kept quiet. I was working hard at keeping my eyes focused and not letting the colors swim from object to object as I looked at them.

We started walking toward the orchard where the cattle were out. The farm was an intricate network of tractor trails and cow paths, which, even after a week of fair weather, remained muddy in spots. Walking on the dirt I felt connected to the earth. Gravity and inertia seem visceral, powerful forces, but when we set off across the field, the matted underbrush broke that connection. Under the noonday sun, we hurtled through a dense latticework of grasses, hay bent over nettles, and small bushes that hugged the ground. The surface we walked on felt spongy and brittle at the same time, like the crusted ice that forms on snowpack when the weather turns cold after a rain shower. The surface gave way, but we almost never broke through. Walking on this underinflated air mattress left me feeling muddled and disjointed. Jude led on intrepidly while Ronnie and I struggled to maintain headway and balance.

We crossed a little rise, and suddenly the cattle came startlingly close: huge, white megaliths, 2,500-pound bulls that seemed larger than my Volvo. Picture Arnold Schwarzenegger as a cow with a pink muzzle leaning forward and flexing his pectorals, then pump him up to ten times his size and you may get a sense of these muscle-bound beasts.

I waved my hands as though at chicks heading for their roosts. Jude turned toward me. The sudden movement sent his ponytail on a graceful arc through the air. His raised eyebrows reminded me of the plan, and chastised, I spread my arms to become more fencelike. Ronnie's experience with animals was limited to horses and beagles, and she, too, took her cue from Jude, not tempted to use the soothing voice and handful of grain that she would have offered to bring a renegade thoroughbred back to the barn. The cattle now either steadfastly ignored us or gazed at us defiantly. Jude plotted a return course for the beasts, and we arrayed ourselves in a battle line, three or four yards separating one from the other.

The air seemed thicker as we approached, compressed as we pushed it against the cattle. We moved forward shouting and yipping. The cattle too made a bit of noise, grumbling and lowing, shuffling their feet. My eyes were open so wide, the muscles in my forehead ached. I could smell the cattle as we approached, and if their snorting was any indication, they could smell us, too. Miraculously, the beasts began to give way. A moving fence, we shepherded them back to their home turf and then idled about a bit in that special aura that recovering from a disaster provided.

Just as my hallucinatory warning lights were starting to dim and my anxiety to retreat into a manageable state, Jude rounded us up to repair the electric fence. I imagined flashes of electric shocks, like the lightning bolts in a Saturday morning cartoon: Felix the cat with hair on end, eyes bulging and tail stiffening as shock waves pulsed out from his cartoon silhouette. We survived the electric fence acid test and returned from the boundary with the developer's land, past the orchard back to the big farmhouse where Jude's mother, Mrs. Miller, had a dinner of roast beef and Yorkshire pudding waiting for us.

How can I describe what it was like to eat Yorkshire pudding while I was tripping? It was a bit like walking on the spongy field. It left me unsettled and off balance, queasy and at the same time fascinated.

I still think of Jude's farm as a real farm. His family had a tractor and cattle valued as brood stock, while we raised baby chicks and washed chicken shit off eggs that we packed in boxes for supermarkets in New

York City. He would argue that I lived on the real farm because it actually provided my family's livelihood. I loved our farm and I hated it. As I grew up, there was always more work and more responsibility, always some task I could take over to free my father or my mother for other, more important work. My only safe escape was schoolwork. Over the years the whole family began to hate chickens, but somehow I still have a soft spot for baby chicks.

The Stein Sort

∞

*The trouble with the world is that the stupid are cocksure
and the intelligent are full of doubt.*

Bertrand Russell

It was summertime, but in the Big Horn Mountains that stretch across
Montana and Wyoming, there was snow in the air and Lifeline radio
on the airways. We had been driving for 14 hours, two Catholics and
two Jews in a new sedan from one of the General Motors divisions.
Whenever the mountains blocked out the local radio stations, the
Fundamentalists were the only ones left on the radio. It was before the
Fundamentalists had allied themselves with the right wing of the
Republican Party and brought Ronald Reagan to power, but their
anti-Darwin crusade was already in full swing. It was 1972, and barely
finished with adolescence, we were off on tour. For Ronnie and me it
was our first summer together, our first long trip. She was already closer
to me than any person I had ever known. I had sometimes been more
honest with her than I had dared to be with myself.

Bob was a friend from MIT, a short, dark Italian genius, an intense
young man, brooding but warm with a quick smile. His girlfriend,
Helen, was new to Ronnie and me. We had met her once or twice, but

our interactions had been limited to small talk, greetings, smiles, and nods. We were planning to pick her up at her parents' house, but instead she had us meet her up at a rest stop on the New Jersey Turnpike. Puzzled by her motives, Ronnie and I exchanged glances but kept quiet. We didn't want to upset Bob, and we didn't want to do anything that might ruin the chemistry of our little troupe just as we were starting our adventure. Were the directions to her home that complex? Was she embarrassed about her parents? Was she afraid that we would embarrass her or that Bob's beard would scare her parents? We put her backpack in the trunk and set off. After a few hours of driving, she asked us to stop so that she could make a phone call home.

"Um, hi, Sis. Tell Mom and Dad I love them, but I decided to go. They can find the car at …"

Helen had called her sister from a roadside phone booth to let someone know where she had gone.

I could hear her sister shouting at her over the phone: "I'm not telling them that! You tell them! They'll kill you. They'll kill me if they think I helped you! I wish I were going…."

For several days we looked anxiously out the back window, expecting the police to arrest us for kidnapping. Helen's parents knew vaguely about her boyfriend. But they had never heard of Ronnie and me. The days passed and the miles rolled along, and eventually we calmed down and started being paranoid about more normal things like whether the cops would find the tiny stash of marijuana stuffed into the aluminum frames of our backpacks. We put 12,000 miles on a brand-new car that summer.

In the faint glimmerings of an early-morning sunrise on the Atlantic, we headed west in search of blazing sunsets. We cruised through the eastern states with their mix of farmland and industrial conclaves. After crossing the Mississippi, endless flatlands streamed past our windows. Corn and wheat stretched off toward the horizon in every direction, the raised highway a ridge running across the plains. The wonder became tedium, but eventually the surface of the land began a slow undulation: the foothills. We passed through the Badlands of South Dakota, the land of the Lakota Indians and the American bison. We had been adjusting to this new landscape when suddenly we were negotiating tortuous bumps in the Earth's crust named after sheep, the Big Horn Mountains. Before us was a flying buttress set in front of the great divide that splits the continent.

Drawn toward a moonscape called the Badlands National Monument, not a monument built by men but an eerie place set aside by the government in 1939, we wandered in mountains that were towers of shale. Steep ravines cut through striated sediment. The area had been a huge seabed until the sediment that had lurked beneath a shallow sea was pushed up into the dry air. Now streams cut meandering channels through the soft rock of the monuments that rose up. They were not mountains thrust up in volcanic chaos but sculptures chiseled by the fickle waters. Sand and clay and volcanic ash combined in diverse recipes, each layer marking a millennium in a different shade. Fossils of sea creatures pulled from the South Dakota landscape were on exhibit at the visitor center.

We were traveling from national park to national park in search of the nation, bound for Yellowstone with a trunk full of down and nylon and plaid shirts.

Ronnie was behind the wheel smiling and speeding along the mountain highway. Bob and Helen slept fitfully in the back. I had one eye on the road while the other peered out the side window, down the ravines that started just where the roadway ended. I was troubled by visions of careening over the edge, the rough and tumble of free fall, dust rising from the final impact. In New Jersey, they had guardrails on exit ramps. This was ridiculous; it must have been 800 feet to the first ledge that might break a fall. Ronnie giggled whenever my hand reached up to grab the dash. I wished we were still in Kansas.

"And now, another in our ten proofs against evolution!" An eager broadcaster spoke to us over Lifeline radio.

"Consider the archerfish; this little fellow is a freshwater fish no more than six or seven inches long. The archerfish cruises the waters of Java. Now all God's creatures are blessed, but few are as remarkable as this little fish. Friends, if I told you this fish was a hunter and lived off insects, you would say, 'So what?' Any fly-fisher in America knows about fish that feed at the surface. But the archerfish swims just below the surface and shoots a jet of water up at its prey, knocks it down, and then snaps up its dinner. It can hit a mosquito six feet away with the accuracy of a long barrel Smith & Wesson. It can knock a spider out of its web five feet above the stream.

"God gave us the archerfish as indisputable proof of his glorious hand in the creation of all things large and small. Ask a godless evolutionist who believes that men are descended from apes, the evolutionist, accursed in the eyes of God, the heathen who has forsaken Jesus Christ our Savior. Ask this heathen who may be teaching in our public schools to explain the archerfish, and he will be dumbfounded. The Bible tells us: 'And God said, Let the waters bring forth abundantly the moving creature that hath life, and the fowl that may fly above the earth in the open firmament of heaven. And God created great whales, and every living creature that moveth, which the waters brought forth abundantly after their kind and every winged fowl after his kind and God saw that it was good!'

"Yes, friends, God created the archerfish to make his majesty plain to us and to confound those evolutionists."

The regular DJ came on and told us we could write away for the whole pamphlet that explained all ten proofs and would in general maintain us on the path to righteousness.

Ronnie and I laughed uproariously. She pounded the steering wheel in disbelief. I gasped as the car fishtailed briefly. In the back, Bob woke up in a haze and asked what the hell was going on and where the hell were we? I explained about the archerfish and the Big Horn Mountains.

Helen said that the nuns in her Catholic school told the same story as the man on the radio. She and her classmates were taught evolution in high school biology but were told it was a heathen belief, and students knew it was not their place to contradict the nuns. Bob groaned wearily. He knew that there were some in the church who still preached against evolution, but most of his conversations with priests in and out of the confessional had concerned faith and hormones, not evolution.

At my yeshiva high school, our biology teacher was a college professor who also taught at Yeshiva University. He was getting us ready for the New York State Regents exams. Even though it was a religious school, he used a modern text with sections on Lemarck and Darwin. When I asked about the seeming disparity between the biblical creation story and the theory of evolution, the rabbi who taught us Talmud in the morning explained that the seven days of creation could be viewed as a metaphor. Each of the seven days of creation may have been an eternity, but for God eons passed in a single breath, in the time it took us to fill our lungs. God took part in every decision, to make light, to separate the land from the waters. For a while I thought of God as the president of a small corporation, unable to delegate.

Helen said that as a girl she felt sorry for God. He had to worry about everybody and everything. He reminded her of her mother. Helen had more siblings than you could count on both hands. Her mother was a god in her house, worrying about all her children.

"Why do all these folks have such a hard time accepting natural selection? I mean half those cretins are farmers, and they breed cattle and horses." Helen looked out the window at rock faces screaming by us.

Ronnie piped in: "Because nobody wants to believe that people are animals and that having animal desires is normal." I forgot she had my life in her hands and kissed her on the neck.

We were preaching secular humanism to one another. Some see it as its own religion, a belief in the natural order of things. I had given up my search for holiness, and the mantra "Truth is whatever theory best fits the facts" had rushed in to fill the vacuum. Yet for me, the fundamental problem remained: If there was a God, how did He come to be? If there was no God, what was the origin of the dark matter that scientists say exploded to create our cosmos? The photons that rush at us from the sun, the network of neurons that support consciousness, and the archerfish are all wonders. Yet nothing seemed so improbable as the simple fact that matter existed in the void, that there was something, anything—stars, moons, black holes. Nothingness was believable, existence so improbable. Did the master of the universe create us in his image, or did some other miracle leave us wandering about, the culmination of a billion years of evolution? At the time I was afraid that as a species, we were at a dead end, but I still hoped that somehow we were headed for a benign outcome.

Night descended. The snow, a glowing white mask before our headlights, settled as black tears on the rear window. We might have been the last people on earth. Not a car or truck passed by, not a track to mar the fresh snow on the roadway. Bob sat up and leaned forward onto the front seat, dark eyes burning in deep sockets, his bright smile startling against his Mediterranean complexion.

"I used to love those nature shows on TV," he remembered. "Strange animals and weird insects each adapted to its particular environment. Noble beasts, the predators, kill off the small and weak doing the herd a favor. Not like man who killed everything. Even vultures and jackals got good reviews from the narrator. They were like the sanitation department. You might not like the way they smelled or looked, but they provided an important service to the community. They were big on survival of the fittest and the balance of nature. Nature could be cruel, but man was the real monster, the only creature powerful enough to upset the balance.

"Survival of the fittest…fit for what? Fit to survive."

Helen glanced over at him, surprised by his intensity. I wondered if she knew about his brother. Helen had lost a brother, too, an infant, and she sympathized with her mother's grief. Bob's brother was 12 when he died. Ronnie's mother had died when she was an infant, and all of my family, save my parents, had been killed when the Nazis set out to purge the world of Jews. There are those who die as innocents before *they* lose a loved one. But if we live long enough, we all come to live with death. Years later, that sinister thief would reach out to steal from me again.

Back on our road trip, Bob's voice trailed off, and he stared vacantly at the lights and controls on dash. I thought he was thinking about his brother, who had died suddenly in a tragic medical accident. The 12-year-old boy had undiagnosed diabetes. He was very sick at home one night, and Bob's parents took him to the hospital. A few hours after admission, a nurse gave Bob's brother a shot of insulin that put him into insulin shock. He died immediately. His parents never recovered. Bob was 14 when his brother died, and for years he suffered through nightmares in which his brother appeared sitting on his bed and talking to Bob.

Helen jumped in with a tirade on the environment, on how short-sighted and generally fucked up people were. It was the kind of speech we were all good at, full of righteousness; we were too young to have screwed up badly ourselves, so it was easy to cast stones. Perhaps she had missed Bob's mood or this was her way of trying to help him out of it. She seemed to get lost on the surface of conversations. Bob thought she was warm and sensitive; at least, that's how he described her the first weekend she came to visit. I caught myself thinking she must have warm thighs and sensitive breasts but chastised myself, knowing I was not being fair to her or Bob.

After a long climb, we seemed to be on our way down. Ronnie was a good driver. She would steer around the curves and brake on the short straightaway, but it made me a bit uneasy that she laughed when the car picked up speed. The snow stopped and the headlights showed a white ribbon curling first around an outcropping and then an abyss. Bob and Helen had dozed off in the back.

Ronnie whispered:

"Have you ever taken acid when it was snowing?"

"Nope. I did play in some old snow once when I was tripping on the Appalachian Trail."

"Isn't it amazing?"

"What?"

"Snow. A giant flake, a filigreed crystal settles on your hand, and before you know it, it becomes a drop of water running through your fingers." She screwed up her face in a petulant frown.

"Of course, when you're tripping, everything is full of wonder. Have you still got the shell we found that had the map of the universe on it and all the colors of the rainbow?"

"It's on my desk."

"It made some clam a good home once."

"It's so easy to get lost when you're high. Remember Michael Stein? He was tripping and sorting apples. Someone was baking, and the good ones were going to be saved for snacks and the rest were going in the pie. He would pick out two apples and feel them in his hands, look them over real close, and put one in the good pile and the other in the bad pile. He kept reaching for them two by two until we came upon him stuck in a quandary. He had been sitting for quite a while with one apple in each hand, perplexed with two apples both so good he couldn't bring himself to put one in the bad pile. When we asked him what the problem was and it dawned on him how silly he'd been, he started laughing so hard, he was useless for hours. Some of us were computer geeks and had studied algorithms a computer could use for sorting: the shell sort, bubble sort, insertion sort ... The MIT guys in the house gave him an ad-hoc patent and named the sorting technique after him: the 'Stein Sort.' It may not have gained wide appeal, but I didn't think he did all that bad. After all, for every apple in the good pile, there was a worse apple in the bad pile."

Ronnie laughed and jabbed me in the ribs, a reward for my poor but honest tone. I grabbed at the dashboard, reminding her that she held my life in her hands.

For me, the Stein Sort seemed closer to the true path of evolution. Not some choreographed ascent toward perfection, but small accommodations to circumstance and environment. The creatures that survive to reproduce were not always the best but possessed some features that helped them through; they were just a bit lucky about timing and competition when circumstances raised them up to see who would survive and who would perish.

∞

Several days later we were in the desert of eastern Washington driving southwest from Spokane. The sky was ocher, when you could see it. Yellow particles filled the air. It might have been a strange impenetrable fog, but the wind hurled the sand at the windows so that it sounded like a hailstorm. It was hot, but opening the windows filled the car with dust so thick, it was hard to breathe. Thunder bayed and lightning shot red jolts through the dust clouds. I felt like we were on the set of the *Martian Chronicles*. In the middle of a thunderstorm we prayed for rain.

"Jesus Christ!" Helen muttered, face pressed against the window. "Do you believe this? It's just the way I pictured hell. When I was walking back from the bathroom at the rest stop, the sand was flaying skin off my face and arms. For a moment I thought, any minute the Earth will open up and I will find out whether there is fire in hell."

Closed up in Detroit's finest car, a present from Ronnie's father, the car dealer in Scranton, we were forsaken, lost for the moment in the maelstrom. Lifeline radio led us away from foreboding: another in a series of remarkable adaptations, creatures so weird, creatures that relied on such arcane and surreal gimmicks that they stood in defiance, a Fundamentalist's rebuke of science with its cold logic, smooth arcs, and geometric splendor.

Days later, we camped in the Redwoods. I remember the shrieks and giggling, nylon tents beneath an ethereal canopy. In the morning, when Bob and I walked to fetch some water, he told me about one of his teachers.

"In high school I had a teacher who was obsessed with survival, man against nature, man struggling against a hostile environment. Most of the books he made us read were about men trying to overcome nature, fight the sea or the desert or the leviathan."

I wanted to see my dad's survival story in terms of the heroic battle championed by Bob's teacher, but I could not. Dad had struggled for survival, but his struggle seemed less noble, more protean. Dad was not the hero of some classic bout against nature or evil; rather, he was someone who had managed to squeak through cracks, to step aside when the hammer fell on the anvil. He had clung to life, his courage and cleverness manifest. The true wonder of his achievement would only sink in slowly over the years.

Bob continued: "It's sad. People have such awesome power, and we build bombs and strip malls. We could blow up the planet or cover it over in concrete. I wonder where Noah's ark will land after our version of the apocalypse." Bob shook his head and placed his hand on the trunk of one of the redwoods. The tree reached up into the heavens.

Looking up I thought once again of Michael Stein and a dream he had shared with me. In his dream he had died and was in a reception room. The receptionist was busy making copies of paper files and Michael wondered out loud about people using copy machines after they died. The receptionist looked up at him and said, "Oh, yes. We buy them directly from XeroxAfterDeath." She was proud that they bought from the source and not from a middleman. He wondered at the reach of modern corporations ready to sell to our friends and our enemies, even to the dead. Eventually she told him to go down the hall to where the hallways split and choose whether to go to heaven or hell. She warned him to be careful about which he chose since the decision was up to him alone. There were two corridors leading from that room. They were clearly marked heaven and hell. The copy room woman told him to choose where he felt he belonged and scurry along ... it was an honor system. When he got to the divide, he looked up at the signs and, pleased with himself, set out down the corridor to heaven.

There were classrooms along the hallway. He looked into one and a guy at the whiteboard was placing Hebrew letters on a musical staff. As he walked down the hall, he became worried. He often made mistakes, and maybe he had read the sign wrong. He walked for a little while, but there were no more signs. Had he made the wrong choice? He hurried back to where the halls divided. He checked the signs, and reassured he set off again. Long strides, he walked briskly, but as he got farther away from the fork in the road, his steps became tentative, the path gave no hint of its destination, and the nervousness set in again. Had he made the right choice? Could it be this easy? Once again he turned back.

When I heard the dream, I thought it was his version of purgatory, a bit of painful wandering while his soul prepared for heaven.

The lesson he took from the dream was that the way was open, but few of us have the courage to walk down that corridor to heaven.

Richard and
My New Vocation

∞

In the fall of 1972, after a cross-country adventure that put more than 10,000 miles on the new Plymouth Duster that Ronnie's father had given her to celebrate her graduation from Boston University, we were back in Boston. I was moving furniture to earn some money. Ronnie worked the night shift at King Bagel in Brookline, and day-old bagels became a staple in our diet. I was still living with the folks that I met through "Judy the Menace." I had a degree in history but no career plan. I thought vaguely of going to law school or business school, but neither excited me. I was treading water, marking time until one day my housemate Richard suggested that instead of doing unskilled labor, I go to the Massachusetts Institute of Technology (MIT) and learn a trade.

Everyone had a nickname back then. We called Richard "Huckleberry." "I'm your Huckleberry" is a quote attributed to Doc Holliday, the legend from the Old West, meaning "I'm the right man for the job." It can also mean something small or insignificant. In the crowd of MIT geniuses ready to pontificate on almost any topic, perhaps Richard had a smaller voice. Still, he drove around in a massive Mercedes with leather seats, and he always had the most beautiful girlfriends. I'm not sure where Richard got the name, but for me it implied a sweet-hearted country boy, less cynical and more compassionate than the students from the cold cities of the northland. Richard came to

MIT from Tennessee. He could come off like a hayseed, barefoot with straw in his hair, but his parents were Northerners who moved to Oak Ridge, Tennessee, to work in the nuclear research program there.

When Richard suggested MIT, it was like he was reading me an advertisement on a matchbook cover. I wonder about the new generation, youth who never smoked cigarettes, who use matches mostly to light candles or an occasional firecracker or a cannabis stick. Have they seen those "matchbooks" with advertisements for correspondence schools for aspiring artists, secretaries, or detectives? Richard was prescient. A few years after our conversation, ads for computer programmers appeared on matchbooks.

People smoke far less these days, and the few matchbooks we handle are from weddings or bar mitzvahs or restaurants where smoking is forbidden. In 1972 matchbooks were still ubiquitous, often with ads printed on both sides for everything from beer to support hose and a host of academies that promised training that led to a career.

Become a SPECIAL STUDENT in Electrical Engineering at MIT and you too can make $10/hr. PROGRAMMING COMPUTERS in your spare time.

It seemed absurd and unlikely when Richard started lobbying for the idea. Still, the very absurdity of the idea drew me onward, and I found myself talking with an admissions officer at the end of a marble hall in one of the numbered buildings that make up the MIT campus.

After looking at my SAT scores and my mediocre transcript, he said, "If you think you can do this, I won't stand in your way!" I took two courses in a provisional enrollment.

At MIT I felt like I was walking into a science fiction movie with geeky guys, loose wires hanging from racks of electronics suspended over lab benches, vast chemistry labs full of glass beakers that held agents and reagents, and metal cylinders that held gases or liquid nitrogen. Still, in many ways it was like any university with large lecture halls and kids carrying notepads and backpacks full of books. I was turning over a new leaf. I had a second chance to see if I could put my brains to use. It was a less cynical world, a world where kids who had been the smartest in the class were suddenly just ordinary students struggling to keep pace. The odds were pretty good that someone in your class would be nominated for a Nobel Prize. I was terrified and amused to find myself in their company. For the first time in my life I was older than most of the people in my class.

Like the MIT buildings, the courses had numbers, not names. I took classes in course six, electrical engineering. Course number 6.251 was an introduction to computer science, such as it was in those days, punched cards and card readers that had not changed significantly since Herman Hollerith used them in the 1890 census. The old round holes had been transmuted to tiny rectangles so that the cards could hold more data. They became a central part of my life for two semesters.

We were learning to program computers, and a major part of our coursework was programming problems we needed to solve. It is hard to fathom now, as I send video messages and Instagrams to my nephew from my iPhone, but it was a time before keyboards were attached to computers. We sat at keypunch stations and punched up card decks that got submitted to the computer through a card reader, and we got back a printout as a result. Computer screens were just arriving on the scene and reserved for the air-conditioned room that held the beast. Access was limited, and we had only five or six runs to get all the bugs worked out of our programs. Students complained that this was not enough access, that runs were being wasted because of errors made when they punched up the cards. Professor Donovan was amused but unsympathetic. He later became infamous as the professor/entrepreneur who shot himself in the leg in an attempt to discredit his son in a legal battle. That day he held up a stack of cards and turned me into a two-semester legend. "If it's so hard, how did Mr. Kirschenbaum get it right the first time through?" My new career path was confirmed.

I had not been the best of anything since high school geometry. But as in so much of my life, I was floating on top, not like the cream in a milk bottle but more like an insect that had dived into the lemonade. I was no electrical engineer. In most of the sciences I could barely follow the conversations going on around me. But Richard had given me a shove, and I had stumbled into a career in a field that was expanding, a universe undergoing its own big bang. Transistor radios had been a hot high-tech item in the late 1950s and early 1960s, but then Moore's law took hold and the high-tech world began churning out PCs, cellphones, laptops, iPods, and iPads in a gang bang clusterfuck of semiconductors strewing data in unimagined symphonies over the Internet.

The technology that we find embedded in our lives is the result of an oscillation between what is possible and what is popular, between what fills a need and what fills a void, between what can be imagined and what can be produced, and underneath it all is the test of what the market will bear when perceived cost and perceived value overlap. Bubbles sometimes appear as monopolies. One company's overwhelming market share perturbs the curve, but mostly in the world of technology, some breakthrough brings us a new class of products, and progress is manifested through ongoing innovation and a search to drive down costs.

I marched along with the industry. My first job was at Keydata, one of the first companies in the "time-sharing business." Keydata had a large mainframe computer that customers could access over a network with slow teletype-based terminals. The applications were commercial: inventory management, accounting, etc. Customers could use the Keydata applications rather than having to buy their own computers and hire staff to manage them.

My main project was Instinet's electronic stock-trading programs for institutional investors including banks, mutual funds, pensions, and insurance companies. Instinet's service allowed its customers to bypass Wall Street brokers and specialists. It used Keydata's services to automate buying and selling of equity securities on an anonymous, confidential basis.

Today, when most cellphones have high-resolution, touch-sensitive screens, it's a little hard to fathom a time when there were no screens or monitors on computer terminals. In 1973 we used teletypewriters, a keyboard, and scrolling paper. We typed a command and the central mainframe typed back at us, usually at about ten characters per second.

I was a programmer. Writing programs consists of constructing the steps the computer needs to take to make something happen, and in those early days, programming began on paper.

Think of breaking down a task such as getting out of a parking space:
1. Open car door.
2. Get in.
3. Close door.
4. Insert key.
5. Turn key.
6. If car won't start, go to "starting diagnostics."
7. If car starts, check mirrors and adjust if necessary.
8. If there is no one in front of you, go to "starting your trip."
9. Otherwise check space behind you.
10. Put car in reverse.
11. Turn wheel toward ...

The "starting diagnostics" subroutine would check, among others, the battery and gas gauge and, once you started the car, send you back to step 6 to continue working on getting out of the parking space.

Our old egg grader program might look like:
1. Lift gate so that egg rolls down to pickup position.
2. Pick up egg.
3. Move to first counterweight.

4. If egg is heavier than counterweight, release the egg so that it rolls down the table.
5. If it is not, lift egg and move to next counterweight.

At Keydata, building a program to trade stock required designing a user interface to determine:
1. What the user could do: check prices, sell stock, buy stock
2. What the user needed to type at the keyboard to make each of those things happen
3. What the program typed back to indicate success or failure or to ask for more information

Once there was a plan for the user interface, the programmer had to figure out how to get the computer to do all those things. For example: The user can ask for a quote by typing a "?" followed by the stock symbol and then a carriage return. "?IBM" asks the program to type back a current quote for IBM's stock price. The programmer has to construct the steps the computer needs to take and interpret what the user typed.

A crude approximation might be:
1. Read the line.
2. Does it start with a "?"
3. If it does, then take everything until the end of the line and treat it as stock symbol.
4. Look it up to see if it is valid. If not, type back an error message.
5. If it passes muster, send it off to a subroutine that gets the current price.
6. Store the price the subroutine delivered.
7. Get the current date and time.
8. Format a line to print on the teletype.
9. Print "Date, Time, Stock Symbol, Price."

And the teletype prints something like: "02/18/1974: 11:23 AM – IBM - $234.50."

The stock market was crashing in 1973 and 1974. The same query would have returned a price over $360 for IBM in February 1972. Technology was evolving, and the teletype world of Keydata was quickly becoming out-of-date. I started looking for a new job. Richard helped me get my next position at Intermetrics, a company founded by folks from the Draper Lab at MIT, who had worked on the APOLLO moon-landing program. Intermetrics built compilers and other system tools for computers. Compilers are programs that translate high-level computer languages like COBOL, FORTRAN, C, and PL/I into object code, the instruction set a computer processor understands. I worked on HAL, a computer language that Intermetrics designed for NASA, and later on HAL/S, a version designed for the computers on the space shuttle. Another part of the company worked on military software and eventually focused on ADA, a language commissioned by the U.S. Department of Defense (DOD) to replace the dozens of languages used for DOD systems.

HAL was named after Hal Laning, one of the founder's colleagues at the Draper Lab. ADA was named for Ada Byron, Countess of Lovelace, daughter of Lord Byron, the Romantic poet. Lord Byron left Ada's mother soon after she was born, and Lady Byron, in an attempt to short-circuit any inherited poetical tendencies, made sure Ada was trained in music and mathematics. Ada died of cancer in 1852, that is, she died of the bloodletting her physician employed in an attempt to cure her. Ten years earlier she had translated a work on Babbage's Analytical Engine. Babbage had invented the idea of programmable computers, and Ada suggested a set of instructions for the computer that would generate the series of Bernoulli numbers, becoming the world's first computer programmer. Years later, reading Nabokov's novel *Ada*, I remember thinking I could have used a compiler to translate some of the more challenging chapters into a language my untutored processor could understand. His complex allusions cast in Russian and French, snaking through beautiful English prose, sent me lurching about with my *Oxford English Dictionary,* looking for translations to words that sometimes were newly minted puns or anagrams coined by the author.

I was seven years old when the Russians launched Sputnik, starting the "space race." It began my love affair with science and science fiction. Like millions of others, I went out into the front yard and looked up into the sky as the satellite streaked by, a tiny moon, a round ball with antennae, a spider missing four of its legs. Some of the work I did at Intermetrics went into spacecraft that hurtled out toward the planets. The computers on those early spacecraft were cumbersome and slow. They had very little memory. I found that I had a talent for packing programs into small spaces. I am also good at loading dishwashers. Maybe it began with packing eggs, or perhaps watching my Allied Van Lines crew chief deftly pack furniture into moving vans had rubbed off on me.

My friend Tony Flanders wrote a history of Intermetrics that you can still find on the Internet. We both worked in a division headed by Dan Lickly. To quote Tony:

> *Dan's group was that rarest and most enviable kind of organization: a functioning anarchy. Things got done because everyone wanted them to get done. Dan spent most of his time in his office with his feet on the desk, reading magazines. If you went in to ask him for direction, he would listen carefully, and then, nine times out of ten, snort and go back to his magazine, implying that it was up to you to make the decision. If not for Valerie, his secretary, things would have deteriorated into total pandemonium. As it was, we tolerated a high degree of chaos as the price of freedom.*

Dan had worked at Draper Labs on reentry software for the Apollo moon-landing program. He was also the pitcher on our company's fast-pitch softball team. He had a gift for hiring people who were smart and interested in making things happen. Computing had a short history in the 1970s, and computer science departments had just started to appear at engineering schools. Dan hired an eclectic set of folks. Personal recommendations carried a lot of weight with him. Once he hired someone, he gave him free rein. Many of my roommates wound up working there, part of a large MIT contingent. I even helped Ken

Nappa, my old yearbook mentor from high school, get a job in the division.

Today, with casual Fridays and "fun consultants" helping improve the atmosphere in the workplace, I think back to Raymond Spears. He was part of the Caltech contingent at Intermetrics. His long hair and beard didn't really set him apart from the rest of us, but Ray almost always walked about at work barefoot. We had a lot of folks who would make good fodder for situation comedies, but Ray stood out. When he was told he needed to go to Florida to do some on-site work for NASA, Ray disappeared for three days. People panicked. Where was he? Had he booked a flight? Well, Ray had grabbed a backpack and hitchhiked from Cambridge to Cape Canaveral. I wonder if he had packed shoes. I used to get postcards from him and his boyfriend, with their picture standing at some landmark from the site of each year's solar eclipse. Nowadays it is email. One year it was from the Burning Man Festival in the Nevada desert.

Dan's group had some hippies and some geeks, a couple of evangelical Christians, and a high degree of tolerance for diverse outlooks. It was also a hardworking group with high standards for the software we produced.

I found I had another talent. I could bridge the gap between the weirdos in Dan's group and the rest of the company. For John Miller, our company president and a West Point graduate, walking into Dan's part of the building must have been a bit surreal. John always wore a business suit. He was tall, well scrubbed, and genial, with the posture of a military man. He was rarely seen in our quadrant and almost never stopped to talk to Dan's troops. Our part of the building was a bit of a circus. The narrower halls had handprints on the walls near the ceiling left by folks learning to ride a unicycle. Offices were sometimes decorated like dorm rooms. In some of the conference rooms there were dents in the wall where flying juggling pins had gone awry as people practiced tossing them back and forth to one another. I have to admit, I was one of the jugglers. I still have juggling pins in my closet, and I occasionally find myself juggling oranges as I wait in line at the checkout counter.

John always dressed meticulously. He was tall and had a majestic bearing, erect and proud, his balding head gleaming in the sun streaming through the skylights in the main corridor. Yet somehow he felt comfortable with me. My Jewish Afro did not put him off, and the blue jeans and flannel shirt were OK with him. Maybe it was because he had seen me dressed in a suit for a client meeting, wearing shoes with my suit instead of sneakers. We did not have access to the computers from our offices. We still wrote code in pencil or marked up printouts before sitting down at the terminal areas to interact with the mainframes. One of the terminal area activities was called the "pencil skill game." The pencil game, hmm. I do not really remember it as a game, just something to kill time while waiting on a slow time-sharing connection. We learned to throw pencils so that they would stick in the acoustic tiles that made up the dropped ceiling of our offices. I was sitting at one of the computer terminals when John walked up. He looked at the ceiling with dozens of pencils embedded at odd angles and shook his head. "Do they do that on purpose?"

These terminals also connected to precursors of what was to eventually to become the Internet and the World Wide Web. For several years the tubes we stared at were text-based, but eventually graphic color terminals started appearing. They could display characters in different colors, but more amazingly they could also display images.

Over time terminals were replaced by PCs.

The IBM PCs had been around for a while, but they were these clunky expensive things useful mostly for text processing and spreadsheets. They were so expensive that when the new Intel 80286 processor came out, Dan and my old roommate Jude and a few others started a company called Applied Reasoning that was going to sell replacement boards for PCs so that people could take advantage of the newer processor without spending thousands of dollars for a new PC. It was an ill-fated venture. The cost of PCs dropped precipitously, and the rationale for keeping your old one and trying to juice it up disappeared and so did our company.

Sometimes necessity drives innovation, and often innovation flies off on its own leaving things in trash bins, but occasionally it brings unexpected benefits. All of this innovation operates within a constraint system of what is possible today, what people can imagine in the near term, and envision in a more distant future. The hardware drives the software, and then the software drives the hardware. Everything gets faster, smaller, and cheaper. The high-definition TiVo box I bought in 2009 is a digital video recorder with a million times more storage than the computer on the first probes we helped NASA send out into the solar system.

After Applied Reasoning, my next stop was Data General, a company that still made computers in New England, before everything moved to California and Asia. Suddenly, I was in corporate America, not quite with an insurance company, but managers were expected to wear ties and talk about the bottom line.

I did not last long at DG. Richard saved me. He was working at the Lotus Development Company famous for the spreadsheet software, Lotus 123. When I was hired, Lotus was beginning to lose the spreadsheet wars to Microsoft's Excel. A new product, Lotus Notes, an email and "groupware" software, was becoming more and more central to Lotus company strategy. Lotus was just coming to grips with rolling out "Notes" internally as the company email. Richard was in charge of getting Notes up and running. The same fellow who convinced me to go to MIT hired me at Lotus to, at least in part, make sure Lotus itself took advantage of the "groupware collaboration" capabilities of Notes. Lotus bought IRIS, a small software house, to get Notes and then, when IBM acquired Lotus, it bought Notes.

At Lotus, one of my friends pointed me to a new piece of software called Mosaic, the first web browser. I used it to start poking around this new thing called the World Wide Web. Mosaic had a graphical user interface, but the websites I found were still mostly text. It was 1995 or 1996 when I stumbled on WebLouvre: "a World Wide Web exhibit" that invited me to:

- Visit a French medieval art demonstration
- Explore a collection of well-known paintings from famous artists
- Take a tour around Paris, the Eiffel Tower, and the Champs-Élysées

As I explored the collection, image after image appeared on the screen: paintings by masters from Rembrandt to Mondrian, Matisse, and Klee. As I clicked through the site, I felt weightless, giddy, floating in the ether. A paradigm had shifted underneath me as I squirmed in my chair.

Many of my friends still viewed anything that smacked of corporate governance as part of the establishment. It was OK to be an engineer, but anyone climbing up the management ladder was suspect. Richard may have climbed into this category. He went to MIT's Sloan School of Management to get his MBA. He was a good manager, concerned about the troops, but also clearly aware of corporate goals. Lotus was not the "controlled anarchy" of Dan's group at Intermetrics, not quite a new age company, but it tried to be hip. "Hip" feels like an old word, those "hep cats" jiving. But some of the synonyms capture the mood of the place: up-to-the-minute, informal, trendy, cool, styling/stylin', with it, in, happening, now, groovy, funky, sharp, the in thing, phat, tony, fly.

Looking at them now, the adjectives seem a bit over the top. IBM bought Lotus before "phat" and "fly" hit the mainstream vocabulary. Lotus, struggling to be a hip company, grew into a sizable corporation that was subsumed by a well-run megalith. When I joined Lotus, you were truly hip only if you were part of product development. The sales force, the administration, the folks doing product support had less cachet.

Working for Richard, my little group had developed Notes applications. I made presentations and trained various work groups inside the company. In my wanderings, I had stumbled into a new job with a great title: Product Manager for Advanced Technology. It was 1992. I had a huge corner office that looked out at Boston, across the Charles River. The office was far more impressive than the job warranted. Still, I did get to go to trade shows and talk to clients about emerging technology like Video Notes, a kind of business YouTube that was about a decade too early for what the infrastructure would bear (the networks were way too slow then for video).

Later, I would join Richard as one of the partners in The Jacobson Group, a "groupware consulting company" that specialized in Notes. My largest client was IBM's Management Development group.

I had studied history before coming to Cambridge and finding Richard and MIT. The first histories are the histories of tribes. The members reinforce tribal identity with stories and myths from the past. Then the history of individuals takes over, especially in the West: kings, generals, business leaders, artists, and inventors. Modern treatments of history are rich with social movements, ecology, and geography. Richard was a prime mover for my career, which had a geographical nexus in MIT's Technology Square, where KeyData, NASA, and IBM all had offices in the same complex.

My father never really understood my work. In his immigrant English he would say: "He works by computers." He was in his late eighties when he first sat down in front of a PC. It was in the office that he and my brother shared in their construction business, a converted 1950s single-family house. Dad had retired, but he still worked on a few projects in the central Jersey countryside. Dad had learned how to get stock quotes from the Internet. He was delighted.

"You should see. I give a 'kvetch' and it shows me everything."

Sam and Marion

∞

When I try to understand Ronnie's life, I find myself thinking first about her father, Sam. She basked in his love. Her burdens assuaged, her edges softened, an infant's radiance gurgled and cooed when she held him in her thoughts or found herself in his presence. Sam loved his daughters, but heartbreak tangled his steps and melancholy infected his humor. Sam had also had a true love, a fairy-tale love, but like so many of those fairy tales, dark shadows waiting nearby, a warning to those who heard the tale.

Marion Mittleman was one of the local Scranton girls. Sam Lebensbaum was young and handsome, a sharp dresser, witty, a college graduate, a man about town. It was the eve of America's entry into WWII, but for a while Marion was just a college girl in love. She was living at home and so was he. They dated. They spooned. Then Sam joined the army.

They wrote to each other incessantly. She saved his letters and he saved hers. Whenever the army moved him, Sam sent bundles of her letters back to her and asked her to keep them for him. He carried all their letters with him 50 years later when he came to Massachusetts to be near his daughter.

Marion's nickname was Mink. Like her namesake, she bore shiny brown hair and a sprightly, mischievous demeanor. She was living in the dorms at the beginning of the fall semester in 1943.

Marion

Just got back from the movies with the class. I'm sitting on the bed trying to put my PJ's on and write at the same time. Light's out. Gee, it's dark in here. Wonder where you are, what you're doing, what you're thinking of. Good Night. —Mink

The world was at war, but an innocent, unembarrassed love still flourished. The tenderness in Sam's and Marion's letters makes them painful to read. They are mushy, even sappy, and gloriously unaffected. But there is humor and irony, too. Sam's letters reveal pride in the money he won at playing poker with the boys, sarcasm about his role in the army, and a teasing sexuality; there are cloaked and uncloaked references to intimacy and lightweight barbs tossed out to provoke jealousy. Also a recurring hint of uncertainty creeps in.

Of late your letters sound platonic. Have you renewed warm friendships with old acquaintances or have you acquired new ones? You just don't act like my gal. Hope I'm wrong.

I know you love me.

Do you ???

Do you ??

Do you?

Sam and Marion were like so many during a war that tore millions of men from their homes.

Five minutes before lights out and while I sleep, I'll tenderly hold your sacred possession and make believe you are alongside me. God's gift to womanhood, Sam.

I thought of buying a music box, but somehow it seemed more appropriate for an older person (you and I can make our own music—Remember?) Don't give up hope, flowers and music may drop in unexpectedly someday. All of me. —me

I picture him on guard duty at his base in Georgia. Hours of tedium, hazy white sun, humid heat dulling the senses. Sweat dripping in the armpits of his uniform, the occasional visitor to be challenged and vetted.

While I was on security duty last week I had the strangest vision. (It's not like me because I'm not sentimental). There you were in your grey plaid skirt and vest with a white blouse (eagle on the sleeve) sitting in the restaurant in Wilkes-Barre. Suddenly you said: "Sammy, I want to call my mother." You made the call to say, "Sammy passed for the Army." Tears welled up in your eyes, but you said, "I'm not crying".

In the meantime all the people in the restaurant gazed at us wonderingly. I'll bet they thought we were a love sick newly married couple. You know. I can recall every incident that happened with and between us since we met, yet I can't recall yesterday. See you in nine days. Love, Sammy

The pages are dotted with humor. In a unit preparing for an amphibious assault, Sam jokes that he is getting ready to invade Goat Island near Niagara Falls and secure it from the Canadians. But even that story is overlaid with hints at Bridal Falls and honeymoon couples. Sometimes he includes jokes that could have come from a Borscht Belt comic.

A friend of mine told me about this sailor who was doing the breast stroke until he got smacked in the face by a cold wave.

There was a woman who complained in court about a thief whose hand crept up her leg and took money from inside her stocking.
  The judge asked why she didn't resist.
  She replied (pouting), "How was I to know what his intentions were?"

Sam, the soldier, surrenders: *You won the battle. It was a tough fight while it lasted, but you won the battle sugar. I'm convinced. I'm defeated completely and totally without you.*

In one letter, Sam had tucked in a folded-up picture of a Vargas girl in a bikini, her fingernails painted a bright red. A finger was held to red pouting lips, the woman's wide blue eyes asking for quiet. Beside her were written these words:

Bob writes me from the tropics
And beefs about the heat
Ned writes me clear from England
Where taverns are his meat
Jim writes me from an air base
And his gags are fresh and smart
But I'll never spill what I hear from Bill
He writes me from the heart.

In the same letter Sam voiced concerns about not getting time off to go to the chapel for Yom Kippur and trying to make sure his mother would not find out.

Sam suffered some injuries over the course of the war. He wrote from a San Francisco military hospital teasing Marion about the nurses and the WACs (Women's Army Corps) who visited the soldiers.

Maybe it's because your picture is staring somewhere in my direction. You seem so close and yet I can't put my arms around you. I believe

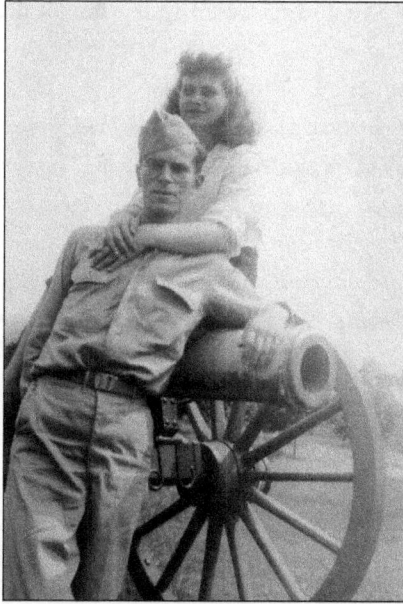

Sam and Marion

I worked up an awful fever just thinking about you. The nurse will be here shortly to take my temperature. Hope I won't shatter the thermometer. Fond caresses! Sweet Dreams. Your Lover, Sammy

Marion's letters are a little less tongue in cheek.

I haven't had a letter in days. If you stopped writing because you didn't feel like it I won't be responsible for my actions. I have your picture in front of me and, as I write, there you are smiling at me. Honey, maybe God will be good to us and it won't be long before you're here, really here, smiling at me. Sometimes when I'm in bed and can't sleep, I wonder if you're thinking of me. Wonder whether you love me as I love you?? If my prayers are answered, honey, you'll be a happy man. I pray that throughout your life your fondest hopes and dreams are fulfilled whether they include me or not. I love and miss you. Mink

Sam was in the San Francisco military hospital because of a leg infection.

> *I hope I didn't scare you when you called. Friday evening the doctor walked into my ward and casually told me: "Tomorrow I'm going to do a sympathetic block on you. If it works out it will reduce the pain and swelling in your legs." I wasn't quite sure if that was an operation, but he said no it's just a spinal. … then the nurse brought me a printed form which I had to sign:*

While cut open during the operation if the doctors thought it was advisable to remove any part of my body they were at liberty to do so!

> *You can understand why I thought that he would operate despite what I had been told. I refused to sign the form. The nurse assured me it was only a spinal. When I asked the other nurses what was in store for me they were somewhat evasive. They gave me a green pill to "help me rest." I was asleep when they came in to tell me I had a phone call from you.*
>
> *At 5:30 in the morning they woke me to get me to take another pill. I refused and by 7:30 the whole staff knew I had refused the pill. At 8:45 I was given a fresh gown and my head was covered with a clean white cap like the caps maids wear when they are dusting and they put me on a table and wheeled me into the operating room. You can see how my imagination worked, more and more I believed they would do more than just a 'block.' It's not that I'm afraid of an operation, but I hate to have a so-called fast one pulled on me. I just like things to be on the up and up. They were collecting clamps, sterile cloths and other instruments. The doctor began scrubbing his hands then put on rubber gloves and a mask over his mouth as the nurses, also wearing masks, painted my back.*

Sam came out of the operating room in a cold sweat, with parched lips, dry heaves. Finding his legs temporarily paralyzed did not improve his

Ronnie and Marion (Sissy)

faith in doctors. He struggled to recover for years after the war ended, enduring chronic health problems and shuttling from one military hospital to the next.

But Sam and Marion stayed connected. Their love held on, and they eventually married. Rhonda was born just over a year later, in 1951. They were a happy couple, a young veteran with a new business, a college girl with her new blue-eyed infant. Just two years later Marion died giving birth to her second child.

The little girl was named Marion, after her mother. But tears welled up in everyone's eyes when they spoke her name, so they called the infant Sissy or Sis. She even signed her Father's Day cards "The Sister."

Sam's true love had died. He was crushed. He focused his love on his daughters, but somehow Sissy remained in the shadow, smaller, quieter. Rhonda's cards for Sam's birthday and Father's Day were hand-made. Sissy's were from Woolworth's. Sam saved them all. Rhonda inherited the ability to love unconditionally. For Sissy, life has been harder.

I fell in love with Rhonda, that poor motherless child. Reading her parents' letters, I understand where she inherited the genes for romantic love: mooning eyes, an emotional focus that rushes toward its target like a flooding stream. In that torrent, in that love storm, I floated not like a weathervane tossed about in the wind but like a compass always aligned by a powerful magnetism.

When his wife died, Sam was still a young man, but he never remarried or dated openly. Perhaps he was loath to find happiness, to betray the dead. The evil stepmother was still a dominant stereotype. Perhaps he feared for his daughters' happiness. Single-parent households were rare, and faced with caring for an infant girl as well as a toddler, Sam took the girls and moved in with his wife's parents, the Mittlemans. When I first met Sam 20 years later, he still seemed like a visitor in their house.

Grandpa Mittleman was an earnest working man. He was quiet and reticent, and his English was clumsy. I almost never heard him speak. He was kind to the girls, but their attention focused on Grandma. Over the years, she grew heavier and less mobile, yet she remained a force in the household, cleaning and cooking. She put on weight and gravity pulled the flesh down. She rarely left the house. By the time I met her, she looked like an overweight penguin, her gait a side-to-side shuffle.

In the house politics, Rhonda allied with her father and Sissy with her grandmother. Grandma was industrious almost until she died. She kept a clean kitchen, did the laundry, and cooked the meals. The girls were largely excluded from the basic chores.

Sam worked as a used-car dealer. He was a sociable fellow in the marketplace, but he lived mostly in a society of men. It's said he had a girlfriend for a while and that they would meet at her apartment, but it was not a public affair, and I am certain he never spoke of it to the girls. I heard about it from people on his wife's side of the family. As they told the story, they somehow implied that he was cheating on his dead wife. Was he taking advantage of her parents who helped to raise his daughters while he took some solace elsewhere? Why keep it secret? Maybe she wasn't Jewish, and though he lived a secular lifestyle, was that still an embarrassment? Perhaps he simply did not want his daughters to know.

His wife's sisters lived nearby, and though Sam's mother was still alive and his brothers lived in town, the girls grew up in the Mittleman clan. The Lebensbaums were like relatives from some distant country. Sam's brother Irving was a simple man. He might have been considered slightly retarded. His older brother, Al, had married an Irish girl, Rose, and moved to Baltimore. He was such a good-hearted soul, it was hard to censure him, but for the Mittleman clan, there was still some discomfort with Al's marriage outside the faith.

Aunt Sarah and Aunt Dottie, their mother's sisters, were the closest to mother figures the girls had. Sarah was small and taut, with a high-pitched voice, earnest but with a tinge of sarcasm if you listened for it. Dottie was softer, more debonair, more at ease with the ways of the world.

Ronnie and I were driving to Scranton for my first visit. It was early 1973. We were on the Massachusetts Turnpike about an hour out of Boston with four or five hours of driving ahead of us. She was trying to prepare me for her family, for her grandmother, but especially for her sister. Sissy was shorter than Ronnie with a smaller frame, but the same bright eyes. Ronnie explained that she was very thin, a fussy eater, and that she had a chilly relationship with their father. It was her way of telling me that Sissy was anorexic. At one point she had become dangerously underweight. At five feet two inches, she had weighed less than 70 pounds. She looked like one of the starvation victims from the Holocaust. She thought she was just fine, but the family was frightened. Against her strong objections, the family had sent her to an institution to help her deal with her anorexia. She never forgave her father for locking her up for treatment. After being released, she carefully managed her weight to some threshold set by the doctors. When I met her, I think she weighed 85 pounds. Anorexia is a complex syndrome, but her history made it easy to jump to conclusions. Her mother died giving birth to her. As an adolescent starting to develop sexually, the starvation held off any signs that she was becoming a woman. No hips, no thighs, almost no breasts. It also was a way to be in control, to assert herself against a household where her grandparents were obese.

Had I not been prepped for the meeting and had I not known that Sissy was 20 years old and enrolled in a local college, my first impression would have been of a fairly normal girl, a prepubescent 12-year-old. Trying to do right by Sissy was a burden her father would carry all his life.

Sam always bemoaned the fact that he was not closer to us, but he stayed in Scranton trying to take care of Sissy, tied into his car business and the Mittlemans. In early 2000, he was aging and living alone. The grandparents had died. Sissy had moved to Maryland to teach in a Montessori school. When we finally talked him into looking for assisted living, he was ready to consider moving to Massachusetts. He was coming here to live out his last days. We tried to make him feel welcome and at peace, but fate follows its own schedule and there is no deadline for *tsuris*.

Ronnie

∞

Ronnie's family moved to a "better" neighborhood when she was in high school, but as a child in the 1950s, she had lived in Scranton's South Side "flats," a working-class neighborhood in the flood plain between the Lackawanna River and Nay Aug Creek.

Before our first visit, Ronnie had drawn me a map of the block she lived on as a kid: It showed Munchak's Funeral Home, the beer garden, the barbershop, the Catholic Mission.

"We lived two flights up in an apartment over Munchak's Funeral Home. Our front yard was the concrete sidewalk where my sister and I wheeled our doll carriages and rode our bicycles.

"Sometimes we visited our friend Joe West, the barber, just two doors down the block. His comic books were really good. Not romance like Cousin Leah read, but *Tarzan, King of the Jungle,* and *Superman.* He gave us presents, brightly colored plastic combs tucked into vinyl sleeves with his name on them in gold print. He had two barber chairs. If no one was waiting, he let us spin around in the extra chair until we were thoroughly dizzy little monsters. Then we'd stumble back out onto the sidewalk and stagger around.

"The Catholic Mission showed movies, but we weren't allowed to go there because Grandma said the nuns could turn us into Catholics if we weren't careful. But when they showed movies and if Grandmother was upstairs, we would risk it.

"Grandma said the mission kids were dirty and had bugs in their hair. If we went too close, we would get bugs in our hair, too. I dreamed about thousands of bugs crawling on my scalp.

"On sunny days we went skipping down the sidewalk playing 'step on a crack, break your mother's back.' Even as a five-year-old I knew it was not really true. And, anyway, *my* mother was in heaven and out of harm's way. She watched over me. Dad said so.

"But if Mom was watching over me, what would she think if I purposely or even carelessly stepped on a crack? Would she be insulted? Angry? Disappointed in me? I tried never to step on a crack even when we weren't playing. It was the only thing I could still do for her."

Ronnie was in her twenties, but when she told me the story about the cracks in the sidewalk, she became a schoolgirl again, blue eyes shining, curls dancing around her ears. Her eyebrows, a little too dark for her face, could make her smile seem demonic.

Scranton had been in decline Ronnie's entire lifetime. The anthracite capital had fallen on hard times as coal gave way to other fuels. The population was cut in half between the end of WWII and my first visit in 1973. I remember Grandpa was a taciturn working man. Tall and still solid when I met him, though he died just a few years later. Grandma was the center of the house, just over five feet tall, with sloped shoulders and full breasts almost always hidden behind an apron. Her daughter had been dead more than 20 years, but she still carried the weight of the loss, even when she smiled at her grandchildren.

The apartment was sad, with aging wallpaper, old furniture, the wood carefully polished, the upholstery frayed, covered with blankets so that the dog could jump up without doing any more damage. Ronnie's father had his own apartment, but I didn't see it until his health took a turn for the worse years later and he was preparing to move in with his in-laws. Ronnie and her father had a special relationship. When he looked at her, he glowed like a man being handed his newborn infant for the first time. Sam's clothes seemed a bit faded, his belly soft. He appeared sober and careful when speaking to adults. A bit of wry humor was on tap for his friends, but for his daughters he had a separate voice.

Sam and Ronnie

I think Ronnie took from her father her ability to love unconditionally. I am in his debt. His love for her was without restraints. They
were a mutual admiration society. For him she remained a princess, an
angel, all her life. When she walked into the room, when she called on
the phone, his countenance changed. Sam was a cautious man, a bit
cynical, beat up by the fates—a beloved wife who died in childbirth,
old war wounds that made each step unsteady. Yet, when he was near
Ronnie, even when he spoke of her, his face would light up and his
voice would soften.

He had taught her to love, and the fates let that radiance, that
blinding light, shine down on me. I bathed in its glory. What did I do
to deserve her? It was not a reward but a gift, a treasure that I stumbled
upon. I was 22, a young man still always in heat, looking for a warm
embrace, for passion, for relief. But somewhere in that creature being
led through life by his gonads was another who searched for romance,
for a soul mate.

Mercifully, in college I did find the occasional young woman who would diminish my sense of sexual hopelessness. Yet I still felt like a pretender, a beneficiary of a sexual revolution spawned by others. Sarah, my brief flame on the kibbutz, gave me hope, but with the few other girls that I dated, I was trying to find a way to make love, not believing I could fall in love, not believing I could be loved.

Ronnie was not eager to get in bed with me, and I would soon discover that she was a virgin. Not quite the anachronism it seems to be today, but still unusual for a college graduate in the mid-1970s, in a big college town like Boston. We were both shy, both introverts. When I looked at her, I found myself lost in the wonderland of her azure eyes. I had fallen off a cliff and floated in a daze, unconcerned with gravity. Still, my heartbeat quickened. I had to look away before I could speak. Thoughts would not organize themselves when locked in her gaze.

Amazingly, I soon found that I could talk to her and laugh with her about high school, the days full of yearnings, full of hormones. I had despaired of finding someone who would love me if they saw me as I was. I had been a teenager with acne. A boy who got braces late in his teens and refused to smile and show the metal gleam, the little freight train of teeth in metal jackets, rubber bands providing traction for an agonizingly slow realignment. When I look at old photos, I look fairly thin in high school, but I held on to the image of a chubby kid wearing "husky" pants, plump cheeks looking out from my bar mitzvah photographs. Even after my bones stretched out into a six-foot frame, the belly looked back at me. I was jealous of the athletes in the locker room with their flat abs and bulging biceps.

Unlike her anorexic sister, Ronnie had a more typical history for a woman in the second half of the 20th century. Her ongoing struggle to lose a few pounds left us with a shelf of weight-loss books that traced the history of fads and "best practices." Weight Watchers, Dr. Stillman's diet, set-point theory, aerobics, the Pritikin diet, *Beyond Pritikin, Fit or Fat,* and *Fat Is a Feminist Issue* were some of the places we traveled in search of a more perfect body.

When I met Ronnie, she was a recent BU graduate but still carried most of the "freshman ten." I thought she looked great; I have always been more drawn to fleshy Renoir women than to Twiggy types. Over the 30 years that I knew Ronnie, she bounced around between 115 and 155 pounds. At her thinnest she reminded me of her sister still finding fat on a trim and healthy body. She would ask me if she looked fat and then ignore my response.

Were her breasts too small? Did people notice that one was slightly smaller than the other? I worked at convincing her that she fell short of Reuben's excesses, looked more like Renoir's bathers, the full thighs and bottom an erotic wonder to me. Fleshy, buxom actresses like Marilyn Monroe and Jane Russell had been the archetype for female beauty. Now the women's movement was encouraging women to build strong bodies. Diana Rigg and Jane Fonda became the new icons. Ronnie became an aerobics queen, a dancer, a confident feminist. She even dragged me to some dance classes and we became jitterbug jujus. We spent a brief period in an acrobatic swing dance troupe, and she loved to fly through the air sailing across my back or landing on my shoulders, spinning on the dance floor as though she were still in Joe West's barber chair. Each phase was a new wonder, though I felt a bit of nostalgia for what was left behind. Feminism and dancing eventually brought Ronnie to a point where she was relatively happy with her body.

She struggled with her weight, and she struggled with her hair. I can still hear the voice of one of my mother's friends, a heavy Yiddish accent. "Darling, you have such nice curly hair!" Nevertheless, Ronnie wrapped the shiny auburn mass around her head, tied it up in a long ponytail, or worked half a dozen other ways to straighten the hair so that it would hang down to below her kidneys. My hair, a mass of unruly curls, would never succumb to the polished look of the Brylcreem man. The "little dab will do ya" didn't work for me, and so I thought: "The gals just won't pursue you." By the time I met Ronnie, the braces had come off and hippie hair was in fashion, my Afro part of an entrenched counterculture. It took a few tears, a few years, until fashion or feminism allowed Ronnie's locks their freedom, and my black curls could mix with her brown ones as we shared a pillow.

A compassionate listener, Ronnie was ready to suspend disbelief and keep her sardonic side in check as friends shared their burdens.

Richard's wife, Barbara, was struck with a mysterious disease. Crippling pain crushed her, and she would find herself writhing on the floor. The doctors were stumped. Was it psychological or physical? Barbara pushed on all fronts, desperate for relief. She sometimes stopped in to visit coming from therapy and talked to Ronnie. Ronnie listened to Barbara recount her therapy, a story of a foreign land with strange people. Not comfortable with a psychiatric vocabulary, Ronnie persisted with an active, empathetic presence, ready to share the weight of the sufferer's burden, helping just by listening, great big blue eyes watering slightly as she helped them endure.

Ronnie read voraciously, often absorbed in two books at once. When she found an author she liked, our bookshelves soon contained the collected works: Gabriel García Márquez, Jean Rhys, Cormac McCarthy, Ian McEwan, Anne Rice, and Penelope Lively were among them. A panoply of contemporary authors occupied the shelves beside Faulkner and Hemingway and Twain. Occasionally she would insist that I read one of her new "finds." I remain in her debt.

Sunday mornings I would invariably find Ronnie in the study with her *New York Times* crossword puzzle and the *Times Book Review*. She loved language and art. Understated, frivolous, carefree, yet she possessed a fierce dignity about her person, not born of pride or arrogance but rather from a faith in the dignity of all living beings. This loyalty to herself Ronnie extended to her friends. She had a way of making people feel special. When you talked to Ronnie, you always had her full attention. She took joy in small things and never took herself too seriously. She loved to laugh. Her smile would melt your heart and light up the room. We shared a brand of humor that ranged from a caustic deadpan to a warm, almost melancholy mirth.

While my folks kept poking at us trying to get us to dress up, to stop wearing our torn jeans, Ronnie's dad was happy to see her no matter what she was wearing. Ronnie told me a story about going out to a fancy restaurant with her dad and her friends, Pearl and Colleen.

"The place had white tablecloths and two wine glasses at each setting. Colleen was in her hippie summer phase and walking around the city barefoot. It was a little gross. Her feet would be black by the end of

Ronnie

the day, but it was part of her 'freedom of expression' thing. Anyway, the maître d' was upset about it and said they had a strict policy against seating anyone who was barefoot. Dad tried to offer the guy a few bucks, but he wasn't having any of it. 'No shoes. No seats.' Dad asked him if sandals were OK, and the maître d' said yes. Dad dragged us back to his car where he pulled out some cardboard and string. He had Colleen stand on the cardboard and drew an outline of her feet. Then he took out a Swiss army knife he always carried, and we made Colleen a pair of cardboard sandals. The jerk in the restaurant raised his eyebrows and wrinkled his nose, but gave us a table." The triumph, the pride in her father, came through in her voice every time Ronnie told the story.

When I met her, she wasn't a girly girl. No nail polish, no high heels or flouncy skirts. Makeup was a smear of lipstick reserved for Halloween and a few other special occasions. But there was no mistaking her femininity. If anything, Ronnie was a girl comfortable in a phase before getting all dolled up mattered, not trying to be a doll but still playing with dolls, with rubber stamps, with colored pencils and India ink.

It wasn't until we started dancing that she reached out toward a different look, a different way of presenting herself. For a woman, dancing swing and jitterbug without a skirt and heels meant missing half the fun. Pants were briefly a statement of liberation for women, but pants, except for maybe hot pants, were not true to the nostalgia, the raucous revelry, that swing music inspired. You spun to have your skirt fly up, to tantalize with athletic legs, stockings, garters, or panties if you dared. The stance you took in heels forced energy up from the toes through the calves and thighs to the rump, the sexuality an implied and explicit part of the art form.

Dancing helped Ronnie become more comfortable with her body. She had always been shy, a girl without a mother unsure of herself when she was not among friends. Not one of those "liberated" women who swam naked or pulled their T-shirts off at rock concerts. Even in private, in our bed, she agonized over her breasts, yearning for some fearful symmetry, a goal outside her reach. I tried to convince Ronnie that her breasts were beautiful, each one a marvel, a delight, so little different that she had convinced herself of some disparity only after hours of study in front of the bathroom mirror.

In the 1970s, Ronnie belonged to the Boston Women's Graphics Collective. They were artists whose work focused on feminist issues and more broadly on sources of pride for women. Forty years later, I found a piece of Ronnie's from that period while visiting an old friend of ours living on St. John in the Virgin Islands. She had invited me to dinner at her house overlooking Rendezvous Bay. Ronnie's silk screen print of an iris hung on the dining room wall. The 30-by-40-inch silk screen of the flower was spare and beautiful with text in English and Spanish: "Goddess of color, *arco de Colores*." The friend served a nice risotto, but the iris held me in its grip. I smelled the solvents Ronnie used in her studio and saw the rainbow of colors on her paint-stained fingers, my own goddess of color.

∞

In 1976, after living together for five years, Ronnie and I decided to get married. The wedding ceremony was at the MIT chapel. The chapel is circular, intimate, a medieval fortress with interior walls of undulating brick. A shallow moat surrounds the building. Slits, like those for archers, channel light reflected from the moat. A metal sculpture cascades from a large circular skylight down to a small, unadorned marble altar. My parents were in the front row with Ronnie's family. They seemed a little uncomfortable—they would have preferred a synagogue—but they were beaming. That day the air-conditioning was not keeping up with the midday sun.

Ronnie in her wedding dress, gleaming hair and glistening eyes, had an almost transcendent beauty that does not belong to the current time. She had lost so much weight trying to look her best at the wedding, she was thin, almost frail. At the rabbi's suggestion we had fasted that day, waiting to break bread and drink wine as part of the ceremony. The fast is like the one on Yom Kippur in which all sins are forgiven. I remember sweating in my white suit, anxious about our parents and the others that had come in from out of town. Barbara, Richard's wife, still takes delight in the image of Ronnie in the chapel. Barbara remembers her swooning at the wedding altar and my catching her. It was as an "exquisite image that carried with it aspects of your relationship. Not her weakness, but that there were deep currents, nonverbal, that kept you in sync with each other on your path through life. It showed when you danced, a lovely sense of frivolousness or lightness. I liked visiting you guys. The disarray was welcoming like a sign that said, 'You can bring your mess here, too.' You were connected at such a core level, that of course, the moment she fainted, you were there to support her." Barbara chuckles, "If it had been me and Richard, chances are, I would have hit the floor."

I remember walking arm in arm up to the altar, the rabbi waiting for us in ceremonial robes. There was a slight tug on my sleeve. I thought she was being romantic, but as I tuned toward her, she clutched desperately and then went limp. I grabbed her and managed to get my arm around her waist so that her head was on my chest as she slumped to the ground. A moment's panic until she opened her eyes. I looked up and the rabbi was gone. Oh my God, now what? How will we ever get out of here? But after a small eternity he returned with a glass of water and the ceremony proceeded. The vows were in Hebrew. "Today you are made holy to me according to the laws of Moses and Israel."

We went off to Spain and Portugal for our honeymoon and returned to wedded bliss in our rent-controlled apartment in Huron Village in West Cambridge. I was working at Intermetrics and Ronnie was doing odd jobs in retail and trying to make some money printing silk-screened T-shirts.

She eventually enrolled in a program that taught computer programming, sponsored by the Job Training and Performance Act (JTPA), which replaced Nixon's Comprehensive Employment and Training Act (CETA). The program was run by George Lukas, who had worked with Wally Freuzig on Logo at Bolt, Beranek, and Newman. BBN is a high-tech company famous for pioneering work developing the Internet. Logo was a software project rooted in a constructivist educational philosophy that believes that knowledge is created by learners in their own minds through interaction with other people and the world around them. This theory is most closely associated with Jean Piaget, the Swiss psychologist, who spent decades studying and documenting the learning processes of young children. In the mid-1960s Seymour Papert, a mathematician who had been working with Piaget in Geneva, came to the United States where he cofounded the MIT Artificial Intelligence Laboratory with Marvin Minsky. Papert worked with the team from BBN, led by Wallace Feurzeig, that created the first version of Logo in 1967.

Ronnie was mystified at first but soon became one of the stars in the class and eventually worked with George Lukas at a company he started called Data Solutions. She was good at it, but it was not her calling, and after a few years she gave up working with computers.

Ronnie loved to make art with others. She stopped silk-screening prints and T-shirts in part because of the nastiness of the chemicals used in the process and in part because she never saw herself as an artist with a capital A. She did not see herself as someone whose work would stand out calling for attention from a wide audience. She found a compromise in "mail art."

Art that floats through the post, for some a hobby, was for Ronnie a passion. She delighted in creating letters and postcards decorated with drawings and colored-in images that came off of rubber stamps. Her

Ronnie in her studio.

correspondence, like that from some earlier century, yielded devoted friends that she never met. Their bodies never crossed the transom, but their art, photos, words made them real. The letters she received, beautifully decorated in styles that ranged from folksy to surreal, made going down to get the morning post a true adventure. Throughout her illness our mailbox was filled with beautifully decorated messages of caring and humor.

In the 1990s most of her collaboration took place at monthly meetings of her Stampers Anonymous Club, a group devoted to art made mostly from rubber-stamped images. Their bible was *Rubberstamp Madness,* a magazine devoted to "rubber addicts," which eventually ran a feature on Ronnie and her mail art. She also joined others in serial mail projects in which each person contributed a page or object. The Zeti project was one of my favorites. Everyone involved created some artifact recovered from the Zetis, an imaginary civilization whose history and culture took shape as the project traveled through the mail from one artist to another. She left behind some beautiful hand-bound books built from pages contributed by artists from all over the country.

In the late 1980s we bought a condominium near Harvard Square, the top floor of a three-family house. A decade later, we bought the second floor and combined the two units and undertook massive renovations. Part of the plan was a new workspace for Ronnie's art with built-in tables and shelving. We decided to live in the place while the work went on. At first it seemed like a good idea. Most of the work was downstairs. An array of plastic sheets and duct tape managed to keep most of the dust contained, but as the reconstruction work proceeded, our living space got smaller and smaller, and for the last month we lived in our 10-by-12-foot bedroom eating takeout and showering at the health club. The work ended, and Ronnie was delighted with her new studio.

Auschwitz

∞

In July 1998 I was in Poland, looking out at the evening sun from our hotel on the banks of the Vistula River. The river was tranquil, and the city of Krakow looked ancient and peaceful, but my thoughts were in turmoil, my emotions churning. This narrative is difficult for me, and if it seems at times brutal or callous, please forgive me.

Ronnie and I had traveled to Poland to join my parents and my brother for a family visit to the old country. It was my father's idea. I think he saw it as part of reaching closure on his life and his past. His name, Godel, comes from the Hebrew "big man." In his youth, my father's friends used the diminutive Godela (little big man), which somehow suits him better. In the camps one of the Jewish guards called him Gedaliah, after the Hebrew governor in the time of Nebuchadnezzar II, in 587 BC. During his reign, the Babylonians had laid siege to Jerusalem for more than two years and eventually breeched the walls and sacked the city destroying the First Temple, the one that Solomon built.

Every worst woe befell the devoted city, which drank the cup of God's fury to the dregs.

We visited my father's hometown, Wyszogród, along the Vistula River, just north of Warsaw. Jews lived there as early as the 15th century and a famous stone synagogue was built in the 18th century and had stood for 200 years. Dad spoke with awe of the place with its baroque architecture, the biggest building he had ever seen in his youth. The Nazis destroyed it all in 1939. What had once been a mostly Jewish town with an active commercial district was now a sleepy farming village.

To me, it looked like other small towns we had passed through. It supported a small network of houses, a petrol station, a few rundown stores, and an empty square that held a bar/restaurant. Together, they warranted a name on the map. We eventually found the house that he had lived in. The woman now living there gave us a warm, somewhat stunned, reception. Her just grown daughters milled about. One had a young child in tow, smiling and a bit confused. She invited us up to a small but well-kept apartment on the second floor. The entryway on the first floor was a communal mudroom with an uneven stone floor. My brother, Ben and I, both six feet tall or taller, stood like miracle-grow plants looming over my five-feet-five father and my five-feet mother, my video camera an added distraction.

My father must have felt a bit like I did when I went back to visit my old grade school. He marveled at how small the rooms were and how many people had lived there. Like all of us, he remembered home as the biggest part of his childhood. The woman's mother appeared from down the hall, and she and my father reminisced in Polish. I understood not a word. There were questions about a person, about a place, some recognition of common memories. "*Tak,* yes, yes, no, I don't know."

"Come have some tea."

"No, *Genkui,* thank you, thank you."

As we drove around town, I could see that Dad was disappointed because much of the Jewish part of town had been leveled, the commercial district gone. The market that once held stalls for dozens of vendors was now an empty square.

We found the Jewish cemetery. It had been totally destroyed. The headstones had been ripped out of the ground and used as paving stones by the Germans; the gravestones made roads for their Panzers. You could still walk on the paths that had segmented the graveyard.

Some survivors had erected a monument, an obelisk some eight feet tall with an inscription in Yiddish. They had cleared the paths, but most of the grounds were now once again overgrown. The Catholic cemetery just across the street stood pristine and bedecked with flowers, a sad contrast. One other headstone still stood in the Jewish graveyard, a massive boulder with a flat surface, a memorial to someone's parents. The stone's huge mass was daunting. They would need a backhoe to move this one.

On this midsummer day, true nightfall would not arrive until just before midnight. On the drive down from Warsaw to Auschwitz and Birkenau, at a rest stop on the highway, we met a group of American teachers on a Holocaust learning tour. My father knew the tour leader, Mr. Meede, a survivor, who was working to make sure that the Holocaust was not forgotten. The teachers were from all over the United States, most of them non-Jews. One of Mr. Meade's assistants was from Philadelphia. She had graduated from the University of Pennsylvania just two years before I did. We chatted about the great Northeast, Philadelphia's multiethnic equivalent of New York's Long Island.

The signs led us to Oświęcim, Auschwitz, just like any other tourist spot. My father had first returned to Auschwitz 12 years earlier, in 1986. After my parents sold the farm and Dad launched a successful new career building homes, my mother started taking trips to Slovakia. Every few years, she and some women friends traveled to the spa and mud baths at Piešťany. She wanted my father to join her. My father insisted that if he went back to Eastern Europe, he had to take her to see Auschwitz, and so, on their way to the spa, they stopped at the camp. For decades, they had argued about who had suffered more during the war. When they returned, the arguments ceased.

Our driver dropped us off and went to park the minibus we had hired. We entered the camp and began touring the barracks. Some 27,000 inmates were once housed there. My father pointed out each of the three barracks in which he had lived. He pointed out the laundry where he had worked and the building next door that had housed whores for the Polish guards and the German SS. The grounds were clean and well kept, just as they had been during the war. There was

Godel and Bronia enter Auschwitz

more grass now between the barracks where the men had stood for their daily roll calls. Men had swept the streets each day, and like the chain gangs that patrol U.S. highways, they had stabbed stray paper and cigarette butts with sharpened sticks. Somehow, the initial impression of the camp was not nearly menacing enough.

We walked through the infamous gate with its *Arbeit macht Frei* sign, where a prison orchestra had played Strauss marches as the prisoners went off to work. The streets were now lined with tall and graceful trees; the barracks were solid brick, three or four stories tall, with wood flooring. Superficially, it looked like the military barracks it had been before the war.

The place is organized as a museum with exhibits in each of the barracks. Since childhood I had seen the films and heard the stories about the camps and the selection process. Take everything from me and then take my life. Had I been inoculated against the horror? The piles of broken eyeglass frames, mountains of boots and children's shoes, mounds of human hair, pyramids of lipstick cases and shaving brushes:

Ronnie was aghast. Tears stained her cheeks. For me, the volume was overwhelming, each artifact a marker for some poor soul. Still, the detritus remained somehow distant and insulated behind the plate glass, the contents labeled in four languages.

The pictures of inmates that lined the halls tugged harder but were somehow too innocent, the shaved heads with their ears sticking out and wide-striped uniforms with numbers sewn on the breast. The low numbers marked them as early arrivals, a time when they still took photographs. Many of them were Poles and other non-Jews arrested for their political beliefs or their resistance to the Nazi occupation. Everything was numbered, pictures, clothes—the people, too, were numbered with tattoos on their arms.

Looking at the pictures rekindled my amazement at my father's determination to find a way to survive. Many gave up hope. Dad told of a man he knew from his hometown. "One day I was standing by a guy from home. He was a wise guy at home. He liked to drink, to smoke cigarettes. He was standing with me in the hall, and he was in a bad way. 'Godel, I am not going to survive here. I don't have cigarettes. I don't have bread. What is my life? I go tomorrow.' The next morning, he went to where they were collecting the people who couldn't work, to the *musselmen,* and they took him right away to the gas chambers."

You could tell when someone had arrived by their number. "What number?" was one of the first questions my father asked the occasional survivor we encountered. You could guess at who they were among the visitors. The older people stood out in a crowd that was quite young. Auschwitz is a popular school trip for older teenagers, especially Israelis, but we also met groups from Poland, Holland, and other European countries.

As we walked through the camp, my father retold some of the stories I had heard over the years. Most concerned hunger; struggling to get enough to eat was a constant battle. He told of stealing sweaters, socks, gloves, and other clothes from the laundry. He would take the stolen goods to workers that traveled outside the gates who might be able to trade clothing for a crust of bread or some potatoes. He had a partner in these enterprises, a fellow who worked a different shift and could take care of the goods or help in the marketing.

Moving from barrack to barrack, the tension mounted. My hair rose up on the back of my neck. Auschwitz was mostly a work camp, but it also held torture dungeons and a block that Josef Mengele had used for his experiments in human sterilization. We turned a corner and came to the "Killing Courtyard," the yard with the "Wall of Death." Sometimes the wall was a backdrop for firing squads, and sometimes individual SS officers dispatched death sentences with their lugers. Gunshots rang out, bodies crumpled. Along the side of the courtyard, hanging yardarms stood where corpses or the near dead once had hung as warnings to the rest of the inmates.

As we entered the final barracks, the ones used to perfect the IG Farben gas Zyklon B, I realized that my mouth was parched. I could not swallow. The watchtowers, the barbed wire, the electric fence, the brick killing rooms with observation glass for spectators made me gag. I was furious, raging, horrified. I felt disgusted with the human race, our miserable species. It seemed easier to forgive the barbarians, the wild hordes, full of lust and greed, who pillaged and plundered. What had happened here was an organized effort by an advanced civilization, cold and calculated, with enough support from the general population to work steadily at genocide for half a decade.

As we passed the infirmary on our way out, my father retold the story of his brief stay at the camp hospital.

"Every day they woke us at 4:30 and threw us out of bed. We went waiting in line for the toilet, one next to the other, trying to keep warm. They gave us coffee. They gave us a piece of bread at night. Some people kept it to have with coffee. At 7:00 I had to go to my assembly for work. One guy had fallen out of line. Maybe he was tying his shoe. I don't know. The capo threw a stone at him and yelled for him to keep up. Instead of him, he hit me. I got hit in the ankle by the stone. I told you this story already.

"When I came out alive from the shower, I was in a hospital. One of my neighbors from Wyszogród was working there, and he said, 'Godel, if you want to live, you must get away from this place.' So when they asked me if I could move, it was like they were testing a horse. They ask me to show I could walk. With whatever strength I had left, I ran for them.

"They let me out back into the camp, but I didn't have any work. I needed to find work. They had some young men who were being trained to be masons. It was wintertime. I went down to check on this work. There were several boys from my hometown working there. I went down to them, but they said to me, 'You are too old.' I couldn't join them."

"How old were you?" I asked.

"I was 26, but I already looked older. They had shaved my head. I had just come from hospital. So I went over to where they were sewing numbers on to the prison uniforms." He points to his heart. "They put one here and one on the pants.

"I saw a guy that I met in the Nowy Dwór ghetto. He said, 'When they ask you for work, tell them you are a tailor.' So they took me. The first few days I was fixing socks. Some of the musicians who played at the gate came in later in the morning. They played in an orchestra at 7:00 a.m. and then they came up at 9:00 a.m. to work on the socks. These were talented, educated people. Not to believe." He had a reverence in his voice. He was an uneducated kid from a small town. These people were intellectuals from the great cities of Europe.

"I set it up with my friend that I would be the one distributing the clothes to the tailors going around with the uniforms and the numbers. I did that for a few weeks, and then the capo came at me and said, 'If you are a tailor, sit down at one of the machines.' I tried for a few days, but I was no tailor."

We entered the block where Dad had failed as a tailor. My father wanted to take us upstairs to show us the place he had worked after giving up on his sewing career, but the museum guard stopped us. Dad tried to give him $10 to let us pass, but he wouldn't take it. When my father explained that he had been an inmate there and that he had worked upstairs, the guard let us go up. Not many visitors went upstairs, and there was not much see; it was dusty and there were some stored files up there, some other junk.

More vivid was my father's memory of the place: "Downstairs they were sewing. Upstairs they were tearing up clothes from the baggage taken from the incoming prisoners. I did this for my father. He made hats. We cut up old clothes and made hats from the material. I was a specialist. I was two times, maybe three times, faster than the other workers. Anyway, that became my work. I started to steal stuff. Every day I'd take something, a pair of pants, a sweater. I sold or traded the stuff to the Poles that were working around the camp." A capo, a *Donjivan,* he looked at me. He knew I was stealing. He said, 'You eat. I need to eat, too.' I used to bring him every day some food, some salami, some bread."

"What's a *Donjivan?*" I asked.

"Oh, I don't know how to say in English."

"Tell me in Yiddish."

"He was someone who liked the ladies. He could go with two, three girls at once. What would you say in English?"

"He was a playboy. In English they would call him a Don Juan."

From the beginning of his stay my father had managed to keep some money hidden. For several months he held on to it, concealing it here and there on his person and elsewhere through dozens of searches. The SS had warned that anyone caught with money would be killed. My father's attitude was, "If they kill me, they kill me, but I must take risks or I will not survive."

"I'll tell you a story about hiding money. I had a few marks. I thought maybe it will help me. You could still buy things, a kind of black market, but each day we would go by the SS men, one in Birkenau and one in Buna. If they found money on you, they would shoot you. They always said, 'If we find you are stealing, we will shoot you.' I hid it in my belt. But every day we had to take off our clothes to go through the disinfection, and I was worried they would find it.

"One time I heard a rumor they were going to come through for a search. I knew this one guy. He married someone from my town. He was from a different town, but I knew him. He was a tailor, Wolf. He worked a different shift, and I say, 'Wolf, you keep the money while I am working and I take it back when I come back to the block.' He said, 'No, I am not going to get in trouble with you. No, NO, NO.' I said 'OK, just don't talk nothing.'

"But this son of a bitch told the capo. He said, 'I am not going to suffer for you. The people not suffer for you.' I had hidden the money under the slats, in a bunk in the block. The Germans would never have found it.

"I went to sleep; it was 8:00 or 9:00 p.m. They came into the block and they hollered. '83193, 8-3-1-9-3!' They were calling out my number. What could I do? They dumped everyone out of their beds, the whole block, maybe 400, 500 people. There was an aisle between the beds, and we were all standing there. There was no place to hide. They knew I was in that block."

All the inmates were forced from their bunks, and the capo told my father that everyone would remain standing until he gave up the money. They beat my father. They tied his hands behind him and hung him from his wrists. He was afraid to confess. It was not the torture that defeated him, but the sight of the rest of the block standing during the few hours that they might sleep. "I went down from my bunk, and they came and hit me: here and there once, two times then again." He waves his hands in front of his face. "I didn't say anything. They said, 'We know you have money.' They said, 'Everybody is going to stand all night if you don't give up the money. They are going to suffer for you.' *Ich starb aveck* (I was dying).

"I gave up. They took away the money. They took my belt and my boots. I had good boots from home that I had made myself. They took away my warm boots, and they gave me *hollanderkes*, wooden clogs. They were the worst. Worse than getting beat up. Oy, yoy, yoy." He shakes his head and grimaces. "Those shoes, I got blisters, sores. I went a nice few days with those things until I found some boots. Oy! I remember when your brother came home from California wearing clogs. I couldn't believe it. How can you wear those things?"

"So, how about this guy Wolf. What happened to him?"

"He didn't survive. He was cursed. I was so mad at him, I cursed him. How can a man do like this? You don't have to help me, but why tell the capo? He didn't get anything out of it. He didn't survive. His name was Wolf Friedman. He did not survive. I'm happy he didn't survive."

"Don't say that."

"After what he did, I couldn't look in his eyes. It was a good hiding place. This place in the bunk, nobody knew. How could he give me up?

"Hiding money, you can't believe where people will hide money. In Germany, some people smuggling gold pieces and silver dollars from Switzerland in condom in their *tuches* (bottom). I couldn't do it. They took 15, 20, even 25 silver dollars inside them to Switzerland, to Belgium. Not to believe. It's no way to make a living."

After walking the length of the camp, both of my parents were tired, so we stopped for coffee at the cafeteria just inside the gates. One of the women we had met at the rest stop was there, the Penn graduate who helped run the learning tour. We talked and drank coffee and ate some surprisingly good pastry. Meede and his wife joined us, and we talked about his stay at the camp, his current work, and the time my father had heard him speak in Washington with President Reagan in the audience.

We were speaking Yiddish, my brother and I talking about our yeshiva days in Manhattan, about learning to read Yiddish by reading headlines in the Yiddish paper, bemoaning the fact that there was only one Yiddish paper left in wide circulation (*The Forward*). Mrs. Meede suddenly pulled back from the table and said, "This is too *gemütlich* (cozy, pleasant) for a meeting at Auschwitz."

My brother, Ben, and I sat on either side of my father. We were giants next to the 81-year-old little big man, my mother an even more diminutive bystander. Mrs. Meede looked at Ben and me and said, "Your sons are proof that Hitler did not succeed." There was a tremor in her voice. Her strong emotions and my father's tear-filled eyes brought out my first tears. We left the coffee shop barely able to speak.

The sad truth is that while Hitler did not manage to exterminate the race or kill the religion, he did succeed in ridding most of Europe of its Jewish population. Poland, especially, is virtually devoid of Jews. Wyszogród, my father's hometown, once had 4,000 Jews. None remain. Krakow, whose Jewish section is undergoing a major reconstruction, a resurrection, once had a community of 60,000 Jews; when we visited, there were perhaps 100, mostly old people. The synagogue often had to recruit from among the tourists for the ten men required for a minyan, for public prayer. In Warsaw, Poland's one remaining kosher restaurant was staffed and operated by non-Jews. Ninety percent of all the Jews in Poland, some 3 million people, were killed by the Nazis—more people than those who live in Kansas or Mississippi, and three times the population of Rhode Island.

In 1998, when we visited, there was quite a bit of Jewish tourism in Poland, with trips to the camps a regular activity, complete with little handouts at the Krakow hotels. As we visited Jewish sites, my father would approach people, especially older people, to ask if they too were visiting, where they were from, and eventually, were they Jewish. He met other survivors traveling the Jewish tour route. A few spoke freely about still feeling unsafe in Poland. Their resentment remained focused against the entire nation of Poland, while strangely their fear and loathing of Germans was more personal, directed at individuals and specific groups, at a generation, not a nation. As we toured, we did see swastika graffiti, especially in the poorer suburbs, but most everyone was quite pleasant.

My father was in six different camps as the Germans retreated before the Russian onslaught. He was liberated on a train taking Jewish prisoners from Dachau, Germany, to the Italian Alps. He says he is alive today because the Nazis did not think their own population would stand for wholesale massacre. Even though 80 percent of Italian Jews survived the Holocaust, by the end of the war the Germans were unconcerned with how the Italians might react; they were taking the prisoners to Italy to kill them. There were no large-scale death camps in Germany. Seventy-five percent of German Jews survived. The Poles turned their backs.

Of course, some did help Jews. Hundreds of Poles were killed for hiding Jews or feeding them when they were on the run. Still, witnesses report that far more Poles were eager to be rid of the Jews, to take over their homes and land, and take leftover spoils from the Nazis. My father, while not disagreeing with the sentiment, was more relaxed and easygoing than most, happy to make small talk in Polish to the Poles he met both old and young. He took a certain pleasure in returning a wealthy man with two successful sons.

After leaving Auschwitz, we took the short ride over to Birkenau: the Auschwitz II subcamp was the primary site of technological, industrial mass murder. Birkenau housed the first two gas chambers and four massive crematoriums. My father's family, *my* family, came here first, and only the boys survived to go to work at the Auschwitz camp. Walking through the gate, you followed the railroad tracks to the site of the crematoriums. It is about a quarter-mile trip with rundown wooden barracks lining the way. Some of them had been rebuilt for a motion picture.

The crematoriums were blown up by the Nazis as they retreated before the Allies, at the end of the war. The Nazis tried to cover their tracks. Amazingly, even today you can find websites arguing that the Holocaust is a myth, that not enough coal and coke was delivered to burn that many bodies. These websites offer fabricated statistical proofs and aerial photos that question the accounts of survivors. At first they made me angry; mostly they make me sad.

Still, even while you are there looking at the camp, it is hard to believe it happened. As we neared the end of the tracks, my father spoke again about his mother's last words. "She told us, 'Children, I, with your father, will not survive. Maybe you, if you stay together, you will survive.' During the 'selection,' they separated the men and the women. I never saw my sisters again. They took my brother and me into quarantine. My brother had some open sores, and they took him out the group and to a kind of hospital area. I went after him, and we sneaked around to get back in the line.

"We arrived near Christmastime. One guy, our capo, was homosexual; he had a blue star. Homosexuals had blue stars, communists had red stars, and criminals had green stars. This guy was a good guy. He told all of us in his group, 'Boys, you got two bad months, January and February, 59 days. If you get through these days, you have a chance to survive. Keep moving, do something. If you stay still, you will freeze.' So we worked and we worked."

We stood there, more than 50 years later, on a cool gray day in July, looking from the tracks to the monument built on the site of the first two crematoriums. My father put on his *tallis* and yarmulke and said first kaddish and then Tehillim, psalms read as prayers for the dead. We wept once again for those who had died.

Kaddish, the Mourner's Prayer

Exalted and hallowed be His great Name.

Throughout the world which He has created according to His will may He establish His kingship, bring forth His redemption and hasten the coming of His Messiah.

In your lifetime and in your days and in the lifetime of the entire House of Israel, sword, famine and death shall cease from us and from the entire Jewish nation, speedily and soon, and say, Amen.

The congregation responds: *Amen. May His great Name be blessed forever and to all eternity, blessed.*

His great Name shall be blessed forever and for all eternity. Blessed and praised, glorified, exalted and extolled, honored, adored and lauded be the Name of the Holy One, blessed be He.

Beyond all the blessings, hymns, praises and consolations that are uttered in the world; and say, Amen.

May there be abundant peace from heaven, and a good life for us and for all Israel; and say, Amen.

Cancer

∞

We had been together for nearly three decades and were still encased in our "sweetly conceited establishment." We traded love notes and sparkled on the dance floor. I was a partner at the Jacobson Group, and my commute was a walk across the Harvard campus to our offices in Harvard Square. Ronnie was happily working part-time at Joie de Vivre, a small store just a few blocks away owned by a wonderful woman named Linda Gibbons. I agreed with the description on her website: "a world of delightful items—clever, beautiful and original, as well as just plain wacky! We carry gifts for all ages and interests: wind-up toys, kaleidoscopes, jewelry, flashing rings, clocks, snow globes, music boxes, books, postcards, rubber ducks, singing animals and all kinds of other things designed to enchant, or give pleasure through the unexpected." Ronnie had been a customer before she became an employee. The rubber stamps that Linda sold may have drawn her at first, but the wacky stuff delighted Ronnie and my basket of Christmas gifts always included some treasure from the store's shelves. My office still features a lovely wooden clock rendered as a time bomb: A round clock face sits next to a transformer and a bundle of dynamite sticks.

It started with a pain in her chest. Ronnie was 50 years old, and she had been one of the healthiest chain-smokers on the planet. Her father's experience in army hospitals after WWII had left her leery of doctors. Except for her gynecologist, she rarely interacted with the medical profession. When I convinced her to seek help, her doctors did not find anything wrong with her chest or her heart. The pain persisted, and a year later, in 2001, my wife was diagnosed with lung cancer. A large mass of cancerous cells had spread across both lungs. It was the first year of the new millennium, before the twin towers fell, 5760 on the Hebrew calendar.

Smoking killed her. Was she seduced by the sophisticated women smoking cigarettes in Hollywood films? More likely, it was the kitchen table at the Double-A Barn where she had learned to ride horses. The horse people gathered around a Formica table with metal legs that held cups of coffee and ashtrays. You had to put up with the smoke to sit with the adults. You had to smoke to become one.

Surgery was not an option. She went for chemotherapy and radiation treatments, but the prognosis was bleak. The treatments seemed as devastating as the cancer.

We scrambled about looking for alternative cures. We even went to visit a Russian "healer" who claimed to cure people by laying his hands on them and channeling healing energy into them. Ronnie was skeptical and so was I, but I was happy to try anything that might make her feel better or give us some hope. We were ushered into a small room with a daybed covered in a white sheet. The bed made a crinkling sound when she sat down, and she lifted the sheet to find the mattress encased in plastic like some cheap upholstery. We made only one visit. Ronnie thought the place was creepy.

She was recovering from a round of chemotherapy, and as she lay in her sickbed, the blue veins in her neck were tracings on a delicate pedestal that supported a face whose bones pressed out against the skin. I asked her if there was anything she wanted to do, and she smiled at me and said: "Let's make art!" On that day it meant answering some of her correspondence. Smiling, I asked her which rubber stamps she wanted to use. She sent me to her studio to fetch the stamps, describing them and telling me where I would find them amidst the thousand or more she kept in flat files in her office: 25 drawers each meticulously labeled (words, places, pointers, angels ...). I went into her office to fetch a laptop desk, colored pencils, and colored stamp pads.

I fought off tears as I left the bedroom, in awe of the energy and tranquility she summoned in the midst of her pain and decay. She designed the envelopes, and I helped in marginal ways, inking the rubber stamps on the pads, coloring in some of the images with colored pencils. I stopped to get her some soup and some oxycodone, but she kept at it, writing the letter only after the envelope was complete. She had a little trouble eating the soup and was a bit wistful about the quality of the finished artwork; still her eyes smiled and my heart worked hard not to explode.

The first few months of her treatments passed in a blur. She lost weight and began to lose her hair. I think I still have the wig we bought for her tucked away in one of the file cabinets that held her art supplies. She lived for less than a year after they found the tumor. Time played with my head. On some days I struggled to hold back time as it rushed by me. Toward the end I was often frozen in anguish watching her life seep away. The moments I sat with her as she moaned in pain stretched on and on.

When Ronnie died, I felt like I was left tossing about in an open sea, foaming mountains of blue-green water lifting me and then hurling me down as I struggled through the waves. As I stared into the mirror, razor in hand, scratching away the day's stubble, water kept creeping into my thoughts. Behind me the shower dripped in time with my heartbeat. The seal in the shower's faucet swelled slowly to staunch the flow. I remembered the plumber's warning not to compress the rubber seal, not to twist too hard. Was I twisting too hard? Was there another way to be? Was I skimming across the water, a stone skipping along on the tense surface of a pond, doomed to sink into the dark waters? Was I fighting against fate, leaning forward and surfing the waves in a raging storm? Or was I just a passenger in a boat adrift, floating inexorably in the slow current of an ancient river? The buoyancy of the waters held me up as gravity pulled me down, a steady hand with an implacable grip.

The network of friends and family that formed around me worked to keep me afloat as my soul struggled in life's waters. I was not the center, except perhaps in my mind's eye, just another body on this great raft full of strange tribes, but the world was also a small place with people tied together in small knots. One person had been tied so closely to me that it seemed we had breathed as one. She had lifted me higher than the others, and I had found myself like a cartoon character dancing at the top of a geyser lifted by a surge so strong, it thrilled the soul.

Our friend Pearl helped me with the design for a gravestone. It has a Shaker "tree of life" from a design that I know Ronnie liked. Lebensbaum means "tree of life," so it satisfied my objections to random images of doves and laurels on headstones. When I was ready to send the design to the stone merchant, what might seem a small matter grew to terrorizing proportions. Which first name should I put on the gravestone: Rhonda or Ronnie? It was torture. The name would be etched in stone forever. What would she want? Would her father take offense? Did it matter to me? When we were together, I called her Ron, the other syllable unnecessary. With others, I parroted whatever they expected to hear. Grieving, was I in denial, not ready to put her name on a gravestone? Angst and anger over this quandary rose up before me. We had lived together for 30 years. How could I not know her name? In the end both names went on the stone...

Rhonda
(Ronnie)
Lebensbaum
Her smile opened our hearts

In The Shadow

∞

As the rain and the snow come down from heaven,
and do not return to it without watering the earth
and making it bud and flourish,
So is my word that goes out from my mouth:
It will not return to me empty, but will accomplish what I desire
and achieve the purpose for which I sent it.

Isaiah 55

Isaiah seems so certain, but I am not so sure. My words seem more like dead leaves gathered beneath a thorny bush. The thorns tear at me as I bend down to search among the leaves. I am a faltering shaman, deracinated, extirpated, but still rattling bones, tossing dust into the fire. It is a miracle that words sometimes convey meaning, like the miracle of the senses, but my words lack the magic to bring her back to life. Will Ronnie forgive me for failing in my task? I am not sure it augurs well that I feel the need to ask forgiveness before I proceed, but she will forgive me. She always did.

I tell you about my love so that you can understand the riches I have lost, a love that was lustrous, noble, kind, and gentle. Our bond was a wonder and a burden. We were like sails spreading out wings to sail across the sea, and yet, for each other, we were like anchors, safety in the storm.

Remembering our love, emotions surge back and forth. A fugue whose soaring melody is set against a dark counterpoint becomes a feedback loop, ululating. The quiet oscillation intensifies until it becomes a crescendo, cymbals clanging. Underneath the rage, the low heartbeat of a cello and the plaintive cry of an oboe whisper dread and despair. I am walking through a black canyon. Is that light ahead the Hellmouth or the rising sun?

She was the one who should have lived. She was the better half. Who is that fat man I see in the mirror? An acolyte of a profane culture, I wander about lost in purgatory's wasteland, a vapid technocrat who counted his money and his teeth. I thrash about trying to make time pass, finding solace in solitaire, waiting to retire, waiting to die. I look back at a coward unwilling to struggle with his pain. It cannot be me. It must be someone else. How can he live in the sunlight while she lies in her grave?

My parents' stories were full of death, but, with the bravado of youth, I ignored those harbingers. A few of my college friends died early, one from leukemia and another from Hodgkin's disease, but I had moved to a different city and their deaths seemed far away. Soon death moved closer. Ronnie and I lived in a condo in a three-story house in a quiet neighborhood near Harvard and shared a driveway with our neighbors, Ross and Joanne. Their sons were teenagers when Joanne was diagnosed with cancer. Ronnie drove her to therapy once a week until the angels from hospice took over.

Death's shadow loomed. When Ronnie was diagnosed, waves of terror, denial, and hope washed over us as we took our turn to struggle with the disease. I tried to face the facts, to somehow help in the fight, but too often, I averted my eyes. Leaking wet strands of despair, I was afraid that the truth would leave me comatose, mortally wounded. The agony seemed eternal, but looking back, she died fairly quickly, in months not years.

We had been a *duprass,* a "sweetly conceited establishment." In Vonnegut's mythology, both members of a *duprass* die within a week of each other, but I am still alive. While the world still has some sweet moments, I have given up many of my conceits. Will I love again? Can I still be loved?

After Ronnie's funeral, her father, Sam, and I sat shivah at my place in Cambridge. I tore my clothes and sat on the floor as family and friends came. They brought food and tears. *Nichum avelim* (comforting mourners) is a mitzvah (a good deed). The tradition is not to knock or ring the doorbell but to simply enter a shivah house, and not to exchange greetings but wait for the mourner to initiate conversations. It is the mourner's responsibility to acknowledge visitors. Did I do my duty? I hope I did with my father and brother. The shivah candle burned for seven days. The flame is a symbol for the soul. Some say the flame helps the departed find their way to heaven, but for me that week was a dark blur. Someone organized the food. Someone explained the rituals and organized a minyan so that Sam and I could say kaddish, a mourning ritual.

Each day I woke early and sat on the floor of our apartment staring at the dust floating in the sunlight between the windowsill and the hardwood floor. Did the light that filters through the tiny particles floating in the air or the dust itself hold true meaning? Or was there something else? My first instinct was to run away. I was a coward afraid to face the truth, but where could I hide? Could I still fit in the linen closet where I had hidden from my parents' Holocaust stories?

I went to synagogue each day to say kaddish. One says kaddish every day for a month when a spouse dies. It is said every day for a year for one of your parents. Ronnie would have been amused. It was another thing I did out of respect for my father and the traditions he tried to pass on. Perhaps he did point me in that direction, but saying kaddish also served me. It gave me a destination, a reason to leave the house. As the weeks of mourning crept by, I came to understand that I had to fight with the coward. I could no longer stumble from day to day, pretending it was all I could do to cope. Somewhere there remained the remnants of a soul. Could it begin a new life? I had fallen from a great height, descended from the heavens, not an angel but an alien on a strange planet. Would I rise up from the depths?

My synagogue mourning ended. I sat in the bathtub smoking a cigar, a hedonist in hot water. I lay back wondering why I was chosen to live on, why I wanted to stay alive. We were marching through life, a two-piece band, every day a parade. Sailboats happy in the wind, we were floating in our own ocean, sometimes slipping and sliding, carving through the swells. I still talked to her.

We had the music inside us, and I am lost without you. You were the real thing, even better than the real thing. And now you're gone. I keep seeing you. You are all eyes smiling at me, a sparkling jewel swirling on the dance floor. I wander tearfully through your last days, in awe of your courage and suffering. I cannot believe that you are gone and I am still mired among the living. I hate living without you. It embarrasses me to still be alive. I know you want me to move forward, but passing time is a struggle. Yes, the sun still warms my black clothes, but I shiver as I try to hold back the tears. I had trouble sleeping. Is it OK if I sleep on your side of the bed?

I had taken an old comedian's advice. George Burns talked about the trouble he had sleeping after Gracie died. When he looked over to her side of the bed, his partner in life and on the stage was missing. For him it was an unbearable loss. How could he find rest without her? He struggled with this agony for weeks until he finally tried sleeping on her side of the bed. He wondered at how peacefully he slept until he realized that now, instead of Gracie, he was the one missing from the bed, and that was no big deal. He was tired of himself anyway.

At night I sometimes push my hips over searching for your warm body. Awake, I look at our bed and I can still feel my knees pressing into the mattress. You were moaning in the depths of a coma, as I kneeled with my knees on either side of your chest dripping morphine into your mouth to ease your pain. I can see you dying, but I struggle to hold on to images of you before the cancer knocked you down: walking Roxie, at your desk with your letters and stamp pads.

Ronnie made my friends promise to take care of me after she died. She was worried that I would not get on with my life and that like her father I would remain attached to a love that died. She told my old friend Richard who was driving her to treatment one day, "Kirsch might need some help in moving on after I die." She so seldom asked other people for help. She was so fiercely independent. She needed help to reach beyond the grave.

I try not to rail against fate, to somehow accept what cannot be altered. I feel blessed to have had a true love, a soul mate. Now I am once again alone, and I do not know how to be. Our friends reach out to me, and I try to live among them. They are sweet, but I do not know how to let them comfort me. I cannot weep with them, but I cry sometimes when I watch TV. Lingering despair nourishes my grief. I have trouble with large groups. I am once again the alienated youth, but without a generation to share my anomie. It has been months now. I am traveling again as part of my job. Airplanes take me from place to place. I go to meetings, but at night alone in my hotel room I still want to call home, to speak to her as I did every day we were apart. I still want to hear her voice before I go to sleep.

The central terror of my youth, of a nuclear winter, has faded, but one morning my brother calls me to ask me to turn on the TV. I watch planes crash into towers of steel and glass, and once again the tension rises and oblivion seems closer at hand. The baseball season stops for a week. The leaves abandon their summer homes, and nothing moves through the air but military planes. We face the fallout from our tribal roots, from transgressions embedded in our history: the hatred and perpetual conflict that are the legacy of colonialism. The great powers draw lines on a map and nations are formed from tribes ill at ease with one another. Holy wars still fought over shrines bring us knights fighting the modern crusades. With no end in sight and no end imagined, life moves on. Air traffic resumes, people walk their dogs, and the media goes about its business of making heroes and villains. It touches me in little ways, an extra hour at the airport or a missed dinner with an old friend, when paranoia makes it impossible to meet in D.C. in the midst of an anthrax outbreak. The world's turmoil is once again penetrating into my daily life, seeping in like varnish on unpainted wood. As I watch the nation grieve and turn to anger, surreal images of Ground Zero remind me of my private pain, of the hole torn in my life.

The days grow shorter, and the air becomes dry and crisp. The sun droops down toward the horizon. The oblique angle of the winter sun makes pools of lambent light, but the sun's sharp slant also casts longer shadows. The dark seems close to home, the light mysterious.

I wish now that we had had children so that I could think of us living on in them. The freedom we thought we had bought when we gave up the burden of child rearing seems less real now. The travel and the mornings we slept late seem like a dream half-forgotten as the dreamer wakes, desperate for some tangible memento of the long journey through the night, grasping for bits and pieces, trying to make sense of his dream.

I take some comfort in the notion of reincarnation or its restatement as eternal recurrence, all living things part of the cycle of life and death. Buddhism and many other religions make it clear that we must accept sickness and death as part of life. Death, the price we pay for living.

My friends make sure that I return to work. I try to be useful, to fill my day with activity, to be around people. Can I find a way to not dwell on my loss? Can I live with the horror of Ronnie's death? The small struggles that beset the workplace and the strong feelings they evoke in my coworkers grate on me. They are smart, good people, but if they cannot accept these small wrinkles in their privileged lives, how can I accept what has happened in mine? Like Candide, in some best of all possible worlds, my friends and coworkers know everything could be perfect if someone would just make fair rules and follow them. Their distance from my reality of loss and suffering makes them hard to bear. I find myself in a darker world whose rules do seem clear and terrible.

My friends are trying to support me. Should I light my grief before them like a bonfire? Exposing my pain feels like pouring acid into an open wound. I cry alone and then move among them. Mostly, I do things that make time pass. Sometimes, like Yossarinian's friend, Dunbar, in *Catch-22*, I feel like I am working to extend life by making every moment excruciatingly boring. Each hour passes in painful languor. I dull my mind with morphia oozing from TV and computer screens.

Frustration and anger creep in as grief plots its course, and I float in a familiar world, a management position in a small consulting company. It is a life that includes difficult clients and tough decisions. The anger is new to me. It begins as cold rain, then, like a storm rising over the ocean, it churns up the seas. Waves rise up and suddenly I am flotsam hurtling about in a sea of emotion. Fear and anger, a malevolent distrust of fate and human nature crash against the life raft. Thrown from the raft, I am tempted to lash out with peevish malice, to injure without feeling guilt. Perhaps it is better to hold my tongue, to let the words rot unspoken in my mouth, rather than launch the pointed barbs that pierce the skin and rend the flesh.

Trying to accept what I cannot change, I hide behind a thin mask of normalcy, but I still separate myself from my emotions and my friends. I push them off, or rather I measure the distance and the measuring leaves them farther away. Isolated, desolate, is it fair to show my true emotions? Is there anyone who can look at them and not turn away?

After Ronnie came back from the doctor, we stopped making love. We were in shock. There was something growing in her, a large evil mass spread across both lungs. She had an old-fashioned attitude about sex, the male as the aggressor with the woman seeking intimacy. This pattern held throughout our marriage. Her invitation to make love was never explicit, the signals orthogonal, a good-night kiss that lasted a bit longer or just a rueful smile, a slightly raised eyebrow as I walked toward the bed. I was the one who reached for her. It was her sense of decorum, of modesty. Was it growing up without a mother, with a father who never brought a lover home?

When the treatments started, the idea of making love was pushed further and further away. I still wanted her when she began to lose weight, even after her hair fell out. But she bruised so easily now, and just getting up from bed left her breathless. Months went by and she spent more and more of the day in bed. Most days I worked from home, trying to make her comfortable. Any free time was consumed by researching hospitals and doctors, following up on any hint of a new cancer therapy that might somehow save us. The week took on a new rhythm that centered on her treatments. Devastation followed radiation or chemotherapy, and then she slowly recovered. This theme played on a descending scale. We were in the good part of the week. I was bringing her dinner. It was a constant struggle to find something that she could stand eating. She nibbled at the food and then looked up at me. Her eyes, how can I do justice to her eyes, sad, warm, and hopeful? They were fearful and mischievous, blue searchlights in a misty fog.

"Make love to me."

I had never heard those words from her lips. I smiled and then I cried as I helped her out of her pajamas. Tears fell from my cheeks onto her breasts. She was saying good-bye, but part of her was reaching out for life. She was still alive, still a woman, still in this world.

She fought a few months longer. I can still see her at peace after her final struggle, the heat seeping out of her body as I tried to say good-bye. I want to carry her with me as I try to live the life I have left. I feel guilty about simple pleasures, especially when I find some freedom in being alone. I can now smoke my cigars in the house and the car. I can drink the last cup of coffee and eat the last cookie. But these freedoms remind me that I am without her. And so it will always be.

Can I take heart from my mother and father who survived the horrors of WWII? My mother is ill, and soon she, too, will die. My father is a small man, a tower of strength, curving back toward the earth as gravity pulls on his flesh. His old bones do what they can to resist. We have become closer in the last few years, since Ronnie fell ill and died. He has dropped his air of authority and become more of a peer. More than that, he knows that I, too, have now experienced true suffering and loss. I am no longer a soft-assed American who does not know how fortunate he has been.

Sleep is that special pardon. It is not quite a reprieve, because our dreams follow us into the darkness. Still, sleep gnaws at me, calling me to its embrace. One night Ronnie came to me in a dream. I was in some treacherous place in Afghanistan supervising a food delivery and she appeared. I embraced her even as I thought, "Why have you come into this danger?" I sent her away to safety. When I awoke and the haze slowly cleared, I was glad we had embraced, but I wondered about sending her away. Perhaps it is my guilt over the last hours when I had hoped for an end to her suffering and mine.

Trying to creep back toward the world, I finish my first Harry Potter book and cry. Tears well up in my eyes when Harry explains that his mother's love had protected him from evil incarnate. I think of my mother's love, of her fight against illness, and the smile that came to her face, sneaking past the pain, when she recognized me at her bedside.

Modern man has the burden of Freud and Shakespeare in thinking about mother and son. I think of being pulled to my mother's breast, old enough to be embarrassed by her display of emotion and yet eager for the comfort of that loving embrace. I reveled in the love of mother and wife. Climbing out from under the terrors that my parents carried with them as survivors of the Holocaust, I found another kind of transcendence. I found a woman I could love with all of my being. That she loved me remains a true wonder. It was a miracle, enough to start a new faith.

Sometimes I feel as though I'm walking along the edge of a cliff looking down at a river as it sweeps past an unseen shore. It is not quite vertigo I feel, but I am left rootless and unsteady, afraid to look over the edge. I try to move forward step by step. Is it free will or fate? How much of this path did I choose? I climb down from the cliff and try to enter life's waters. I float on the surging river crouched in a leaky boat with a single oar that I try to use like a rudder, an oar that will not fight against the current.

∞

I am not ready to let go of my grief. I have said the kaddish. I have forgiven God, who remains glorified and sanctified. Those words repeated in the prayer are always spoken in the presence of others. For me God is a shorthand for life or perhaps, more broadly, existence. May its name be blessed forever and ever. Our universe in all its turmoil and horror remains a wonder. We lack control over all its processes and all its awesome complexity—from subatomic particles to the subconscious mind. Our fate is to grope at understanding, and even that curiosity is a holy marvel. Most of us can control a few things, at least most of the time. We can decide to end consciousness, and some people end their lives just to assert themselves against the vagaries of fate.

We rage against the storm, struggling to make order in a world that embraces chaos. Even our all-powerful gods seem ill at ease managing destiny. They find themselves thwarted by their creations. Depending on which tribe tells their stories, the gods seem more or less like us humans. They pout and rationalize. They get angry or sad. They punish. They empathize and forgive. Unlike us, however, they live on. Can we forgive them? It is a lot to ask to forgive them for making death a part of life.

The winter solstice has passed. Soon the days will begin to grow longer, although winter has just settled in. The sun barely warms my face. I work at getting out into the world. I walk about the neighborhood with a fat cigar and a heavy heart. I call my father almost every day. My mother is making some progress with her debilitating illness, but he finds himself trapped into giving care to a woman who is angry and bitter about her pain and fate. She grabs at him like a life preserver in heavy seas. I cannot help but compare her with Ronnie, who worked so hard to ease the pain of everyone near her even as she lay dying. I wonder how I will face my own end. I understand that it is the only plotline, the debt you have to pay. But who will hold my hand as my life ebbs away?

It is late December, and I have decided to go ahead with our annual New Year's Day party. The holiday party is a tradition, a big part of my role in my community. Buying champagne for a party, I know that I cannot celebrate the New Year, but perhaps others will. After visiting the liquor store, I drag fluids up the stairs, returning to that primal role of the water carrier. My father was the water carrier for his family. He carried two pails on a wooden stick slung over his shoulders on his way back from the stream. He told me of the day when he began spinning and the buckets began swirling outward like those Ferris wheels that turn sideways at high speeds. At first the water stayed in the pails and he kept spinning faster and faster, laughing giddily. Then he looked up to see his father, who stared at the nearly empty pails and, with stern words, sent him back for more water.

Climbing the stairs with the champagne, a rumor of vertigo makes every step an adventure. For months I have been trying to walk with my friends, but all too often I slip. I stumble and fall out of the crowd. I find myself once removed, an observer. A hesitant traveler, I am still skeptical of any attempt to make the journey. Time passes with or without my consent. Alone beside the abyss, I walk in death's shadow.

The phone rings. It is my father calling to wish me a Happy New Year.

Tisha B'Av

∞

Every person should have two pockets.

*In one should be a piece of paper on which is written,
"I am but dust and ashes."*

*In the other a paper that says,
"For my sake was the world created."*

Rabbi Simcha Bunam of Pshis'cha

Mom was distraught and disoriented in the recovery room at Mt. Sinai Hospital. In her postoperative psychosis, she called out to people long dead and did not recognize the living who came to visit her. The surgeons had removed tumors from the back of her throat. She was wearing an oxygen mask and receiving intravenous fluids. I can still see her struggling with one of the nurses. She pulled off her mask and screamed out in Yiddish, "Help! Help! This one is coming to kill me."

Mom had been a powerful woman, not tall but solid, with wide shoulders and hips and an ample bosom. She had told me stories about smuggling contraband after WWII. I had often imagined her bravely riding atop boxcars, bacon strapped to her belly, her dark hair blowing in the wind. She now looked so frail in her hospital smock, gray roots taking hold beneath her bleached blond hair. Over time she made a recovery, a survivor once again, but she never quite made it all the way back.

When my wife died, the dynamics in my small family changed. My parents once again moved closer to the center of my world. I was a survivor too now. I felt like the cancer that had killed Ronnie attacked us both and I was left behind.

On a late summer afternoon, a year after my mother's surgery, I was sitting in my parents' living room in New Jersey. The day was warm but not oppressive. We were looking out the sliding door that opened to the rear patio. Clouds were building in the blue sky, creating a foreboding dance, water vapor accumulating in larger and larger piles. Later, they would block the sun, looming low to the ground, carrying with them the menace and relief of an afternoon thundershower.

Memories create feedback loops; one reinforces the other. They vibrate, they howl, rising above a heavy counterpoint; they carry treasures and torment, a web of connections that may be just enough to temper loneliness. Angry, kind, and gentle, a wonder and a burden, memories bind us, one to another, links in a chain, a pattern that repeats from father to son, from mother to son. The chain stretched taut can serve as an anchor, safety in the storm, or a choke collar imprisoning us, grating, wearing away the flesh.

My mother was having trouble organizing her memories. She seemed lost in the soft, murky clouds that signal early Alzheimer's syndrome, clouds that had started forming after her operation.

"You're not wearing stockings."

"Yes, Mom. See, I'm wearing these flip-flops."

"So you don't wear socks?"

"Not with these sandals, no."

"You don't have socks."

"I have socks. I wear them with other shoes."

This conversation became a theme for the day. Perhaps not wearing shorts made flip-flops a fashion faux pas. Dad broke in to ask her whom she was talking to.

"I'm talking to my son."

"What's his name?" Dad pushed on her, laying bare her bewilderment, still hoping a glimmer of light would shine through her occluded eyes.

"He knows his name."

"Yes, but can you tell me his name?"

"Why should I tell you? He knows his name. He can tell you."

She still had an amazing facility for deflecting inquiries like a petulant schoolgirl being teased by older classmates.

My father and I went out to sit on the front porch watching the Hassidic kids walk by with their yarmulkes and long sideburns. We talked again about the last years of his life in Poland, and then he asked me what I had done on Ronnie's *jahrzeit,* the anniversary of her death. He looked at me and then looked away. A year had passed, but time had warped for me. Each day carried the memory of holding Ronnie in my arms, her agony ended, her heart stopped, her body cooling as I knelt over her.

Jews, when they mourn for a dead relative, visit the grave and say a prayer on the *jahrzeit,* meaning literally a year's time. We keep this anniversary based on the lunar Jewish calendar. My wife, Ronnie, died on Tisha B'Av, the ninth day of the 11th month, which, in the Julian calendar, sometimes falls in July and sometimes in August. Dad was being kind asking about her, checking in his oblique way on my state of mind, giving me a chance to talk, and I was grateful. But a little part of me remained the teenager in rebellion, suspicious, wondering if he was steering me, pushing an agenda, getting me ready for mourning duties for my mom and for him. Then I thought that I was being unkind.

Tisha B'Av is a major fast day commemorating several disasters that befell the Jewish people, especially the destruction of the first temple in 586 BC and the second temple in 70 AD. It has not been a happy day: All Jews were expelled from Spain in 1492 on Tisha B'Av. The First World War began on Tisha B'Av in 1914, when Russia declared war on Germany. During the Holocaust, the deportation of Jews from the Warsaw ghetto began on Tisha B'Av.

I told my father that I visited Ronnie's grave, a sad place, and not only because it is a place of death. The graveyard lacks character or natural beauty. Near where I live, Mount Auburn Cemetery is a beautiful place. Like the best urban cemeteries, it is a park with old trees and shrubs, a few ponds, winding lanes, a place to walk and enjoy the spring blooms. The dead rest beneath their sculptures and headstones in a place where nature still exhibits cycles of rebirth. But Mount Auburn is not a Jewish cemetery. I had asked Ronnie whether she cared about where she was buried and she thought our parents would want it to be a Jewish cemetery; her only concern was that we also reserve a place for her father so that he would not be buried alone. I had put it off. Jews bury their dead quickly. But I could not bring myself to look for a gravesite until the hospice folks started making repeated inquiries, until Ronnie was catatonic and there was no way to avoid the cold clamor of her imminent death. I turned my head from the truth, but also, it is in my nature to delay, to put off action, to arrive just in time or a few minutes late. For most Jews, their synagogue is connected to a graveyard, but neither Ronnie nor I was part of any congregation.

The place I found was in West Roxbury: a narrow field that extends for acres and acres with segments dedicated to different congregations and organizations, a flat and desolate place with a single paved road for hearses and mourners and one or two trees to break the desperate emptiness.

My father asked me if I said kaddish on Tisha B'Av. Kaddish calls on us to glorify and sanctify the name of our Lord, a prayer that forgives God or at least reconciles the mourner with His actions and asks for peace and a good life in all the days we have left.

I told my father that my friend Dean took me to his synagogue to say the prayer. I leaned on the few friends who were connected to a religious community. They helped me take comfort in religious rituals. While there was some part of my soul that must have yearned for spirituality, I went to synagogue mostly because of *Kibud Av*, the commandment to honor my father, to show him respect. He took heart when I showed some connection to our heritage. He was visibly pleased that I went to *shul* on Tisha B'Av.

I explained to Dad that the synagogue in Newton was being renovated and that during construction, prayers were held next door at the

Bet Mayim, literally the house of water, where the ritual bath, the *mikvah,* was located. This *mikvah,* in the basement of a converted suburban house, looked like a small swimming pool or a large hot tub. The sages insist that a new community build a *Bet Mayim* first, before they build a synagogue. For the truly Orthodox, you need a *mikvah* to have a sex life. Couples are not allowed to have sex while a woman is having her period and can resume only after she takes a ritual bath in the *mikvah.* The Hassidim sometimes say they have a "two-week honeymoon" each month, after taking a break during menses, while the uterus gives up its lining. If the number of kids they produce is evidence, the honeymoon seems to work for them.

Prayers can be said anywhere, even outdoors, the prayers more consecrated than the temple. During construction, a temporary ark held the holy scrolls in the living room/dining room of the *mikvah* house in Newton, and we said evening prayers facing east toward the scrolls. On Tisha B'Av, many people came to services wearing sneakers and cloth belts. Before prayers began, those wearing leather shoes and belts took them off. The bereaved give up some comforts. In my youth, I thought it strange, this custom of not wearing leather during mourning. As a kid going barefoot or wearing cloth sneakers was way more comfortable than wearing shoes. We sat on the floor, another reminder of shivah, the days of mourning. The group took turns reading from Lamentations. Jeremiah weeps, and we read his sorrowful words lamenting the fall of the first temple.

> *How doth the city sit solitary that was full of people! How is she become as a widow! She that was great among the nations, and princess among the provinces, how is she become enslaved!*
> *She weeps in agony in the night, and her tears are on her cheeks; she hath none to comfort her among all her lovers; all her friends have dealt treacherously with her, they are become her enemies.*

As we read, I saw my wife lying in her deathbed as I watched the cancer eat through her. Her friends stood by her, but God and her body betrayed her.

The Lamentations also brought to mind my father's stories, of the destruction of his family and the Jews of Poland. He was the fifth of six siblings. For a few years, my father also had a nephew, who would have been my cousin. Dad's sister, Rushka, married in 1938 and moved to Warsaw; her son, the nephew, was born in 1939. Everyone agreed that Dad's sister was a hot ticket. My father said, "She could charm the spots off of a leopard," which is somehow an even more meaningful phrase in Yiddish. When the war started, Rushka and her son came back to Wyszogród, my father's hometown. The child was with them in the boxcar that took them to the camps, the boxcar with its crowded human cargo, Jews locked up for long hours in the dark heat without food or water.

During a conversation the day before Tisha B'Av, my dad mused about the Germans. "At first they weren't so bad. They took over a part of Poland and did what they had to do to administer the territory, but once they had conquered France and were marching toward Moscow, they thought they were gods who ruled the world."

Dad was 23 years old in 1939, when the Germans arrived in Vishigrod. Almost immediately, they began conscripting young Jewish men for labor. The men were sent off in work gangs and might be away from home for weeks at a time. My father would run off into the countryside whenever there was a rumor of a new roundup. He would stay with farmers he knew from the market or at the orchards his father had rented. When he heard that it was safe, he would sneak back into town to see his family and sleep in his own bed.

On one of his visits to town, a German administrator had stopped him. "This German was not a bad man," high praise from my father. My father paused and shook his head slowly from side to side, just barely enough so that you could see the motion. The German had told my father, "Who goes to the work camp this time will not be sorry." It was January 18, 1941. My father heeded his advice and went off to the camp.

At the work camp, the men slept 30 to a room on straw mattresses. Looking back on it, my father said it was not so bad. He was able to go home for the weekend, where he worked with his father and brother making hats so that they still had some money for food. Two months later he understood the German's advice. The Germans herded all the Jews into the town's market square. Families that had people in the work camp could remain; the rest were taken off to go to concentration camps.

At the end of the summer, another roundup was announced. The Germans were looking for anyone without local identity documents. People without these "passports" were to gather at the firehouse. Rushka and her baby, who had fled from Warsaw to rejoin her family, did not have papers. The family was distraught. No one wanted her to go, but the instructions were clear and people knew she was in town. Regina, Dad's youngest sister, stood up and said, with fire in her eyes, "I will talk to the authorities."

The town administrator was a German, Kraus, a miller from the area, the same man who had warned my father about going to the work camp to save his family. Her charm unleashed, Regina's pleadings were successful and Rushka was allowed to stay. They lived together as a family for five more months, until December 1941. Even after my father and his family were hauled off to the ghetto, they worked their cottage industry as *hittlemachers,* making hats, and had food to eat.

Rushka's husband made suitcases, a very popular commodity for a population of refugees. Some would find passage to safety, but most people were being forced to abandon their homes, "resettled" by the Nazis. My father shakes his head, a wider movement, as he tells the story.

"Stupid people, they packed like they were going on vacation to a resort."

As soon as Rushka's husband made a suitcase, it was sold. He had food, some coal for heat, and he wanted his wife and child to be with him. Rushka went back to Warsaw on the train, and no one in the family ever saw her again.

On December 12, 1942, just after Rushka left, the Nazis rounded up all the Jews in Vishigrod, with just what they could carry. It was a story that repeated itself throughout the war. In 1942, my family, the Kirschenbaums, took quilts and sewing machines, some food and clothes and moved to Nowy Dwór. In the Nowy Dwór ghetto they were given a single ten-foot-square room for seven people. For weeks, there were no facilities for bathing and no way to wash clothes.

Regina did some seamstress work for the wife of the chief of police who, after weeks of pleadings, found them two larger rooms. Eventually the women found a laundry they could use. Again, my father shakes his head. "They brought me some clean undergarments, and I went outside to change and shake the lice out of the dirty underwear. You would not believe it. The lice poured out like rain." He looked at me with wide eyes as I winced. The chickens sometimes had lice on the farms, so I had an all-too-clear picture of the little beasts.

As the Nazis concentrated Jews into smaller areas, people came from other ghettos. Families that had been rich waited in line for soup; former lumber barons, men who had owned power plants, factories, and department stores, stood waiting for a handout.

My father and his brothers cast about for some way to make money. They had tossed a sewing machine into doubled-up pillowcases to take with them to the ghetto, and they located some other hat-making equipment in an abandoned shop. They found an unheated room they could set up in and started making hats and caps. Soon they employed four *hittlemachers*. It seemed like something in their genes, this entrepreneurship, this drive to make a living. While others despaired, they found a way to engage in commerce.

In April 1942, typhus broke out. My father got sick, then *his* father, and then his sisters; my aunts and my grandmother all were struck by the fever. If one survives typhus, the illness usually lasts 14 days, 14 days of bad diarrhea, high fever, and delirium. Rifka, a second cousin, came to take care of the others while they were sick. Yadja, another sister of Dad's, had the worst fever and was severely dehydrated. The family took her and Regina, who was also doing badly, to an overcrowded makeshift hospital.

Regina recovered and came back. My grandmother and Regina wanted to go see Yadja. The rest of the family knew she was dead, her corpse burned in a pit with those of the other plague victims. No one in the family wanted to tell the two women that Yadja had died. They kept putting it off, keeping the illusion, letting the two women imagine that Yadja would return. This seemed a kindness. Or perhaps the others could not bear watching the women grieve.

My father explained that periodically the Germans made "selections." As he spoke, my father's voice went cold. A long silence followed the word "selections." For me, the word had once seemed benign, almost positive: Being selected was an honor, the best students chosen for admittance to a university, the best athletes chosen for a sports team. In this "selection," the Nazis took orphans first, then the poorest of the poor, those without protection. They came to take my father's mother. They took her out into the street with others who were old or infirm.

"*Raus. Raus!* Out, out. Old people out on the street."

My father sometimes used the same German word "*raus*" to rouse us from our beds on school days. It is not my favorite word.

Once again Regina, full of optimism and audacity, followed after her mother looking for some way to use her charm to save her. She had found work as a dressmaker for some of the Germans who had local girlfriends. She recognized one, an SS man who was keeping guard on her mother, and went to him pleading. He kept shaking his head "no," but she persisted and eventually he pointed at an old bombed-out building. The roof had been blown off, and piles of rubble covered one of the first-floor windows.

"Take her there and wait until dark and then you can take her home."

They hid in the bombed-out structure and eventually found their way back to the rest of the family.

One Friday, they had finished work and closed up shop for the weekend, a Friday like any other Friday in the ghetto. Many people still were doing what they could to keep the Sabbath. They said their prayers, but the next Monday the selection grabbed them all and herded them onto boxcars for the train ride to Auschwitz-Birkenau.

I have heard the story so many times. My grandmother gathered the family together on the train to Auschwitz and told them, "Your father and I are finished. *Halt de kinder zusammen; efscher vil zie eberleben.* (You kids stick together; maybe you will live through this.)"

Godel was the only one to survive.

∞

Only a few Kirschenbaum family photographs survived the war. A formal portrait of my father showed a fit young man with a full head of hair. I would never have recognized him had I not seen photos of him from his days in Munich after the war. In my mind's eye he remains the bald farmer in gray work pants, sunburned head, bowlegged with a potbelly, his dentures making him hesitant to show more than a close-lipped smile. He had one photograph of Regina and one of Rushka. The one of Regina showed her and a couple of her girlfriends, smiling and looking stylish in long coats and modest heels on a cobblestoned street. The other was a formal portrait of Rushka. A serious face, hair pulled back, looked back at us through warm, dark eyes. The photograph had only recently found its way to my father.

The process of tracking down people and their stories never seemed to end for the survivors. Frantic activity immediately after the war became an embedded component of survivor culture, extending for decades. Chance encounters might lead to someone who somehow overlapped with your hometown or distant kin. Any new acquaintance, any new piece of evidence, triggered the search for information about the people who disappeared in the maelstrom, for artifacts from a shattered world.

Forty years after the war, when my parents retired and became "snowbirds," spending winters in a high-rise condo in southern Florida, another set of connections surfaced. One of these was a man who had once dated Rushka.

The young Jews in the first half of the 20th century, even in the country towns, were better educated than their parents. The revolution in Russia and the social upheaval all over Europe surged across the Polish countryside. For many Eastern European Jews, politics, whether to the left or right, had Zionist overtones. Most young people belonged to some social club that had a political bent. Rushka's boyfriend, Jossel Putterman, was a socialist, maybe a communist in his youth. He was a tailor. The Jewish word is *schneider* (cutter), someone who cuts cloth. My grandparents did not approve of the match. They thought he was too radical, too wild. My father used the words "not settled," implying that the young man lacked a secure way of making a living. They had a youthful, covert romance until he decided to fight the fascists in Spain. He took her photograph with him but never returned from the conflict. Caught with socialist literature, he paid off some official and escaped from Warsaw to Belgium and eventually became part of the Paris underground.

More than half a century after the war my father bumped into Putterman, Rushka's boyfriend, at a bar mitzvah in New York. He was still living in France. The bar mitzvah gave him an excuse to come to the United States for a vacation. At the bar mitzvah he told my father that he had a picture of Rushka and my father asked him for it or a copy. He agreed but never sent the photo. My father wrote him asking again for the photo, but his requests were never answered. When word came that Putterman had died, my father gave up on ever finding the photo. He was sitting by the pool in the winter sunshine, the high-rise condos behind him, a straw hat protecting his bald head, when a woman approached him. It was Putterman's sister-in-law carrying an envelope that Putterman had given her on his deathbed with instructions on how to find Godel in Hollywood, Florida.

We were sitting on my parents' porch in Lakewood as Dad told me the story. My mother had come out to join us. A slow trembling animated her hands on the walker as she shuffled slowly toward the threshold. For her it was a small mountain ridge, followed by the precipice of the single step out to the porch. My father and I both got up to help her navigate and then settle into one of the porch chairs.

"That's a nice car."

"Thanks, Mom. I've had for a while now."

"It's a nice color."

My friends and I call it my midlife-crisis car, a coupe, something between a muscle car and a sports car, too much horsepower, leather seats, yet somehow, as a childless widower, less shameful than owning an SUV. The firehouse red no longer embarrassed me. I had almost stopped making midlife-crisis jokes when I gave someone new a ride in the car.

My father looked on a bit sad but still curious, puzzling out what he could of her thought processes.

"She always wanted a red car," he said in Yiddish.

In 1953, my parents had just moved onto the farm and they decided to buy a new car. My father was still unsure of his English and had never bought a car from a dealer. He asked the Jewish agent for the feed cooperative, a man who had helped him get started on the farm, to come with him as counsel and translator. My parents and the agent set off for Pine Belt Chevrolet. (We lived in the northern part of Jersey's Pine Barrens, the Pine Belt.) Henry Ford had a reputation as an anti-Semite, and Jews seemed to prefer GM cars. My mother was immediately drawn to a bright red 1953 Bel Air with a bright white stripe along the side. The red-and-white interior was an old ice cream parlor just missing the soda fountain. My father never had strong opinions about color and was ready to go along. But the agent pulled him over.

"Don't buy such a car. Not a red one. People will talk. They'll say, 'Who is this big shot, with his red car?' You are new here; don't send the wrong signals."

They settled on a beige Bel Air sedan with a red stripe, but when our farmhouse needed paint, we wound up with dark red shingles and white trim.

Passover

∞

It was early afternoon the day before Passover. Mom was standing at the counter in an old beige bathrobe making matzo balls. It was good to see her out of bed and in the kitchen. This was the first Passover since Ronnie's death, and the first in 30 years that I had come alone to my parents' house for the holiday.

Dad was setting the table. Mom was using a hand mixer on the matzo meal when I arrived. It was a comforting scene after the trauma of Mom's illness. The tumor had been safely removed, but she had not fully recovered from being hospitalized. A fall and hip fracture had not helped. I had become accustomed to Mom's problems with Parkinson's disease, the determined way she worked with trembling hands as she prepared food. Dad had taken over most of the cooking, but Mom, now 85, had rallied for the holiday. I felt lucky to still have them; so many of my friends had lost one or both of their parents.

My brother and I and Mom's friends had convinced her that letting Dad get out a bit would be good for him and would make him better company for her and everyone else. My parents had hired Denise, a Trinidadian woman, to assist them. Denise helped my parents get through the day—administering pills, bathing Mom, doing laundry, keeping her company the few hours a week that Dad left the house. Mom had accepted Denise, in part because she could not imagine my father being attracted to her. That old people still felt sexual jealousy made me slightly queasy until I realized that, for teenagers, I was way old in my middle age. Thinking of me having sex probably left them feeling grossed out. Several years earlier I had been surprised and embarrassed when Mom had complained about Dad's "unmanliness" after his prostate surgery. Even as a child, I had had trouble imagining my parents having sex. Now that they were in their eighties, it was impossible. (I had never followed up to find out if Dad had recovered his sex drive.) Hearing Mom complain about how Dad looked at other women almost made me giggle the first few times. He was 86, but I guess a man that age in good health with a mind that still worked was a rare commodity. Now Mom's girlfriends (most of whose husbands are dead) were the competition.

My parents had moved off the farm in the 1980s and now lived on the north side of Lakewood near the town line. Their house sat on a suburban plot, well back from the street. A fruit tree, already in bloom, stood in the middle of a circular drive. I had used a clicker to open the garage, squeezing between stinky garbage cans, my parents' Oldsmobile, a freezer, and extra refrigerator, and climbing a couple of stairs to a door that opened into the kitchen.

When I walked in, Denise was standing near Mom in the kitchen. The electric stove separated them. A pot of chicken stock was on the front burner struggling to come to a boil. It all seemed nearly normal and only became a bit odd when Mom turned to look at me as I offered greetings. I find it hard to raise my voice enough to be heard by people whose hearing is diminished. I have the same trouble in a crowded bar. I am by nature soft-spoken, but over the years, between being forced to do a bit of public speaking and having a whole generation become hard of hearing, I was slowly learning to crank up the volume. As Mom turned toward me, the background noise changed slightly. No one noticed at first in all the fuss of greetings after a long absence. Phit, phit, splat. The hand mixer tilted as Mom turned, and the beaters slowly edged out of the batter and started flinging the mix out of the bowl.

Wet matzo meal hit the ceiling. It was like an electric shock. The hair on the back of my hands stood up, my eyes widened, and my pulse

Bronia in her kitchen

accelerated. One by one all of us—Denise; Dad, who had just walked in; and I—morphed into action. We were like cartoon characters, jumping up in the air, our eyes turning into exclamation points, our legs whirring trying to get traction. Loose bits of matzo meal were sucked into the vacuum left in our wake as we surged toward Mom.

The batter was beige and chunky. It was like some off-color oatmeal run through a fan, spraying over the cabinets and kitchen windows, a geyser erupting from the mixing bowl. "Oh my Lord," a smile, and the beginnings of a laugh from Denise before she checked herself, knitted her eyebrows together, and put on a polite grimace, rushing to help with the cleanup. I hurried over to count Mom's fingers, to make sure she hadn't lopped off any in the mixer. She stubbornly held on to the hand mixer even after I pulled the plug to make it stop. She was *oy yoying*, although she looked more puzzled than upset. "*Oy yoy, oy yoy, vus hat passiert?*" loosely translated from the Yiddish: "Uh oh, what just happened?"

I tried to get Mom to sit down in her recliner in the living room, but she wasn't having any of it. "If not me, who will make the *kniedlach* (the matzo ball dumplings)?" The "if not me" construction always reminded me of the Hebrew song: *If I am not for myself, who will be for me? If I am just for myself, what do I have? If not now, when?* My dad offered me up as the cook. Mom was not happy with the idea and became increasingly agitated. I tried to move her, but she shook me off. She looked so frail, I was afraid to hold her wrist too firmly. Eventually she agreed to sit down and insisted that Denise drag in a high chair that usually serves as a step stool. Mom positioned it so that she could oversee the activities. She was like a magistrate on her high bench with the plaintiffs before her.

She loved to prepare food almost as much as she loved to push it at her family and guests. "Do your mother a favor, eat something, darling!" My mother was from the old school: She did not rely on recipes but rather on all of the senses—from taste and smell, to look, touch, and hearing. She would listen to how it sounds when you tap or briskly move a fork through matzo meal. Sadly, most of her senses were falling into disrepair, but they had started out so much more acute than mine that they were still sharper, even in their diminished state.

I have trouble sorting through which parts of my parents' behavior were common to immigrants, to refugees, to Europeans, to Polish Jews, or to poor people who have become middle class and which parts were simply dispersed through the population. My parents were from Poland, but they did not consider themselves Poles. The "Polackem" were the ones that delivered them to the Nazis, the ones who harassed them and ridiculed them, who worked as trustees in the camps, the ones who turned their backs on them and pretended not to see. Every so often a Pole appeared in their stories as a friend, a saint, someone who tried to save lives, a person so rare that he could not be grouped with the others, the way the Bible or the Koran cannot be grouped with other books. My parents' inner circle was that small group of Jews who remained in Europe and somehow survived WWII. They called themselves *greeneh*, greenhorns, newcomers, new to the herd, trying to learn the language and the ways of these United States. Even the Jews who arrived before the war were grouped in with the *Americana teychaster* (American asses), who did not know how bad things could get, people who took things for granted like being able to find food and drinking water. The inner circle was now drying up; my father complained about how few were left to sit with him in synagogue on *Shabbos*.

My parents still agonized about what others would think of them. I had always found this odd. How could people who had been hunted and imprisoned, dispossessed, scorned, and expelled need to work so hard to conform to a small town's expectations? Perhaps they were surprised to find themselves with any sense of community in their new world, or maybe it was just their original small-town upbringing reasserting itself. My father had made a curious accommodation to Jewish orthodoxy that never included strict observance. For example, driving a car is forbidden on the Sabbath, but he would drive his Oldsmobile to get to synagogue. He was embarrassed to drive the car on Saturday, ashamed of what his more religious neighbors would think. On his way home from prayers he would sit idling on a side street waiting for a break in the parade of Hassidim. When the coast was clear, he would make a dash for the garage.

It was easier when we lived out on the farm. The 50,000 chickens demanded work every day. Maintaining some arbitrary set of commandments seemed a luxury reserved for city folk. For my mother, conforming to Jewish orthodoxy was mostly about keeping the house as a showcase, looking her best when she went out in public, and keeping us and our clothes clean and in good repair. Not that clothes had to be high fashion or even fashionable; they just had to be new. Mom never understood about faded jeans or the fascination with castaway clothing that took over youth in the 1960s and 1970s. I was perplexed at the intensity of my parents' desire to be presentable and upright members of the community. Their wariness of strangers and secretiveness seemed much more understandable in people who had been hunted and imprisoned.

I started in on the matzo balls taking instruction from Mom on what to add to the meal and how thick the mix should be. When she was satisfied, I washed my hands again and began forming up balls of carbohydrates. My brother calls them Jewish cement: matzo meal and cold water. Wadding them together was a little like making snowballs, and my thoughts drifted back to when I was 12, standing on top of the ridge at the old gravel pit lobbing snowballs at the 18-wheelers on Highway 9. I was tempted to try juggling the matzo balls because they sat nicely in the hands. Juggling teaches you to appreciate the specific gravity of objects: Some float in the wind, some bounce off the fingertips, and some settle nicely in the palms. Tempting as it was to set the matzo balls in motion, I didn't want to clean up any more stray matzo goop.

As I dropped them into the boiling chicken soup, they sank to the bottom. They lurked there until some geothermal mechanics released them from gravity's hold and they popped up to the top, floating and bobbing in the broth. Mom kept poking me, telling me to add more matzo balls to the soup. She looked small and frail, her thinning hair was dyed an ash blond. I have early-childhood memories of her hair being rich and black, but much clearer memories of being conscripted to help her with the home bleaching and dying. Mercifully, by the time I entered high school, I was spared peroxide poisoning as social pressure forced her to the beauty parlor where all her friends were moving through the colors of the rainbow.

Dad had done the Passover shopping. He had even bought the gefilte fish. He was also in charge of cooking the meat. I joked with him that as the main cook for the meal, he should be doing the matzo balls. He was proud of coming to grips with cooking in his advanced years. "I 'learn me up' how to do everything." After 50 years in America some of his English still came out as badly translated Yiddish. Until Mom got sick, they had fit smoothly into gender roles that matched up well with 1950s TV. I had bought into that Wally and Beaver worldview at the time. It certainly fit my family. I loved my mother, who had a big heart, but I respected my father who was smart and could do complex arithmetic in his head. She always insisted that she was my father's equal, but he never took it seriously. While he was willing to recount the horrors of his youth and the war, he never complained of his fate. My mother, on the other hand, through most of my youth had an unending list of complaints: her mother raising her alone, the better prospects she gave up to marry my father, the endless work and drudgery, the smell and filth of being stuck on the farm. She always found others to be jealous of, what they had and the life they led. For all her whining, she had a warm and friendly temperament and an easy smile. When we were young and even on that Passover, her boys were an endless source of wonder and satisfaction to her.

As my parents saw it, outside the family, almost no one was to be trusted, especially in business dealings. Everyone who could would steal from you. For years Mom resisted hiring household help. She did not want a stranger in the house; she was worried about her jewels, and she was probably a bit worried that it would distract my father and push her ever so slightly away from being his main focus. Their wariness of strangers and struggle to preserve their good name and image in the community made for a strange array of secrets. I remember coming home from college having turned 20 in my junior year and my mother sitting me down in the kitchen of our old house on the chicken farm. We sat at a gray Formica table with metal legs. She was 52 years old, and we had never had a sit-down one-on-one conversation. She was always working in the house or around the farm, always in motion when we spoke. When we sat down, it was almost always as a family, eating dinner or watching TV. She took my hand and she had tears in her eyes. She looked up at me and told me, "Your father didn't want me to tell you. He doesn't like people to know, but your father is not my first husband. I was married to a boy in Poland before the war."

Not quite 20 years old she had married a boy named Mendel from her hometown. It was a love match to a handsome boy. They had a few happy months, and then suddenly he was sick and died a year later from polio. She had been a poor girl living with her mother and step-father, abandoned by her father. She was now suddenly a young widow. Learning of her earlier marriage, I was stunned; pillars anchoring my world crumbled. It was like learning that atoms are not solid. Over time, I managed to reassess my parents' relationship. But as I sat there with my mom, reality seemed less substantial.

On this Passover I was thinking of the loss of both of my parents' families. My maternal grandfather had escaped to America to avoid the draft. When he did not return, my grandmother remarried and had two boys with her new husband. Mom doesn't talk much about her stepfather or her half brothers. They were much younger than she. I think she felt like an au pair in the new household. Her mother and the boys were killed trying to run away when the Germans came to take them out of the ghetto. Her new stepfather ran off, too, and made it into the woods, but he died later in the war.

All together I had six aunts and uncles I never met. None of them survived the war. When my father's family was herded together and driven out of the ghetto, they spent two-and-a-half days crammed into a cattle car without water or food. Dad was parched when they let them out to exercise because they were changing trains. He searched every-where for drinking water. Not finding any and desperate, he drank standing water from ruts in the train yard road.

"It was foul and brackish. The water smelled like diesel fuel. I can still smell that diesel stink." His eyes drifted away, and he paused to shake his head. "Hunger is terrible but the thirst… I was so thirsty, I would have drunk anything."

My father lost three sisters and a brother. He often tells the story of saying good-bye to his mother. How she took his hands and told him, "We are old and there is no chance for us. You and your brother are young; you still have a chance to live." His sisters went with his mother and died in the gas chambers. His brother got sick in the stock car they were crammed into. Later on he fared badly in one of the "selections," when they picked out and killed the men too weak to work. He died soon after entering the camps.

My parents' view of the world crystallized during the war. Their attitude toward America is rooted in the war as well. Everyone wanted to be freed by the GIs. They treated you well. After all, they were not starving like the Russians. They had a refreshing attitude. They were shocked by what they saw in the camps, horrified, nauseated. The Russians had already buried 20 million of their own dead; they did not have much empathy to spare.

Refugee camps became the great lost-and-found emporiums for the tortured souls of a continent. Hordes of displaced people milled about, each carrying his or her own story of terror and survival. Many, especially the Jews, understood there was no going back. But tired of living in camps, my dad had struggled to get back to his hometown in the postwar chaos. Along the way many hazards waited. Food was in short supply. Highwaymen with guns occasionally confronted him along the way. My father, at five feet six inches and 130 pounds, tried to make it clear that he was more trouble than he was worth.

"So you have a pistol. You have a pistol and you say you *will* shoot me…. OK. Go ahead. Shoot! You're not the first one who could have killed me. I've seen more dead men than you've seen live ones. Go ahead, shoot, or leave me alone." (I still find it hard to believe that this same man would later agonize about the torn blue jeans I wore to the mall.)

After trekking on foot most of the way from a refugee camp just south of Munich, Dad reached his hometown in Poland. He found almost no Jews left in the town. Suspicious Poles who had moved into Jewish homes and taken over Jewish enterprises made for a poor homecoming. He eventually came to understand that the zone occupied by the West would be better than that liberated by the Russians. The Russians still needed relief themselves and had much less to spill over for helping refugees.

Returning to Germany, where his few live friends had resettled, Dad soon became engaged in a brisk commerce in Munich. The loot of the dead along with a U.S. surplus from a superheated wartime economy traded hands in the postwar chaos. The reparations folks, who had a great German name, *Wiedergutmachen* (make it good again), helped with a stipend, and there was plenty of only slightly bombed-out housing. When asked what he did in this period, Dad would reply, "*Ich habe gehandeld*." He handled goods. Dad became a partner with a watchmaker and jeweler, Felix, whom he had met just as the war was ending. They traded watches and silver or gold and occasionally contraband items restricted by rationing or high tariffs, like saccharin or silk.

He saved his money and still lived well. By the time I was born, in 1950, the Allied occupation was ending and the Cold War was in full bloom. Refugees were dispersing to start again in some new country.

For my parents, the big decision was between Israel, which my father preferred, and the United States. My mother had located the father who had abandoned her years earlier. He was in New York City, and she wanted to go see him and introduce him to his grandson.

For Passover, my father had set the table in the dining room, with the Rothschild china that my parents brought with them from Deutschland. Mom had purchased the standard four sets of dishes. Two pairs, one for the whole year and the other reserved for Passover. Each pair had one set for meat and one for dairy. The meat dishes for Passover were bone white with gold trim. Fifty years later they still looked new. The whole trousseau had been packed into large pine crates six feet long and four feet wide that came over with them on the boat to New York City. When I was growing up, I used one crate to create a fort in our basement; it was still part of my rainy-day games when my brother was born in 1955.

Mom sat patiently at the Passover table dressed in a clean white blouse and dark slacks. Denise had helped her dress and put on her makeup. She was wearing red lipstick and blue eye shadow, which made the white bags below her eyes look even paler. My mother seemed to concur that all was in order. She nodded her head in approval, but this may have been the Parkinson's. She had rallied enough to grill my father about what he had already put out on the table, how the meat was doing, and the whereabouts of the fish and the wine.

Dad was tired. Just dealing with Mom's illness was wearing him out. The holiday preparations had pushed him toward his limits. Still, he seemed in good spirits. He told the story about going to market with his brother twice and was about to tell it a third time when Mom stopped him. The first night of Passover had fallen on a Thursday in my father's 14th year, in 1931. As it sometimes happened in the spring in those days, there were two midweek markets on the same day in different towns. He and his brother got sent to the one farthest away while his father and older sisters went to the near one. A lone donkey pulled a cart with goods from several families, and the boys walked alongside the donkey for the seven miles in each direction lest the donkey give out and they get stuck having to carry the stuff home, jumping on the cart for only a few minutes on the way home when exhaustion set in. Dad returned home bone weary but managed to wash and change in time for the meal. He had to ask the questions. "Why is this night different than all other nights?" Usually, this responsibility provoked enough anticipation to keep him anxious until he discharged his responsibilities.

Dad always smiled when he told this story; he would pause to smile, each time in the same place. His family did not have enough chairs for everyone, and some of the family sat on a bed that had been pulled up to the table. He had fallen asleep almost as soon as they sat down at the table, and his father began the ritual of reciting the benedictions and telling the tale of the escape from slavery. When his turn came to ask what was special about this night, his father had to wake him. Each time he tells the story, he remembers how pleasant it was to wake up with his whole family around the warm holiday table smiling at him and his little nap.

Back in New Jersey, the table was set, the soup and matzo balls were ready, and it was now time to tell the Passover story. The Jews were not the only ones with stories of death and dislocation. Denise had her own stories. Two weeks before Passover, she had disappeared, leaving no note, no phone message. A week later she returned. I asked my father why she had left, and he said he had no idea.

I was curious, but at first she would not answer direct questions. She shook her head from side to side. I kept after Denise trying to unravel the mystery. Eventually, she told me she had to deal with a family problem. We might have left it there, but I think Denise needed to talk to someone and I was the only one in the house not wearing a hearing aid.

She left to help her cousin, who was in trouble, all sorts of trouble. His stepfather, John, was a strict man and didn't hesitate to use physical discipline. No one in Denise's family liked him. He had been known to beat his wife, Denise's aunt, who had since left him. Denise's cousin made a terrible choice, a pact with the devil. He lived in John's house and put up with his cruelty in exchange for free rent. It was not the house though; it was a car, John's old Pontiac, that did them both in.

The 19-year-old cousin had borrowed the Pontiac without asking permission. When John found out, he began cursing. Then, first with an open hand and then his fists, he struck the teenager again and again. It drove the young man over the line. The teenager's anger boiled over. His stepfather had gone too far. In frenzy, the young man reached out for a hammer. Tears of sorrow and rage streamed down his face as he struck his tormentor. Was it murderous intent? An unholy fury unabated, he stuck out at his oppressor until a blow to the head finished the man.

The young man sat for hours with the body on the kitchen floor, in shock, paralyzed, despondent. What had he done? What would he do? He was the only one left in the house. His mother had moved out long ago and lived in another borough. He had no friends he could trust to ask for help. As nightfall set in, he moved the body into the bathtub and cleaned up the kitchen.

He did not know what else to do, so the next day he got up and went to work. Two days later one of the neighbors stopped in to inquire about his stepfather and the young man told her John had taken a trip to visit relatives upstate. Three days after the killing one of his John's pals stopped in because he had missed bowling night. His bowling buddy got the same story, but the man wondered out loud about how he took that trip because he had just seen John's car on the street. Later that night the kid went out and moved the Pontiac to a spot several blocks away. Overwhelmed by what had happened, he never managed to come up with a plan for getting rid of the body. Days passed.

Another lost soul living in impossible conditions. I wonder if he slept, if he ate his Cheerios in the morning before going to work, if he used the bathroom where the dead man lay festering in the tub. Did he brush his teeth in the kitchen sink?

Almost a week later a policeman who knew John came by because he had seen John's car with a bunch of tickets on it in its new locale and wanted to warn John that it would be towed. By then the odor of the decaying body filled the apartment and made the cop suspicious. He asked about the smell, about why John had left his car so far from the house, and the kid broke down and told him the whole story.

Denise shook her head and wrinkled her brow at how that old Pontiac had caused all this trouble. She raised her eyebrows, and her eyes met mine for a moment. Borrowing the car had provoked the fight, and the parking tickets on the car had led to his arrest. That damned car! Even though she was from the Islands, she reminded me of the old Mississippi Delta singers and the mysterious blues they sang. Songs filled with implied contradictions and curious juxtapositions, a wistful amusement at a tragic tale. The calm voice, the quiet in the eye of a hurricane, an old black man singing a parable, a story that passes along a bit of wisdom that prepares you for what the end's going to be. Folks that sing the blues combine paradox and parable. You sing a sad song and then smile. Things may not turn out so well, but you live with that and still keep on keeping on. You take comfort in accepting sadness, build strength. In my youth this seemed the heart of wisdom. Nowadays I might see it in a Buddhist light: Pain is everywhere, but suffering is what you take on for yourself.

Like my father, my mother hated being dependent on others and she hated being left alone. So much of her life now consisted of waiting and watching time slip away. She got along fairly well with Denise. They had become used to each other. Mom, who for years had refused to hire a live-in companion/aide, now seemed to accept the situation, despite some lingering concerns about having her jewelry stolen. Even so, she resented my father's independence. She grudgingly conceded it was his right to go to synagogue on the Sabbath, but she complained about his "bumming around and abandoning her" when he made visits to his old office and the business my brother had taken over from him a few years back. Dad needed to get out. He missed the action and stopped in to check on current building projects. Sometimes he sat at the computer *kvetching* the mouse to check his stocks and making small talk with Barbara, the office manager. *Kvetch* is a loaded word in Yiddish. It is from the German word for "press" or "crush," but it is also slang for someone who is a whiner and always complains. Mom viewed Dad's one- or two-hour excursions as heartless abandonment. Was she *kvetching,* too? I thought I understood her jealousy of his relative fitness and independence. She started being cranky about it years ago, in her seventies, after her third accident when she lost her driver's license. My brother and I tried to get her to sign up for a car service, but she insisted on making my father be her driver.

As Mom grew weaker, especially after the cancer surgery, she became more despondent and fell even more squarely into a victim's role. Watching her suffer was heartbreaking, but I couldn't avoid comparing her whining and histrionics with my wife's grace as she struggled with cancer.

Mom's surgery had left her with scar tissue inside her palate, and she could not fully open her mouth. Her food needed to be cut into small pieces that would pass her lips. Denise helped her cut up the matzo balls. Mom was on good behavior at the holiday table. Tonight, she did not ask anyone to taste her food first to make sure she was not being poisoned. She did not rail about how everyone wished she were dead. We rushed through the text. I asked the questions, and Dad recited the answers from the Haggadah (the telling): this poor bread that our ancestors ate and these plagues that were visited on our enslavers, even a bit of reminiscing about how the famous rabbis of the Middle Ages interpreted the texts. I had liked studying the Haggadah in school, but for most of my youth, I had found the actual reading from it at the dinner table tedious. Like some grumpy pet waiting on the humans, I was hungry and the telling stood between me and chopped liver.

The story is of surviving slavery to make a new life. Dad read from the Haggadah. He answered the four questions. Why do we eat matzo? Because we left Egypt in such a hurry that bread dough didn't have time to rise. The story also tells of the plagues that eventually convinced the pharaoh to release the Jews. The ancient Jews had marked their doorways with lamb's blood to escape the tenth plague in which the firstborn of every household died. I had often thought that my parents should abandon the text and tell their own stories. Their doorways were marked with human blood, and whole families were slaughtered.

My mother had hidden in a snowbank, with no gloves and torn socks, in the dead of night, listening to the German patrols that were searching for the partisans after someone had seen her troop running from a nearby barn. The Germans were close enough so that she could hear every word. *Wenn ich euch finde Juden, werde ich euch totschlagen!* (When I find you Jews, I will kill you dead!) Death lurked in every doorway, in every shadow. Each day was a test.

In Auschwitz, Dad had pilfered small items and bartered them. He had combed the garbage for anything that seemed remotely edible. Somehow he lived from day to day. While marching out to a work detail, the foreman, a criminal who had been pulled out of prison to boss work gangs, would throw stones at the feet of those who seemed lethargic. He called out someone else's name and heaved a rock in his direction, but it struck my father squarely in the ankle. He started to limp immediately, but still he went out into the fields. After a day of digging drainage ditches, his ankle was too swollen to support him. When he reported for work the next morning, they pulled him aside because it was clear he could not walk. They set him down under guard to wait for the ambulance truck. My father was desperate. His brother had been "selected" for death because he had open sores on his feet, and now his own foot was injured and he had become unfit for work. He was sure his hours were numbered.

He climbed into an ambulance, a panel truck with wood benches and a red cross painted on the side. It was taking him from the work camps to the border of the extermination camps. He shook his head as he told the story. There were four other young men in the truck. They were German Jews, "nice boys, 80, 90 pounds," gaunt, their muscles withered, their eyes bulging in their heads. *I am finished,* he thought. He took out a small crust of bread and some saccharin he had hidden in his clothes. He wanted to have a sweet taste in his mouth before he died. He sat praying with his whole body shaking forward and back on the wooden bench. *God help me.*

They took him to the camp hospital at Monowice, a nearby facility. They took his clothes, and a male nurse examined him. My father pleaded with him.

"Please sir, help me. I am a young man. I want to live."

"I cannot do anything to help you."

239

An SS officer met the truck and told him he would need to strip and take a shower before entering the hospital. Most of the men knew about the gas chambers. The inmates had heard about the "showers" from the poor souls whose job it was to drag out the bodies and move them to the crematoriums. When he heard the word "showers," his hair rose up on the back of his neck. As he and the others on the ambulance truck waited their turn, my father made his peace with God. I can still see his face when he first told me the story, eyes moist, eyebrows lifted, and the rumor of a smile on his lips.

"They took all our clothes, and we went in to the shower, naked just like the day we were born. I was so skinny, you could see my ribs poking out. They painted my number on my chest with a grease pencil. They closed the door behind us. I stood for a long time waiting to die and then just to see what would happen I reached for the faucet and turned the handle…" He paused to shake his head slowly.

"I turned the handle and water came out … water … cold water." As he told the story, his hands went out to his sides, palms up as though testing for rain. He looked up with a glassy-eyed smile.

"I thought, 'I am still alive.'"

Rosh Hashanah

∞

The early September night was warm and sultry in the part of summer that lingers after Labor Day. The long drive from Cambridge through Connecticut and New York was yet again taking me back to my roots in the Garden State. The ancestral vine grew for centuries in medieval Poland. Uprooted and hacked to shreds, it stayed alive in postwar Germany, long enough to make its way across the Atlantic, to New York, before putting down roots in New Jersey soil.

I was returning home to celebrate Rosh Hashanah, the New Year in the Jewish calendar, and the first of the days of judgment and repentance. My mother had died in February. She was 86 years old when cancer and Alzheimer's disease took her from us. Now my father and I were both widowers. This would be the first Rosh Hashanah without Mom. My father, my brother, and I were still saying kaddish, still grieving. I cannot bring myself to compare my grief for my mother with the pain and loss of my wife's death. It is always tragic when anyone you love passes away. Is it less troubling when an old person dies? Is it better or worse to watch a long decline or a quicker passing?

Trying to accept what I could not change, I tried to focus on the living, especially on my father, who had not lived alone for more than 50 years. Mercifully, the Polish woman whom we had hired to help take care of Mom in the last stages of her illness had agreed to stay on as my father's housekeeper. Christina was a godsend. Christina (Krisha in Polish) had come to the United States to find work. There was a rumor she was also trying to get away from her husband. She had been diligent and compassionate taking care of my mother. My father had become comfortable having her in the house. This was fortunate. I am not sure that my brother and I could have talked him into hiring a live-in housekeeper if he didn't already have one.

I dropped my luggage at my brother's place. Ben is a native, born in New Jersey, just like Bruce Springsteen. Born to be wild, he was now the father of two, living on a five-acre estate outside of Freehold. I was born abroad, the son of refugees in postwar Munich. I had a wild streak, too, but mostly I had a problem with authority, stubbornness tempered by an immigrant's wariness. I had the caution of strangers who wandered in a strange land, strangers without a homeland, without some other place that must take them in if they return.

Many years later, in his Florida condo, my father and I would talk about personality types, and he would compare me with my brother. Some people had no *sitzfleisch,* no flesh for sitting. My brother could not stand still. He needed almost constant movement and activity, attributes that annoyed me when he was a kid and amaze me as an adult. Dad said I was not like him. I was a *phlegmat.* We were speaking Yiddish, and I was not sure what the word meant. After a little back and forth, it became clear that he was referring to my phlegmatic tendencies: apathetic, self-possessed, sluggish, even-tempered. The adjectives rang true, but I still hate to think of myself as full of phlegm. Words have special powers for Jews. God created the world by speaking the words "Let there be light." The Jewish mystics, the kabbalists, took special delight in deconstructing the language of the Bible in search of hidden meanings. How would they have interpreted the news that I had a serious problem with phlegmasia (inflammation accompanied by a fever) in my leg on the way home from that same visit to my dad in Florida?

Back in New Jersey, on the eve of Rosh Hashanah, Ben was at a Giants' game when I arrived. Bon Jovi was playing at halftime, and he and his best friend, Elliot, had passes to some backstage partying. My nephews and my sister-in-law, Tobi, were already in bed. In the sub-urban quiet, feeling restless and feckless, I gave M a call, and we headed out in search of cocktails on the beach. She preferred to be called "M," her email moniker. We had met at a dinner at my brother's golf club on my last trip down. Tobi had insisted on inviting M as my date, while my brother had wondered at the choice, given other possibilities. It was the first time I had been on a blind date since high school. My wife had been dead for more than a year, and first my parents and now Tobi were trying to push me back into the social world.

We wound up in Point Pleasant, the beach town that still holds most of my early memories of sand and seashells and playing in the surf.

They had cleaned up the boardwalk in the decades since I had last walked the weathered timbers. This late in the season most of the Jersey shore had shut down, but some of the standard boardwalk kiosks were still open: Kids were squirting water at a target trying to inflate a balloon until it burst, dreaming of water fights with the garden hose. There was still salt water taffy, but the roller coaster was closed and many of the stores had given up on nighttime hours. Walking along, we both won-dered at how earnest we were in those early years, lusting for the prizes, desperate to win as we played Skee-Ball or, like these kids, trying to be the first to explode balloons with water pistols.

Now the prizes looked like the clutter that sits outside trailer parks, abandoned in scrub pine bushes and burnt-out grass. The prizes may have been tacky, but the ocean air was still soft on the skin and the sound of the surf eased through the subdued hubbub. The boardwalk, a clean, well-lighted place, gurgled with the ferocious energy of children out late with their parents. Little Thors banging hammers tried to launch rubber frogs onto lily pads in a quest for booty. M walked carefully on the boardwalk planks. She was wearing high heels with toes so pointed a wicked witch could be wearing them. A short woman, she had mastered the skill of moving about in this western version of bound feet.

We found an open place on the beach. Nearby a couple of imported palms were planted in the sand. A thatched roof over the bar and Kon

Tiki lights all tried to bring the tropics to New Jersey. The palms would need to be moved south or indoors to survive the winter, and the staff would need to find new jobs. The waitress warned us that there was no glass allowed on the beach. So we drank margaritas out of plastic cups and stared out into the ocean blackness. Whitecaps glowed in reflected light. In the distance, we spotted the occasional ship steaming by. On the beach, modern beachcombers worked scanned the wide expanse with their metal detectors, another generation in search of treasure.

We sat for a while, but I needed to feel the sand beneath my feet, to get closer to the sound of the ocean. M took off her heels, and we wandered to a dark spot down the beach a bit. She was much shorter than I, and I propped her up on a sand dune to embrace her and kiss her lips. There is a quality of frankness in the lust of middle-aged people, especially those single and living alone.

Some of my parents' friends would badger me about dating when they saw me. Bella, an old friend of the family, a widow, was another former chicken farmer. In her eighties she was still very active and independent. She had spent time in Israel before coming to the States but was still firmly part of the *greeneh*. She always came laden with baked goods or other treats, her lipstick deep red or purple. She was one of the women who had sparked my mother's jealousy because my father joked with her when she came to visit. He treated her as an equal. She had some of the business savvy my mother lacked. She had taken over running her farm when her husband had fallen ill. One time Bella had sat at the kitchen table when I stopped by to have lunch. As I sat down, she took my hand and looked at my wedding ring.

"It's time to take it off."

"What's the rush?" I almost pulled my hand away.

"The ladies notice these things."

"So?"

"You are still a young man."

I was furiously resisting the symbolism of removing the ring even if I were to start dating.

"My brother and Tobi are trying to set me up with M."

"She's too short for you." Bella knitted her eyebrows casting about for other possible matches.

"A *curva*." Dad chimed using the Polish word that means either slut or whore.

This year my father had been cajoling and strangely adamant about my getting a new suit for the holidays. I wondered who had started him on this obsession. Perhaps it was Tobi, who has a talent for supporting the economy. She may have felt that I was not doing my share to help maintain full employment, especially in the garment industry, both here and abroad. In general, I was lowering the family standards with a decaying wardrobe. She had fingered my aging black silk sports jacket. "The thing is a rag with no structure. It's a bag with sleeves." One night they had tormented me until I had agreed to wear Ben's shoes to the country club because mine were too beat up.

Perhaps it was simply that there was little else to notice in this small-town congregation, or had some of Dad's buddies actually registered that I wore the same black double-breasted suit from Barneys every time I entered their synagogue? In any event, when I realized that Dad was not going to give up his campaign for a new suit, I gave up and went out and bought a new one. As I said, I did it as a mitzvah, a good deed, another example of *Kibud Av* (honoring your father). Something unimaginable had happened to me. Cancer had killed my wife. My father had helped me in my free fall. Having tried, in my childhood, to prepare me for whatever life would bring, he was now trying to help me through middle age.

I was sitting with an old man watching the last years rush by. "*Die Zeit loifed* (time keeps running)" became my dad's frequent refrain, spoken sometimes with resignation, sometimes in wonder.

On Rosh Hashanah morning, I put on my new suit and headed to synagogue with my brother. The synagogue is in Lakewood next to the Bezalel Hebrew Day School (my elementary school); the two take up a full city block on a hill in the geographic center of town. Playgrounds, a basketball court, jungle bars for the younger kids, and an open space where we played *ringolevio* or dodgeball fill out the block. The synagogue is just around the corner from the place where I had danced with the holy scrolls on Simchas Torah. The Beis Medrash Govohah is an exalted place of learning, a yeshiva where scholars from around the world study the Old Testament and the sages' commentaries. In my youth, I would occasionally go to hear a talk by the yeshiva's founder, Rabbi Aaron Kotler, a Lithuanian Holocaust survivor revered as a sage. The talks were in Yiddish as was most discourse at the yeshiva, while the texts were mostly in Hebrew or Aramaic. The audience was full of men in black suits and long sideburns or beards. Rabbi Kotler was already quite old with a long, wild beard and translucent eyes; when he spoke, you could tell he was a holy man. How much of the holiness emanates from within and how much is spread by the awe and reverence of those in his presence? Would you recognize the Pope as a holy man if you met him dressed like a working-class Argentinean waiting in line for a haircut in a small town outside Buenos Aires?

Now, 50 years after the founding of the yeshiva, Lakewood, the "New Jerusalem," has become a stronghold of Hassidic Jews. There are congregations everywhere, not just the Orthodox, Conservative, and Reform trio that most midsized Jewish communities support, but a plethora of Hassidic gatherings, which are spread across town. Black hats and black suits are ubiquitous. Some men wear their pants tucked into black-and-white striped stockings that reach just below the knee. There are bearded men, women wearing snoods or wigs, and, as always, kids in tow. The Hassidim are obeying the first mitzvah: to "be fruitful and multiply." Some have abandoned the lust for possessions; some work in the diamond district in lower Manhattan. You can hear the prayers wafting out of *steibels,* random people's houses where ten or more men have gathered to pray. My father's congregation, the Sons of Israel, is one of few that are Orthodox, but not Hassidic. It consists largely of Ashkenazi Jews, the *greeneh* and their descendants. Greenhorns, new members of the herd, were they still waiting for their horns to mature, to offer them protection?

Dad would be waiting for us. Already in place at his regular seat, he would be making small side bets with his friends about when we would arrive. Orthodox prayer services are similar from holiday to holiday, except on Yom Kippur. Rosh Hashanah services are the longest.

On these holy days, my primary focus had always been on strategies for making the time pass. Lately, the main option for shortening the service was arriving late. (When I gave up smoking, my last excuse for sneaking out for breaks disappeared.) From year to year, my brother and I would speculate on how late we could arrive without incurring too much displeasure. Often, the debate ended in the morning when Ben showed up at my bedside with a cup of coffee and instructions for when I needed to be dressed and ready to go.

My brother and I walked into the synagogue just as the congregation was getting ready to take out the Torah scrolls. They would read from the scrolls the chapters always read on Rosh Hashanah, about Abraham's readiness to sacrifice his son Isaac, about the angel that appears to Abraham to stay his hand, and the ram whose horns are tangled in the thicket. As the segment ends, the ram becomes a burnt offering in place of Isaac.

It was in this "new" synagogue, not our old one, that I was bar mitzvahed. It was designed as an amphitheater, with the women's section starting several rows behind the men's; iron and copper grillwork separate the two sections. (Ronnie had always referred to coming to services as "sitting behind the chicken wire.") A long narrow well forms the center, and rising from the well is the *bimah,* the raised platform where the Torah readings take place. The rabbi and cantor sit in front with the Ark of the Covenant behind them; this is the ark that holds the sacred scrolls.

The scrolls, the first five books of the Bible, are still written by scribes who for thousands of years have carefully inked by hand the same 792,077 letters on cow skin, sheepskin, or parchment. The chest that holds the scrolls always rested on the eastern wall, and we prayed facing east toward Jerusalem. On this Rosh Hashanah my father gave me the once-over, approving my suit. He asked me what it cost and was pleased that I bought an expensive suit; he also pointed out that he would buy three suits for that same price. He nodded toward the eastern wall and asked us what we thought. It took a while to see what he was pointing to, but as my eyes focused, the words stood out in golden letters against the copper-toned wall: "In Honor of Godel and Brandla Kirschenbaum."

He had purchased the east wall, contributing tens of thousands to the synagogue.

"Can you see it?"

The wall was textured with horizontal striping, and the text did not scream out like a billboard, but I assured him that the eight-inch letters were easy to read and that the subdued presentation was in good taste.

My father was not terribly displeased by our arrival time. I had thought we were early. Sadly, we were in time for the sermon, which precedes the Torah reading. Dad told me he had bought me an aliyah, the honor of saying the blessing before a section of the Torah is read to the congregation. Suddenly the new suit came into sharper focus. I tried to refuse, to send my brother in my place, but my father insisted. It was a tradition to give the honor to a visitor, to a guest of the congregation. I gritted my teeth and tried to remember the blessings, but my brother pointed out that the blessings were written out next to the scrolls and etched in glass in front of them on the *bimah*. Even so, I squirmed at the idea of being pushed in front of the crowd. My covenant was with my father, not with the congregation, not even really with God. As my turn approached, my father started on the list of *mesebeyrachs*, special blessings for those who were sick or having difficulties: my sister-in-law, Tobi, who had suffered thyroid cancer; her mother; my cousin Adam, who had been fighting cancer for years. To do this properly, I needed to know their Hebrew names and the names of their parents, fathers for men and mothers for women. I am, for example, *Maier, the son of Godel.* I was named for my grandfather, and my father was *Godel, the son of Maier.*

Pronounced *may'-eer*, as in Golda Meir, I like my Hebrew name. It means "to shed light." But the Americanization, *my'-er*, seemed to scream out Jew boy, especially in high school, when I was working hard to become an American.

My summer 1970 trip abroad made it clear something had to change. My passport had the German spelling my father had used on my birth certificate, Maier, which is a common German surname, referring to the head of a city's or town's government. The Germans thought it funny that I had two last names, and as a final insult, Kirschenbaum, which means "cherry tree," was seen as a childish misapprehension of the German *Kirschbaum* (cherry tree). In college I became Michael and then Kirsch. I preferred Kirsch. I never liked Mike, which rhymes with "kike," but I let my mother call me Mike because I felt guilty about changing my name and she never could bring herself to call me Kirsch. Now most people who know me call me Kirsch, but I still introduce myself to most strangers as Michael. Things became more convoluted when my brother shortened his last name to Kirsch. Surprisingly, my father did not take offense, and that eased a lot of my guilt around my name change. Even so, I was a little squeamish if a woman moaned "Oh, Mike" when we made love, as it became clear to me I was making love to a stranger.

Back in the synagogue that Rosh Hashanah, it was all becoming too much for me; it got worse when my father told me I had to go up afterward to thank the rabbi. I had no love for the guy, and his sermon was atrocious: about us Jews as the "chosen people," denigrating Arabs and harping on self-serving tribalism in its worst form.

When I was a child, the part of the service that had set Rosh Hashanah apart from the other holidays was the blowing of the shofar, the ram's horn, the powerful totem that, like the Scottish bagpipes, struck fear in enemies on the battlefield. The shofars were the trumpets that brought down the walls of Jericho. They were also a tool of the priests who sounded the ram's horn to call people to prayer. In the old farmers' *shul*, the shofar blowing also made for some suspense. Blowing the shofar is a difficult skill, unlike blowing those party trumpets that show up at New Year's Eve events. If you were clueless or out of practice, you could blow vigorously into that old ram's horn without making a sound. The modern congregation was big enough and rich enough to pay specialists and buy first-class shofars. I missed the old *shul*.

I remained nostalgic for the old farmers' *shul*, a small, gray-shingled building on a country road. Built by the congregation on land donated by the rabbi, you might have thought it was one of the single-family ranch houses built just after WWII, although perhaps a bit too square and set on a foundation that raised it too high off the ground to be a regular house. All through my youth our family walked to that synagogue on Rosh Hashanah to begin negotiations with God, to renew our contract with Him for the coming year.

The old synagogue had stood between a chicken farm and a second-growth forest on Ford Road. The farmers were mostly immigrants who lived in our rural patch of New Jersey. There were several towns nearby. I'm not sure which town was closest or rather what qualified as a town. There was a time when a little hollow dot labeled Southard sat on the map just north of Lakewood and a mile or so from our farm. A volunteer fire station and a general store on Highway 9 marked the town, but there was no cluster of houses, no post office. The synagogue was a couple of miles west of Southard.

In the old *shul,* after the Morning Prayer, before they took out the holy scrolls, the *shammos,* the servant of the congregation, would lead an auction for aliyahs. Mr. Laufer, an egg dealer, who bought eggs from farmers and trucked them to New York City, was usually our *shammos.* These aliyahs were honors and good karma. A new person was called up to say the blessing before each section. The first aliyah always went to a "Cohen," someone from the priestly class, a branch of the Levi tribe. The second one went to a Levi, a descendant of Aaron, Moses's brother. The next five and the *maftir,* the final section, went to the rest.

Nowadays the other 11 tribes are grouped together as Israelites. Only the priests and the Levis pass along a tribal stamp to their children. Oddly, becoming a rabbi seems to have nothing to do with tribal heritage. At one time, the priestly tribe had special restrictions placed on them to preserve their purity. They were not allowed to marry converts or divorcees, and certain roles in the service were reserved for priests. They blessed the congregation at the end of the service. As a child, this blessing held a special mystery. You were not allowed to look at those who chanted the blessing. Boys hid under their father's prayer shawls lest they be tempted to look at the priests' hands and be blinded by the transgression.

The auction for the aliyahs was an integral part of the Rosh Hashanah service in our congregation. It never took very long. "Five dollars for *maftir,* ten dollars for *maftir.*" The *shammos* held the auction in Yiddish in a brisk but unhurried cadence. A nod, a wave of the hand, the bidding was subdued, but some of the richer members were nudged if they neglected the bidding. When someone had a special need to improve his karma, like a sickness in the family, no one bid against him. The winners of the auction were called up to the Torah, an honor and a mitzvah.

After the second day of the Rosh Hashanah holiday, Ben, Tobi, and I were invited over to Elliot's house for drinks. Not only were Elliot and my brother best friends, but their inner circle called Elliot Ben's "second wife" because the two were always making plans and spending time together. They are tall, good-looking guys who reached draft age after the Vietnam War. They had caught the end of the 1960s, the part that included sexual liberation and the drug culture, but that had shed politics, the part of the 1960s that was overlaid on the 1970s. They had found financial success in their thirties riding the economic expansion.

Elliot greeted us with open arms. We had planned to arrive after dinner, but his mom was still serving food to a crowd of 20 or so relatives from their extended family. The tables were arranged in an "L" that turned the corner between the eat-in kitchen and the formal dining room. It reminded me of the setup that we had in our old farmhouse for my brother's *bris,* when borrowed tables turned the corner from our dining area and ran the length of the living room.

Elliot's mom, barely five feet, still wore her serving apron. She came after us, trying to get us to sit down and eat, but we were coming from our own dinner and she had to settle for having us taste the *potato-nik,* a kind of potato brownie baked until it was a little crunchy. M was there, too, wearing bell-bottoms trimmed with fake fur and high-heeled boots. Even in boots she was only a little taller than her mom. She was Tobi's best friend, paralleling Ben and Elliot's bond. The relationships between the four of them felt somehow incestuous. Tobi had been working hard to set me up with M, and when I retreated to the deck behind the house to smoke my cigar and sip a single malt scotch, M came out to join me. In my widowhood, in the suburban heartland, I was suddenly desirable. Yet I longed to be alone in the crowd as I had been in my adolescence.

The low-key family gathering got a serious infusion of energy when a friend, Wendy, arrived with some other folks from Elliot's office. She had brought all the fixings for cosmopolitans including a dozen oversized martini glasses with sculptured stems. As the cosmoses kicked in, Elliot escorted a bunch of the guys around the side of the house to partake in other intoxicants. The garage door was open, and Elliot's two Harleys stood like shining ornaments next to a Mercedes.

Back on the deck Elliot was aglow. The newer guests started migrating out to the deck. The women were mostly in their thirties and the men were fortysomethings. The holiday was over, but it was Friday night, and the weekend was just beginning. The table was getting crowded, and M sat in my lap stroking my kneecaps. Elliot set out to explore topics that might get conversations started in mixed-groups.

"It's amazing how you can break the ice just by asking how the ladies have their pubic hair trimmed." Alcohol may be a prerequisite, but it appeared that he was right.

Some of the women guffawed and looked at one another. I was surprised that no one winced, which was my first reaction.

"One of the girls at the office showed me this device she'd bought that you could use to trim the hair and it was guaranteed not to draw blood. It looked like a big eyebrow pencil, but I never figured out how it worked. I mean there are some people who go to a lot of trouble, shaving, waxing, making hearts, and diamonds and angel wings. You'd be amazed."

The women grumbled good-naturedly about what a pain the whole thing was, shaving and waxing, and the conversation spread a bit of titillation, helped along by the vodka. One of Elliot's cousins, Lina, was paying careful attention; she was a little older than Elliot and dressed a little more formally than the other women, a mother of two college kids with her husband, who was sitting across from her and squirming a bit. Clearly she had never given the issue much consideration but thought it was great that women were starting to decorate their privates. Someone remarked that given the color in her cheeks, her husband might get lucky tonight even if she hadn't had a chance to decorate.

At the head of the table Elliot was in full swing.

"So after I see this thing, I had this idea. So people are styling and making shapes, but they could use some help. We could sell a kit with patterns and instructions. I even got a great name for it. Just imagine it on late-night TV: "The Vagina Designah." It could come with videotape. Now you too can have a stylish bush…" He went on for a bit and then turned to the women.

"What do you think?" They were mostly laughing and telling Elliot he should stick to selling mortgages, but he was still milking it.

"We could do surveys and figure out which styles were most popular." The women teased the guys about whether they needed to trim or shave. Stories of shaving testicles invoked the cold chill of emasculation that razors next to testes inspired, but the guys went on good-naturedly, speculating about who had seen the most interesting pussies and how many pussies they were likely to see, about jewelry and piercing, studs in your tongue and whether you took them out to have dinner. Wendy raised her voice to get everyone's attention and reminded everyone about her job. She worked in a gynecologist's office as a nursing assistant. She was mostly there as a second person in the room for exams, a response to lawsuits against gynecologists claiming sexual improprieties.

"I see more vaginas in a week than you'll see in your entire lives, and believe me, some of these images you would rather not have in your fantasy pool."

The phrasing reminded me of my father's story about being threatened in jail. "I've seen more dead people than you have seen live ones."

Years later, the scene came back to me when I paused outside a walking past a lingerie shop in Greenwich Village. "Going commando" had entered into urban slang as an expression for women who ventured out into the street without their panties. In the window, a group of small clear plastic balls held colorful women's thongs, each with the word "commando" printed on the circumference. One thong, a tiny garment, spread out below them. Were they embarrassed to display it on a mannequin's torso? Propped up behind the balls was the slogan:

"They are better than nothing."

Match.com

∞

"Love is when a girl puts on perfume
and a boy puts on shaving cologne
and they go out and smell each other."

Karl, age 5, *superkids.com*

From my third-floor sunporch at the edge of the Harvard campus, I watched a young woman in a short yellow skirt pace slowly back and forth in the late-morning sun. Perhaps she was not *so* young for someone on a college campus, but young enough to my eyes looking out from under gray eyebrows. Was she a professor? A professor's wife? A graduate student? A secretary? A research scientist with legs that said hello from 100 yards, even in low heels? The breeze caught the wide pleats teasingly. The glass front of a nearby office building acted as a full-length mirror. Her yellow outfit shimmered against a black-and-green background, of grass and asphalt footpath, in front of Harvard's Science Center. Even she seemed caught like me by the reflection. Would her skirt behave? Or would it fly up? What was she hoping for? Her blouse was white, but did I see her face? Which hand held the phone and which reached down in reflex to smooth a pleat as the wind cooled her thighs?

I was coming back to life, but I was still floating in a murky haze. It had been almost two years since my wife died, but I was still committed to her, still in love with someone not among us. Dark shadows mixed with lust and loneliness.

After my parents' friend Bella convinced me it was time to take off my wedding ring, I let some friends try their hands at matchmaking. They were trying to bring me back to the world. I was happy to cede to them the vicarious thrills of watching incipient romance. I did not begrudge them the debts they settled by introducing me to their middle-aged women friends. But the romance business was not going very well.

I let myself imagine intimacy, bouncing down the street, a soft breast pressing against my bicep as we laughed over bad jokes or some unlikely common interest. Had I used up my quota of love, the 30 years of bliss that had ended as I knelt over my wife holding her lifeless body still warm on our marriage bed, and her deathbed?

Was I ready for love or lovemaking? I found myself revisiting teenage anxiety about performance in bed. Crudely layered on top of that angst was an old man's concern about hiding the partials that filled in for missing teeth. Should I hide the cup that held my fake teeth and the Efferdent that "killed millions of bacteria" as they soaked overnight?

I had been shielded from concerns about birth control and the negotiations it requires. I had not used a condom in 30 years. Would I still be embarrassed when I walked into the drugstore to buy some? When I finally did so, the variety was amusing, titillating, mind-numbing. They still sold Trojans, but now there were ribbed condoms, flavored condoms. There were the Midnight, Barebacked, and Rough Rider series, promising "max sensation and hot passion." There were so many colors to choose from. Did I need one to match the color of her panties, or was it meant to match my sheets or my skin tone? I didn't need Viagra, but I did worry about maintaining an erection after a couple of glasses of wine. Could I stay in the moment when lovemaking began, when sudden bouts of ennui from unfinished mourning washed over me and left me guilt-ridden, an outsider watching as two people took off their clothes? Did this woman have other lovers? Would I find bliss in the slippery temple, in the warm lust of a feverish embrace?

It was a new world to me. I had been surrounded by the "free love" 1960s, but except for a couple of drunken bouts in college, sex had followed courtship, not coffee.

Was I making love or "bumping uglies" or worse "burying the bone"? The phrase seemed morbid, too close at hand when I found myself with another woman in the same bed I had shared with my wife, the same bed where she passed her last breath moaning not in love's ardor but in pain, pain barely muffled by a morphine drip. I had already been on a few dates when Patty, one of my business partners, pointed me to Match.com. She had enjoyed an exciting infatuation with a woman she had met on the dating website. Patty was working hard at bringing me back into the world. She had booked a trip for the two of us to Iceland and Norway the previous summer: puffins, volcanoes, lava, geysers, and fjords. Six months later, in 2003, she steered me toward online dating. I still wore the beard I had started when I sat shivah for Ronnie, the week of mourning that followed her death.

For Patty, and for me, part of the fascination with online dating was receiving a closer look at evolving technology. Fifteen years had passed since my jaw had dropped as I used my first browser to look at French Impressionist paintings on a new Louvre website. The Internet, once the province of geeks, had exploded. Computers, which had begun as tools for science and then business, had a new branch: personal computers, laptops. Google and Craigslist were already works in progress with Facebook, Twitter, Skype, iPhones, and YouTube still to come. People were just starting to get separate email accounts for personal use so that their business and personal correspondences stayed separate.

I enrolled in Match.com. An automated guru guided me on my quest. The website insisted that I begin with self-examination. First build a profile! Who are you? What brings you to this journey? What are you seeking? How do you attract someone who might be a good match?

Welcome to Match.com, rockstep rocket! You now have access to millions of singles! But who is right for you? To give you some help, Venus will email you a list of singles you may find interesting…

Match.com let you choose a moniker to keep your true identity confidential until you were ready to "reveal yourself" to one of your "matches." I was "rockstep rocket." It seemed silly now. It seemed silly then. Years ago traveling in Spain I had met a young woman who introduced herself as "Ceily." She had smiled and said in English, "In your country that means foolish." The word captured how I felt about the moniker I had chosen for Match.com.

"Rocket" had its origins in one of my first ventures into public space since Ronnie's death. I had been out dancing at the local VFW Friday night swing dances, and one of my old golf buddies had been working behind the counter at the refreshments stand. When I stopped by to get a drink after a fast dance, he said, "I didn't know you could move that fast." I made some joke about the 12-foot rocket that stood like a totem pole in front of the VFW. In other strata of consciousness or unconsciousness, perhaps the work I did for NASA brought rockets to mind. I had written little bits of software for satellites hurled across the solar system like *Voyager,* whose explosive takeoff propelled it onto a trajectory that broke free of the gravitational pull of the Earth to explore the outer planets of the solar system.

Was my love for my dead wife my own gravity threshold? Did I need to become a rocket to break free?

"Rockstep" is a basic step in swing dancing, the jitterbug, and the Lindy ("We flying just like Lindberg did!"). I had missed out on such couples dancing in my youth. Oddly, the sexual liberation of the 1960s had led to a kind of dancing that did not require contact. Some of the folks shucking and jiving and otherwise churning about at concerts and parties in the 1960s and 1970s were sexy, many just moving in their own world, no partner required. Maybe it was a more subtle rebellion against the sexual politics of couples' dancing, in which the male is expected to lead. Or maybe being high or tripping had made staying in step with a partner seem unnerving or unnecessary. The folks dancing in the aisles at Grateful Dead concerts were arrhythmic, and to be fair, some of the music (such as "The Eleven") came in weird time signatures. Anyhow, I was a geek, shy with girls, and my introduction to ballroom dancing at my bar mitzvah had left me uncertain and rebellious. I was still shorter than my mother when she insisted on teaching me to waltz. I was just old enough to be embarrassed when she pressed me to her bosom. It seemed unseemly. I had seen her climb into the Playtex girdle she wore under the full-length white dress she bought for the event. White pearls sown in vertical rows to make her look taller and slimmer rose to her bodice and left little dents in my chin as I twirled in her fierce grip.

Fifteen years later, Ronnie and I took a swing dance class from Bob Thomas and Idy Covington. I stumbled about at first, but Ronnie came alive and I soon found some rhythm and enthusiasm to match hers. She had been a reluctant dancer all her life, moving stiffly through an occasional waltz at someone's wedding or bar mitzvah, moving microscopically at rock concerts and house parties. But once she got past her inhibitions, she was a natural. Her sense of balance had equestrian roots, jumping over fences, changing leads on the fly. Had the aerobics courses she had been taking to lose weight prepared her for spinning like a top?

As we made progress with the basics, a new connection between us jumped to life. While dancing we were focused intensely on each other. I was responsible for her balance, for giving clear leads into whatever move we would do next on the floor. She was poised and eager, a lightning rod for the next lead. We went on to study with Bob and Idy at their dance studio and were both surprised at the progress we made. But what really put Ronnie over the top was the acrobatic swing work we did when we joined Bob's dance troupe. Hip-hip-split, over the back, through the legs—she loved flying through the air. She even got used to the idea that we would become the center of attention when we started bopping. She started wearing skirts of her own free will; she even bought Capezio character shoes (dance pumps with a square heel).

She was dead, but when I stepped on the dance floor, a hot beat could still get me jumping and jiving. On Match.com, I was the "Rockstep Rocket." Looking back at the melancholy photo I posted in my online profile, I would wonder whether I might have been shucking and jiving.

After describing yourself, you had to fill in a profile of who you were looking for: height, eye color, body type, language, ethnicity, faith, education, job, income. Were smokers OK? What about drinking? Someone with kids?

I love swing dancing with an energetic partner, spending time outdoors, sunsets on a warm beach, skiing through fresh snow, reading in a hammock, walking across a lava field to bathe in a natural hot springs. I've enjoyed living in Cambridge and walking to work. I play tennis and golf. I love old movies and film noir, science fiction, Buffy, Faulkner, Kafka, Raymond Chandler and Cormac McCarthy, among others. I studied history, but wound up working in technology and then as a management consultant. I'm working part time and would love to find someone who had time to play and travel. My friends see me as compassionate and sardonic, warm, open-minded with strong opinions, and a soft voice, someone who feels he has been successful, someone who is athletic, who enjoys both being outdoors and curling up on the sofa with a good movie or a good book. Someone with a quick smile and a warm embrace, someone creative and romantic, someone willing to face life's turmoil with a sense of humor and a sense of adventure.

With all my forms complete, Match.com's Venus sent me emails with links to ten women who "matched" my requirements, and my profile went out to Lord knows how many women with similar assurances from Venus that I matched theirs.

Suddenly, I was dating at a furious pace. Coffee or lunch followed by dinner and/or a movie, the occasional exchange of bodily fluids. Too often, a kiss is just a kiss. I was juggling emails and dates, amazed at how ready some of these middle-aged women were for intimacy. I was a kid in a candy store, everything looked good at first. Or was I at a carnival, a place that was fun but a little scary?

Eventually, I did find someone on Match.com. Lynn had been hesitant to join Match.com and skeptical about its possibilities. The photo she posted showed three women on a ski slope, and I had to guess which one was her. She was accustomed to living independently. The manager of a group of graphic designers, she had lived in Nepal and in Berlin. She was fun to be with, had an easy laugh, and liked to cuddle. Could I live with my father's reaction when he found out she was not Jewish? It was a slow romance, but the months passed and she moved in.

My father was chagrined at first but softened over time. Lynn was not Jewish, though she seemed to have a penchant for Jewish men. My brother had already forced Dad to address the issue. After struggling through two Jewish wives, my brother seemed happy with his Italian girlfriend, and my father no longer actively complained about their relationship. I was delighted that my father had accepted Lynn, too. He, too, immediately recognized her warmth and charm, her intelligence, her sincerity, and especially that she made me happy.

Maybe Dad's housekeeper, Christina, had changed his attitude about living with a non-Jew. She cooked for Dad and cleaned the house. In the years since Mom had died, she had become a mother and daughter to him, more devoted than any of his Jewish friends. Christina was a devout Catholic who observed a bread-and-water fast twice a week. It did not bother him that she went off to Catholic mass in the morning. She wasn't stopping him from going to *shul* or keeping kosher. Lynn and I were not going to have children, so the religion of the next generation was not an issue. Most of Dad's friends had died, so being embarrassed in front of his peers was no longer a major concern.

The six of us went out to dinner at my brother's golf club. Dad ordered fish, the kosher compromise when eating at a nonkosher restaurant. He sat there with his two boys. He had worked so hard to make sure we took on our Jewish heritage, I wondered how he felt about our non-Jewish girlfriends. He is a resilient old man. I had changed my name from Maier to Michael to make my secular/business life easier. Now he called me Mike. My brother had shortened his last name from Kirschenbaum to Kirsch, and Dad accepted that, too. We still had our Hebrew names when I was called in synagogue, I was still Maier, the son of Godel.

The women fawned over him. He was still a charmer, and he enjoyed the attention. He ate his fish, and he turned to look at us one at a time and smiled. "Look, it's the Kirschenbaum boys having dinner with our three shiksas." I eyed him closely, looking for any sign of bitterness in his humor, but he was at peace.

"Love is what makes you smile when you're tired."

Terri, age 4, *superkids.com*

Forgiving God
in the Catskills

∞

Dad was wheezing as he went through his morning rituals, shaving, cleaning his dentures. He sat down to put his pants on. He was 90 and we were sharing a hotel room in the Catskills for Rosh Hashanah. I pretended to sleep as he got ready for morning prayers. He liked to get there early, to reserve seats for the family in the Stardust Room. My brother, Ben, and my nephew were in the room next door. It was just the boys.

When my mother died, just two years after my wife, my relationship with my father entered a new phase. Now we were both widowers, and he talked to me as a peer. I was 51, the age my grandfather was when he died in the camps.

Mom and Ronnie were dead. Ben was in the midst of a slow-motion divorce. Neither he nor his wife was eager to sort through the finances, or make themselves marriage targets for their new lovers. Ben and I had girlfriends who were not Jewish. My nephew's girlfriend was Jewish, but she was one of those Russian immigrants who grew up without religion and never missed it. None of the women were tempted by religious holidays in the Catskills.

I smelled Dad's cologne. He took pride in the clean new shirt and fresh tie he had for day two of the holiday. The older crew at the Catskills resort was pretty well turned out, but even here, some of the old folks had trouble keeping food or drool off of their shirtfronts. I was

Ben and Teddy

middle-aged and felt a little guilty about how being among the aged made me feel young.

Dad picked up his *tallis* and headed for the Stardust Room. Most nights, the room served as the cabaret. We were at Kutsher's, an aging resort, one of the few left that served kosher food and offered a Rosh Hashanah program. The Stardust Room, with its flying saucer motif of stars and galaxies painted white on blue walls, featured a dark horse-head shadow that peeked out from one of the nebulae. On Rosh Hashanah the room did double-duty. Services were held in the morning, while at night a stand-up comic took the stage. This was the Borscht Belt. In its heyday, names like Buddy Hackett, Danny Kaye, and Joan Rivers headlined. There was a poster in one corner of the room for an upcoming "Polka Fest," which triggered TV memories of the *Lawrence Welk Show*. My mother had loved the show; she thought that Lawrence was Polish, because he had a polka band. Wikipedia says that he was Russian, from German stock. For me, all accordion players brought polkas to mind, or was it the other way around and all polkas reminded me of accordions? Before Dad left for services, he made sure that I was awake.

"Don't be too late! They blow the shofar today."

The ancient ram's horn was somehow part of our covenant with God. Bob Dylan's "Highway 61 Revisited" came to mind: "God said to Abraham, 'Kill me a son.' Abe said, 'God, you must be putting me on.'" When I had first read Genesis as a child, I had asked my father, "How could someone tie up his child and kill him?" My father had explained that Abraham knew God was just testing him and was not really going to let him burn his son on a mountaintop altar. God does relent. The shofar harkens back to the ram whose horns were tangled in a bush, the ram that Abraham sacrificed instead of his son, Isaac.

My father's faith had been tested by a God that did not relent, a God that took Dad's whole family as sacrifice, burnt offerings in Nazi crematoriums. Dad saw his own survival as a miracle. For him and most of his *greeneh* friends, the survivors, holding on to their religion and traditions was at least, in part, an act of not giving into their enemies, of not letting their enemies completely destroy their community.

"Dad, are you going down for coffee first?"

"No, it's too far. I'll be OK."

"I'll get you some when I come down. Do you want some food, too?"

Yesterday, I had brought coffee on a whim and he drank it thankfully during the rabbi's sermon. He still got around pretty well, but the dining room and the Stardust Room were at opposite ends of the property. The 1,000 yards of extra walking was more than he would pay for a cup of coffee.

"OK. A roll or a piece of cake. Not too much. And, please, this time put it in a bag."

Even though it was a lounge and the worshippers sat at tables in a small amphitheater, Dad's sense of decorum was violated by eating his food at prayers. Perhaps he did not want to offend those who had not had their coffee and who might look longingly at his bagel.

I had struggled out of bed, grateful for the thin sheet of plywood between the bed and the mattress that kept the mattress from being concave. I could not find a new razor blade and on a whim used Dad's

Norelco. I popped off the top and emptied the gray-white beard trimmings. The three floating heads proved surprisingly comfortable and effective, better than my fancy European electric shaver. When I cleaned the shaver, my beard trimmings were almost the same color as Dad's.

Sitting next to my father in the Stardust Room as the cantor led the morning prayers, I thought about our rabbi in the old farmers' *shul*. He drank too much, and his beard was tobacco-stained. He was a gambler and played poker till all hours of the night. There were rumors that he had a mistress in his younger years, but when he prayed on the High Holidays, tears ran down his cheeks, staining his robe. The congregation joined him in tears and wailing as the Unetaneh Tokef prayer was recited. He then became my archetype of a rabbi. The Unetaneh Tokef is a dark prayer with a dark history composed by a Polish rabbi, who was tortured and killed for his faith. "Come let us declare our faith as we pass before the Lord to be judged, who shall live and who shall die, who by sword or plague, by water or fire, by stoning…"

The farmers in our New Jersey *shul* had seen whole cities destroyed, fathers and mothers, sons and daughters, husbands and wives, sisters and brothers sent to their deaths, generations murdered as they watched. In that old *shul*, the dead were gathered among us, a tangible presence. No one was unscarred. Even children trembled. A coda ending the prayer told us that repentance, prayer and charity, reduced the harshness of the decree. They asked for forgiveness, but I marveled that they had kept their faith, that they had forgiven God for what he had done to them. And here in the Catskills, my father was not the only one with a number tattooed on his forearm. The Holocaust had left marks on many in the crowd. The survivors and their families had carried the same burdens.

As we sat in the Stardust Room, Dad asked me if I would be fasting on Yom Kippur, the Day of Atonement that marks the closure of prayers for the New Year. The tenth day of the New Year is the final settling of accounts with God. It is a traditional fast day, one where you take neither food nor drink. I asked him if I should fast, knowing he would say yes. Getting him to say it out loud somehow made it another mitzvah I could do for him. He talked about fasting on Yom Kippur at Auschwitz, how the first year was very hard and he had thought he would pass out during his work detail, how the thirst was worse than the hunger. The second year was easier because he was assigned to work nights, so he could sleep in the day. He had hidden his soup and crust of bread under his bunk, and it had sat waiting for him, waiting for the fast to end.

Rosh Hashanah is not a fast day. And after prayers we joined the crowd heading for the dining room. It was a vast space. The numbered tables, plates gleaming, seemed to extend to the horizon. Gefilte fish, chopped liver, kugel, herring, challah, and bagels were already in place as people found seats. The holiday feast brought back memories of the glory days. The resort was built in 1907. The year after our visit it would celebrate its 100th anniversary. The dining room seated over 1,000. Eddy, our waiter, was a small man who looked like a teenager until you saw his hands and eyes. He and his bus person, Andrea, were from Brazil. Both had been working in the Catskills for 15 years. You can usually judge seniority by how far away the waiters are from the kitchen. Eddy was not one of the oldest hands, but there were newer crews walking past Eddy's station into the deep recesses of the dining room. They carried platters with 15 entrées balanced on their shoulders.

"It's not like it once was." Andrea in a slightly accented voice bemoaned the decline. "Now it's just the old folks."

Last night as we sat at the table, the dead reached out to us. We talked about the Concord, a more upscale resort, near Kiamesha Lake, where our family had spent some of the Jewish holidays, until the resort went out of business. Dad and my brother and I were trying to recall what year the place closed. Our timeline was measured by who was still alive.

"When did we start coming here?"

"Did Ronnie come to Kutsher's?"

"Yes, remember she helped Mom walk to the dining room."

"Oh. Yeah. Mom was still walking then."

Earlier, we had sat in one of the lobbies near a wheelchair elevator, allowing Dad to rest on the way to lunch. He still got around on his own two feet, and today as we walked, he held hands with my brother.

"Remember da Mama?" Dad, a little teary, was looking at an old woman wheeling away from the lift. "We took her just like that…. She didn't like to be in the chair."

"But thank God for the wheelchairs." My brother reminded us of the painful year when Mom insisted on hobbling about, taking ages to get from place to place, a two-person escort required at every stage.

Mom always showed up for meals, especially when there was a Jewish menu.

"Wow, they have gefilte fish."

"Yeah, but it's not like Mom's."

"Oh, look, the honey cake."

"Yeah, but not as good as Mom's."

My nephew Rickie had been looking forward to some honey cake. He loved Mom's. But he had some allergies that made eating at the resort challenging. It was a long list, including milk products. Now it was nuts, which kept him from eating the cake. Mom's cake did not have nuts. Hers was dense, chewy, dripping with honey. Think of fudge brownies: She made something halfway to fudge honey cake. Almost every time I had visited my old college friend Claire, who lives comfortably in Manhattan, she would tell me that one of her biggest regrets was not getting the recipe for Mom's honey cake. "It was amazing. Somehow instead of drying out, it got moister over time."

Dad had taken on Mom's role, trying to make sure everyone ate. Ben and I were good eaters. Tall mesomorphs, Mom claimed that we were finicky in our childhood eating, but we had blossomed. Dad watched us with satisfaction but complained to Rickie that he hadn't eaten anything. Rickie is tall, too, but he doesn't carry any extra weight on his narrow frame. His mother's parents are the Lenches, and while his mother, Tobi, has struggled with weight, his grandmother can still wear the same size-four gowns she wore at her wedding 60 years ago. Dad would say, sometimes jokingly and sometimes not, that she looked starved or withered, but maybe I am being harsh, and skinny is a better translation from the Yiddish.

"You don't eat like a Kirschenbaum. You eat like a Lench." Ben and I were doing our best to uphold the family honor, asking our waiter,

Eddy, to bring out extra entrées, and some potato latkes and schmaltz and some herring to try alongside our three-egg omelets. Plates crowded the table. Ben and I sampled them all, devouring, deracinating, digging through the offerings shamelessly. Rickie was more circumspect, dainty, his plate half full, unmoved by the abundance. In my youth, I had an innate abhorrence of waste and an embarrassment at the gluttony of some of my parents' friends, who piled high their plates with food, as if they were beggars who would never see food again. Their plates looked like dense tropical growth, tendrils of food hanging over the edges as they moved past the smorgasbord. They emptied whatever dry food was on the table into napkins that they took back to their rooms for late-night treats. This repulsion was reaffirmed when I worked as a busboy one summer at a resort on the Jersey shore. As the years passed, my attitude and abdomen softened.

Before dinner, my brother and I had played a round of golf. It was a gray autumn day, damp from overnight rain, but the air was fresh and the fairways a lush green. It was just warm enough for us to be comfortable in long-sleeved jerseys. When I returned to our room, Dad was already dressed for dinner. As I dressed, I asked him how he was doing with Christina (Krisha). She cooked for him and cleaned the house. It was a great relief to my brother and me that he had someone to talk to, someone who made it safe for him to live at home.

"How's Krisha?"

"She's good."

"She's always so happy to hear my voice when I call you and seems so disappointed when you're not home when I call."

My conversations with her are restricted by her limited English and my nonexistent Polish.

"Father, not home. Play cards."

He played cards with "the ladies" now. There were no longer enough men to play poker. They had all died.

"She likes you." Dad smiled at me. "She says you are one in a thousand."

"I told you more than once how great your sons are," I teased him. "But what does she mean?"

Dad's expression became more serious; he looked bemused but did not laugh.

"She means because you are not jealous, not bitter. She likes that you are quiet and don't get angry. She says if every man was like you, there would be no war."

Dad recalled an old Jewish proverb about who is truly a rich man. A rich man is the man who is *Sah-mey-ach B'chelko,* happy with his portion. Ben walked in to see if we were ready to go eat again, and I missed a chance to push Dad on what he meant... Jealous of whom? My brother? His wealth? His children?

Christina's son lived nearby. He came on an education visa and was probably an illegal immigrant by now. She called home most days and talked to her husband, her daughter, and her daughter's husband, who lived together in the same house in Poland. I think her mother-in-law lived there, too, and perhaps others. She had probably sent $50,000 back to her family in the few years she had worked for my father, and in Poland that was a small fortune. Her family members had bought land. I think they were building a new house.

It was easy to imagine why she might have wondered at my not being bitter. My wife died a horrible death as the cancer choked her lungs, but I have worked hard to forgive the fates. My father liked to use the German expression: "*Alles geht vorüber* (Everything goes by, and you can get past anything)," but sometimes I thought of another German expression: "*Alles geht drunter und drüber* (Everything goes haywire and it ties you in knots)."

After dinner at Kutsher's, people wandered about the lobbies social- izing. There were couches and overstuffed chairs arranged so that families could lounge in the semicomatose state brought on by sugary wine and the massive consumption of Borscht Belt food, though, to be honest, I did not see any borscht, though they had served chicken soup and beef flanken and veal paprikash and … and …

Dad ran into some old guys he knew. They are *greeneh,* too. Friends of friends, they were members of the "society" or the "organization," which usually referred to a Holocaust survivor group, but it could be any Jewish organization that Dad supported.

The conversation often began with an old person's Jewish geography, asking about who was still alive and in what state of health, but quickly moved on to children and grandchildren, business ventures, travel, politics, the state of this Catskills hotel.

I drifted toward the Flying Saucer Café, a smaller companion to the Stardust Room. It was a bar/café halfway between the dining room and the larger amphitheater. There was music drifting out. As I walked by one of the larger family groups, an older woman looked at me and said, "It could be John Kerry." They all turned toward me and mostly nodded. There was one young woman, about Rickie's age; her parents were my age and the rest looked like a collection of siblings and spouses from my father's generation. Their accents marked them as New Yorkers, and all seemed to be native speakers. I smiled. I had heard it before.

"I'm not sure whether that's a compliment."

They laughed and argued that he was a distinguished man. I complained that he always looked dour, and even though I had voted for him, I could not remember a single thing he had ever said or a single idea he had championed.

I broke off and wandered into the lounge. A short woman was singing. Her amazing voice, gravel and honey, was belting out rhythm and blues, with some show tunes and rock and roll mixed in. There was a small dance floor. Two couples were dancing, and a few groups of old women sat about. Ben joined me for a drink. "Ask one of the old ladies to dance and make her New Year happy!" He poked me in the ribs, pushing me toward the dance floor. I do love swing dancing, and sometimes the older women have more ballroom skills than the younger ones. One of the women was tapping her foot, expensive shoes keeping a good beat. Her hair was stiff, but her outfit shimmered. I asked her to dance. Shirley did pretty well twirling about, smiling when she got the hang of the stops and gos. She was flushed and breathing hard. I slowed down the tempo and let her collect herself as the song wound down. She went back to her friends beaming.

Since Ronnie's death, whenever I danced, the memory of holding her on the dance floor released a tumult of joy and loss. We were hot stuff when a band was rocking, but it didn't start out that way. Ballroom dance has gender-based roles. Feminism was in an intense phase when we started dancing. Men leading had implications of patriarchy and oppression. Radical feminism, consciousness raising, and women's liberation were a fire racing through the country and especially hot where we lived, in Cambridge, Massachusetts. One of my favorite photos showed a woman working at a construction site wearing a T-shirt silk-screened by the Boston Women's Graphics Collective, the group Ronnie belonged to. Shovel in hand, the T-shirt proclaimed: "Women hold up half the sky," one of Chairman Mao's proverbs.

Getting Ronnie to accept that I was leading on the dance floor was at first a problem. We had faced similar issues when we were learning about white water canoeing, sorting out who would choose direction and tactics for avoiding rocks in the fast water streams.

"Left!"

"Left?"

"No! Right!"

"Right?"

After swamping the canoe a few times in chilly New Hampshire streams, we had learned to trust each other. I would steer from the stern when the water was calm, and Ronnie would call out directions from in the bow when the water became choppy. The struggles over who would lead on the dance floor, and what it meant to feminist ideology, now seem a bit quaint. Ronnie had spent the first ten years of our relationship in a T-shirt and jeans, but she swallowed her wardrobe dogma and bought some skirts and dresses for dancing. She had always been shy, very restrained in expressing sexuality, but dancing had transformed her into someone who didn't mind being the center of attention. If the music had a good beat and there was room on the dance floor, we would fly, her skirt rising in quick turns, her eyes shining, her smile beaming out at the cosmos, electricity passing between us as we moved to the music. Our dancing was a controlled mayhem, and if we lacked the precision of some of the best dancers, the joy and energy we generated often made us stand out on the dance floor.

At the Flying Saucer Café some of the "Kerry" gang wandered in while I was on the dance floor. The young woman pushed her mother,

Susan, along. "Mom, ask him to dance! You'll have fun!" Susan hesitated, and I asked her if she wanted to try. She may have been just a bit younger than the first woman I danced with, but she had the same fancy shoes, glittery dress, and stiff hairdo. She displayed a little more cleavage, and as we whirled about, one of her straps threatened to slip off her shoulder. Ballroom dancing with a stranger begins with a dialogue, but usually no words are necessary: stance, grip, balance. The man's job is to lead and to showcase the woman.

Susan had gotten used to leading herself, but I made an argument for leading. Not a word was spoken, but we did have "a conversation set to music" (credit Arthur Murray). It may have been a long time since she had danced with someone who could provide a strong lead, or who wanted to, but after a few missteps she started to trust me and have fun. She went off happy and sweating and a little disheveled. The band took a break, and I went out to find Dad.

∞

The next morning, I carried coffee, a bagel and a piece of cake to Dad, who was praying in the Stardust Room. It was almost 9:30 a.m., and he had been there for a couple of hours. He was glad to see me, and asked after Ben and Rickie, who had not yet made an appearance. I was pretty sure they would get there in time to hear the shofar. We needed to show up on time for services or "people will talk." Dad was worried that his buddies would tease him about his *yeshiva bochurs* who didn't want to go to *shul*. Somehow this had become less urgent over the last few years. There were fewer people left who paid attention to these things. He had outlived most of his old world friends. It was now my generation's job to worry about these things.

They were reading from the Torah, the chapter about Abraham, the ram, and Isaac (*Yitz-chak* in Hebrew: He will make us rejoice). Dad took the bag of food I had brought him and discretely walked out of the room to have his coffee in the lobby. I was left behind to guard our seats. This part of the service, the Torah reading, had always served as a break for most of the congregation. The kids and the smokers would make a beeline for the outdoors. As I grew older and gave up smoking, I had started to enjoy this segment more than the regular prayers, reading along in the biblical Hebrew that I had learned in grade school, watching the parade of people called up to say blessings.

This break was also when the rabbi gave his sermon. The seats were filling as the time approached for *musaf*, the prayer added on holidays. I looked behind me. The amphitheater café rose in tiers; there were solid balcony walls with tables attached and rows of chairs in the extra space before the next tier. As I scanned the crowd, I saw Susan, one of my dance partners, staring at me, and we exchanged nods and nervous smiles. The other old women I had danced with were also in the crowd, and it felt a bit like high school, furtive glances with hidden meanings.

Shirley's husband was sitting next to her and noticed when we made eye contact. He might have been 80, but his eyes narrowed, and his brow and lips added to the grimace and frown. It brought me back to the Bible. The chapter before the sacrifice of Isaac is about Abraham and Sarah when they lived in the Negev, near the kingdom of the Philistines, during the reign of Abimelech. Even though they were both old, Sarah was still a great beauty. Abraham asked Sarah to tell strangers that she was his sister so that men would not be tempted to kill him and take Sarah as a wife. Shirley's husband was safe. I was not tempted.

∞

After the service, an old woman with her wide walker struggled down the hall from the dining room to the main lobby. There was a little trellis between the doors. This small speed bump made her list to the left. She made it to the lift designed for people in wheelchairs or walkers. She pushed the button, and she waited, and she waited. I asked if she needed help. She said, "It's OK, they will come and help me." And they did. Someone carried the walker and the other person helped her step by step up to the bottom of the stairs. When it became clear that even with help she was not climbing the stairs, they sat her down in a chair and two sturdy young men lifted her and the chair. She smiled and was carried up the stairs.

I walked outside to the back patio overlooking the lake to stand in the sun. In the distance the sky appeared unsettled. Thunder was approaching, and the earth moved under my feet, but it was not the storm. They walked side by side, a massive pair. The smaller one, I guess she weighed about 280 pounds. I swear the earth shook as they moved to cross the patio.

After the ground settled, I overheard one of the guys who had helped the elderly woman up the stairs trying to explain to his little girl about the woman who had struggled to climb the stairs. The child was holding his hand, her head turned up, the tiny chin pointing just above his kneecap, her eyes, searchlights, probing. White leggings reached down to shiny shoes below her little party dress. He bent down to tell her: "Honey, we try to help people. That's what we do."

My eyes became wet, and tears slid down my cheeks. I thought about one of the stories my father had told us when we visited Auschwitz, about an inmate named Avrum. He told it again when Lynn and I visited him in New Jersey. Avrum is a Yiddish variant of Abraham. Did the Bible story bring him to mind?

"This guy, Avrum, gave me the job in the laundry." The laundry job was a blessing, because it was a warm place in the winter and it gave Dad the opportunity to steal clothes. He had a partner who helped him trade the clothes for food.

"This guy who took care of the SS man lived in a small block in the attic. My partner and I would take up rice or macaroni, and sugar to the attic; he would cook it for us. He was a German Jew.

"One time we were sitting looking out the window in the attic. Each of us had a plate with macaroni with a little sugar on it. And Avrum came up behind us. The man had been sick. He looked wasted, *ungedart* (gaunt, shriveled, dried out).

"It was a bad day for Avrum. The guards sometimes came through the bunks making selections of the people who could not work anymore. That day they had picked him out, and the next day he was expecting to go to the gas chamber. He came up behind us. He was in bad shape, skin and bones. He was staring at the floor, muttering over and over, 'It's my last Sunday, my last Sunday.' I tell you, the spoon would not go into my mouth."

The last time my father told this story, Lynn and I were sitting in his kitchen in New Jersey. He coughed, his throat closing again, 65 years later. Avrum had been an animated presence, a leader in his community, and my father did not want to hold this eviscerated image of him in his mind.

"I couldn't look at him. I gave him my plate like this."

Dad picked up a plate from the kitchen table and handed it back over his left shoulder.

"'It's my last Sunday,' Avrum said."

My father shook his head slowly. In the camps, hunger was a constant, food the key to survival. Perpetually hungry, my father saw his throat close up; he could not eat anymore. A sad smile, almost a grimace, crept across his face before he spoke. "I couldn't eat anymore, so I gave him my food."

It was not always possible, but even in the camps people had tried to help one another.

I walked back into the hotel and stopped in to visit Ben and Rickie in their room. I watched Rickie go through a couple of bags of chips and most of a pint of avocado dip and realized he was not really a dainty eater but simply had tastes the Kutsher's kitchen did not satisfy on the High Holidays.

For most people, the kitchen and the dining room were the main reason for going to the resort. The rooms were "getting tired," with old carpets; sagging, lumpy mattresses; peeling paint; the occasional moldy bathroom; and hot water shortages. Ben had stepped into the shower and soaped himself up before realizing that the water was not getting any hotter. He was grumpy most of the morning but cheered up at lunch. A comic at the hotel had joked, "Let me eat in the dining room and I'll sleep under the table."

The resorts were in decline, but in their last days, coming to the Catskills remained a celebration of life for my father and mother. Places like Grossinger's, the Concord, and Kutsher's served kosher food and supported comedians who delivered punch lines in Yiddish. They were places where Jews could gather with their children and grandchildren for festivals that renewed old traditions. Some of the Jews had immigrated before WWII, but many had come after the Holocaust. Now they were old people but still thought of themselves as the new ones in the herd. The *greeneh* were happy to mingle with the others who still embraced a Jewish culture with European roots. My parents and most of the survivors are gone. The hotels aged with them, and most have passed away, but the memories still linger.

Christina

∞

That my father lived into his nineties and still ventured out into the street alone was a miracle. He brings to mind a scene in *Pulp Fiction* in which the hero, played by Samuel Jackson, stands bewildered as a gunman empties a six-shooter at him from point-blank range. Unharmed and nonplussed, Jackson turns to look behind him. Six bullet holes trace his outline in the wall, while he somehow remains alive. My father was that kind of survivor: He stood in plain sight while deadly terrors came rushing at him. All around him people died, but he remained standing.

Late in November, as fall crept toward winter, Lynn and I traveled down to New Jersey to celebrate my father's 91st birthday. We called him shortly after picking up a rental car at small airport near Trenton. On the flight down from Boston, the copilot had doubled as steward on the 19-seat Beechcraft 1900. While going through the safety features of the plane and confirming our destination, he had wondered out loud at why anyone would fly to New Jersey. Almost no one smiled.

Arriving at my father's house in Lakewood, we marveled at the heaps of leaves that covered his yard. They were piled knee-deep along the fence, and Lynn and I agreed to set aside some time to clean up the yard.

Christina had been keeping an eye out for us. When I stepped out of the car, she pushed the button to open the garage door. It was a bad sign that Dad was not at the door to greet us. We found him in his beige leather recliner, the seat somewhat the worse for wear. The TV was on, pouring out financial news in a multimedia stream. The screen was a blueprint for attention-deficit disorder: Market indexes were updated continuously, oil and gas prices scrolled across the top of the screen, world news updates and stock prices streamed across the bottom. In a coup de grâce, the time until the market would close was being updated in milliseconds in a large box in the upper right-hand corner of the screen. All of this made it hard to focus on the talking heads that popped up from time to time.

It had been 66 years since 25-year-old Godel had walked under the now legendary *Arbeit macht Frei* sign that still stretched over the Auschwitz gate.

Soldiers had lain in trenches wearing gas masks when my father was born, near the end of World War I. The only photograph I have of him as a young man shows a serious fellow in a suit. His face is serene, yet somehow troubled. The photo is from 1937. He was 21 and the world was about to explode again, but Zyklon B, not mustard gas, would mark this other world war in the 20th century. It was probably not global politics that troubled him just then but rather his prospects for a career. He had been working at a shoe leather factory stitching leather, and he hated it. He would say, "*Ich habe kein sitzfleisch* (no flesh made for sitting)." He had often used those words to describe my brother. Restlessly peripatetic, both Dad and Ben preferred to be out and about among people. They loved exchanging gossip. They wanted to have a look at what was happening. And they wanted to make something happen. I, on the other hand, could sit still almost indefinitely.

Growing up, I spent hours reading, studying, and watching TV. I loved solving math and chess problems. Dad was good with numbers, too. When I was in grade school, we would play multiplication games whenever we were alone in the car or truck. I was in my late fifties, and my skills had decayed a bit with disuse, but I still remembered the game fondly. Dad would ask me, "How much is 21 x 29? 37 x 52? 91 x 57?" Even when he was in his nineties, Dad could still multiply three-digit numbers in his head.

Sitting in the kitchen, just an hour after we arrived, Dad was telling Lynn stories of people forced from their homes with a single suitcase, dragged off to the ghettos. Suddenly, the sound of leaf blowers roared from the backyard. I leapt up to watch as the garden service guys uncovered the lawn, still very green for late November. Lynn and I looked at each other stunned at how quickly the fates had acted to save us from yard work.

Dad sat in his chair when we moved from the kitchen into the living room, where he now spent more time since his back had started giving him trouble. The disks in his lower spine grated against one another when he walked. He hated it. He could only walk about 300 yards before the pain forced him to stop.

As he would say, he was "in trouble." As I walked over to kiss him, I bumped the chair and he winced. "Careful!" He grabbed his left foot, which was swollen with what looked like an impressive bunion at the base of the big toe. He was disconsolate. We were going to take him out to dinner at my brother's country club and now he did not think he could go. He had been scrambling to get an appointment with his podiatrist, who had an office in Lakewood.

"I should go. He's coming special. I don't want to make him wait."

He put on his new orthopedic shoes. He calls them his *kalyekeh* shoes, footwear for cripples. He confessed that he had been a bad boy, wearing his nicer shoes when he left the house. He was ready to blame his vanity along with the fates.

The doctor's office was on the edge of town in a mini-mall. There were two or three stores nearby that targeted the Hassidic community, including a kosher butcher and a kosher deli. The foot doctor's office was near the deli. The receptionist showed Dad to a chair in one of the examination rooms and asked him to take off his shoes and socks.

"It looks like gout," she said, looking up at me. "Has he ever had gout before?"

A few minutes later the doctor walked in, peeling his coat off as he stepped up to the sink to wash his hands and put on latex gloves. He was from the Bronx with a hard-boiled New Yorker's intensity, the rapid speech and a layer of sarcasm. Scowling, he did little to hide his displeasure at being summoned to the office for some old man's foot problems. Dad introduced us to the doctor. I explained that it's my dad's birthday, and the doctor's manner softened a bit.

I have had foot troubles, too, blood clots and cellulites, but mercifully I've had no experience with gout. Lynn and I asked the doctor about gout, and he turned to us to explain about uric acid, crystals, and arthritis. From that point onward, I had to keep redirecting the doctor to speak directly to my father. After all, I was on a short visit and Dad needed to understand the issues so that he could deal with or, even better, prevent future outbreaks.

The doctor started organizing some impressive needles. Lynn, squeamish, asked if it was OK to leave the room. She could be tough if she needed to be, but she usually turned away from bloody scenes in movies or on TV until someone would tell her the gruesome part was over.

"This one's for the pain," the doctor said as he poked my dad with a needle.

"This one's going a little deeper. It may hurt a bit." Dad winced.

The doctor poked the needles about, separating the gout crystals from the joint. The pain subsided, and Dad smiled. He put on his *kalyekeh* shoes and walked out of the office. By the time we arrived home, he was certain he could go to dinner and we called my brother to confirm the plan.

Dad was becoming more and more comfortable with Lynn. It was easy to be comfortable with her. She was warm and friendly. She had an almost childlike curiosity about people and the world they lived in. She asked questions about Dad's youth and his experiences during the war. He talked to her about his grandsons, my nephews, and how they were spoiled, especially the younger one, who would not be joining us for dinner. He complained that his nephew just liked to play games and sports. When Lynn asked him if he had played sports in his youth, he told her about saving money and forming a partnership with two other boys to buy a soccer ball.

Minutes later Lynn received a call on her cellphone from her old boyfriend, Henry. She moved into another room to take the call, but her voice carried. Dad stopped to listen. When she returned, Dad teased

Lynn, amused at the notion that she was still friendly with an ex-boyfriend. Lynn was impressed by his hearing and his presence.

His foot no longer throbbing, Dad seemed at ease, like a marathon runner who could see the finish line at the end of a long run. He knew he could coast home, that he would finish the race. No one would complain if his last steps were unsteady. Ben called Dad a "hot ticket." Dad flirted with waitresses and would now tell the occasional off-color joke to his sons, even if there was a woman in the room. The dynamics had changed. Dad had given up on reining Ben in. Now Ben pushed Dad around, trying to get him to spend some money on himself and making sure he maintained his social contacts. Dad enjoyed it when Ben teased him about being the only stud at his card games with the old women.

"Your brother's a *lobos,* a wise guy." He was translating for Lynn. "Your brother, he has always got some place to go." While Dad claimed to accept it now, he explained to Lynn that he still could not believe that my brother would leave his business to go play golf for a week in Florida or to go skiing with his boys for a week in Vermont. Dad had never taken off two days in a row until he was in his late sixties. He accepted Ben's way, in part because Ben remained successful in his business despite the vacations, and in part because he understood that his boys lived in a world far different from the one in which he had struggled.

Dad was in a much better mood now that his foot was not throbbing. He talked about *sitzfleisch* again, and I thought about the yoga teacher that Lynn had brought into my life. In many of yoga sessions, especially when working on sitting poses, he would focus on the pelvis, the sitting bones, and the hips, the collection of body parts that is the foundation for the spine. I used to be the golem staring out in space and now I meditate, watching my breath. How much has changed?

Lynn interacted with Dad with openness and curiosity, a sharp contrast to Ronnie's guarded behavior. Over time, Ronnie had turned away from my parents' stories of suffering and deprivation, holding them off because the stories gave their owners moral authority. We were still in a period of rebellion, a new generation trying to assert itself. Was my generation special in its push back against racism, sexism, and commercialism? My parents had been lobbying hard for Ronnie and me to have a family, but she was not ready. Ronnie was afraid of bringing children into the world, and I was unwilling to push her anywhere she did not want to go. Ronnie was dead now, and Lynn and I were too old to make our own children. My father had accepted these facts and was content with my brother's children.

How had the chicken farmer and his son changed? Dad's stories were now precious to me. His goals of preparing me to survive and of pushing me to find financial security and play an important role in the Jewish community no longer dominated our relationship. He was amused that his "communist" son was now a high-tech success story. I saw him more as a man and less as an icon. Yes, he was an Auschwitz survivor, but he was also someone who worried that people would find out that he was a few months younger than his wife. In his eyes, I was no longer an *Americana tuches,* too sure of his place at the top of the food chain. Dad knew that I understood suffering. Mercifully, I had not experienced the extremes that he witnessed and endured, but I did know the simple agony of a man who had lost his wife to cancer.

Part of the birthday present I had prepared for my dad was some film I had transferred to DVDs. I played for him a clip of a lunch with other survivors at Max Frisch's house in Miami ten years earlier. The camera panned the table and my father, Max, and others took turns introducing themselves.

"Look, it is *da mama*." My father's eyes got misty as he watched her on the screen. "We should go to visit her." Dad wanted us to visit my mother's grave.

The graveyard was on the other side of town. The entrance was disheveled, with the caretaker's tools lying about, but the graves were well-kept. We walked over to the family plot: a rectangular slab of marble covered the gravesite with one headstone for the family centered at one end. The family headstone bore the names of those who had died in the war without graves: my father's sisters, his brother, his parents, and Mom's mother. Next to the family headstone, a separate headstone marked my mother's grave. An empty space on the other side of the family marker was reserved for my father.

As we walked toward the grave, Dad pointed out the new housing development across the street from the graveyard. The collection of two- and three-family homes belonged to members of Lakewood's expanding Hassidic population. Dad was a superstitious man, someone for whom the spirits of the dead were very real; he shook his head in disbelief. How could people choose to live next to a cemetery? We said a prayer and left tears and stones behind.

Back at his house Dad retold the story of the two suitcases Mom had brought with her from Lodz to Munich. She had hidden $350 in each, the profits from her sewing business. She arrived in Munich with two suitcases, everything she owned in the world, but when she went to the toilet in the train station, she could not fit them both in the stall. Someone stole the one she left outside the stall. Still, she had a small sewing machine and she still had the dollars that would lead her to my father and his street market currency exchange. Later she would spend some of that money on her wedding trousseau. The china and linen from that spending spree is still in my father's living room in a hutch near the dinner table.

That night Lynn and I stayed with my brother. On the drive to Ben's house we took back roads, and Lynn was surprised by the number of old farms still surviving, tucked in among new developments. The developments have new streets, but the thoroughfares that connect them have the same old names: Lanes Mills Road and Georgia Tavern Road. The names persist, but the mills and tavern are no longer with us.

My brother and I reminisced about sharing the same bed and about the fires our farmworkers had started with careless cigarettes. We marveled again at the evolution of chicken feed, from "scratch" (seeds and kernels) in 100-pound bags that we spread by hand, to the conveyor belts that would later deliver tons of ground mash from a huge bin in the feed room.

Dad, the snowbird, was getting ready to go to Florida. When we visited the next day, he was in the garage getting his Lincoln ready to ship down south. I wondered how many cars would migrate on trailers or trains to new homes in parking spaces underneath condo towers on Florida beaches. Dad's car had a lock combination he would not forget. The cars had a number pad, and you could type in a five-digit password to unlock the door.

My father's Lincoln came preprogrammed with the number tattooed on his arm. Was it a miraculous coincidence, a random number from the factory? Or was it the dealer paying homage to my father or playing with his head? I never sorted it out, but my father thought it was miracle.

My brother and I had trepidations about his driving, even short distances, but he was convinced that he could still drive safely. He was not willing to give up that symbol of independence. He had only had one accident in the last ten years, so the statistics seemed to be on his side. We helped him clean up the car and headed inside for lunch.

As we sat around the kitchen table, he told us again about his first day in America. Dad remembered the conversation with Mom's father, who had met them at the pier:

"You will need to change some money. You cannot use marks and zlotys here."

"Yes, I know. I have dollars," my dad answered.

"You have green dollars?" The older immigrant was stunned.

My father, who had traded currency as part of his business in Munich, surprised the old man with his savvy. Despite his bravado, Dad was ill at ease in his new country. A small balding man who did not speak the language, he was a survivor among strangers. But the survivors found one another.

Members of what Dad called "the organization," shorthand for several different Holocaust survivor groups, had helped him and my mother find an apartment when they first arrived in America. "The "organization" included Jewish Federations and Jewish aid groups. In this instance, it was probably the American Jewish Joint Distribution Committee (JDC), with its long history of humanitarian activity, that had helped my parents resettle in the United States. In Munich, another group, the Central Committee of the Liberated Jews in the U.S. Zone of Germany, the official body representing displaced Jews in the American zone of Germany from 1945 to 1950, had helped Dad find housing there.

Holocaust survivors would continue to stick together, as long as they lived. That was my dad's experience. Dad told us about a New Year's Eve party in Miami, early in the 21st century, that drew some 400 *greeneh*. A few "youngsters" were near 80. Holocaust survivors share similarities with members of many other immigrant communities, providing one another with a support system in a new culture. Survivors are a tribe within a tribe in a country whose ethos works to abrogate tribal bonds. The children of survivors drift apart as they assimilate, seduced or embraced by the American dream. Some cleave to Judaism, to Yiddishkeit. The Hassidim stretch the farthest back to tribal roots.

Winters I traveled down to Florida to visit my snowbird dad. The cement avenue known as "the Boardwalk," on Hollywood Beach, was just a few hundred yards from my father's condo. I was in a middle-class hodgepodge of Russian immigrants and visitors from northern outposts: Canadians, folks from Michigan and Minnesota, and older Jews from New York and New Jersey.

The winter after my dad's 91st birthday, I was nearing 60, but I felt like a youngster in this crowd. On the Hollywood boardwalk, younger folks on in-line skates and skateboards cruised by us, in a bicycle lane. A Hassidic couple passed us in a bicycle cart peddling side by side under a canopy. Her head was covered and he wore the classic black pants and white shirt, a yarmulke perched on his head while his *tzitzis* jangled about his thighs as he peddled. Old men, their bodies in various states of disrepair, walked shirtless in the afternoon sun. Occasionally a fitness buff appeared, also shirtless, tanned and toned. My brother had been trying to get me to do push-ups by teasing me about my old man boobs, but I grumbled and slapped the pregnant belly beneath his muscular chest. We walked along the beach, and he pointed out the old men. Dad separated them into two groups: the guys who belonged to the obesity tribe and those still in shape, with good posture and tight abs. "Which of these bodies do you want to have when you're an *alte kacker?*" he asked.

I went back to Massachusetts to work on my abs, but a few weeks later I found myself back in Florida. My brother had called to say that Dad was in the hospital.

Fluids surrounded his lungs. He was short of breath, and his heartbeat was irregular. He was afraid to be alone at night. Christina had spent the night with him. She slept fitfully on a recliner in his hospital room. She was an angel with blond hair and shy eyes tending to an old man. Christina called my dad her baby. By the time I arrived, he had stabilized. A diuretic siphoned fluid from his body, and an oxygen tank helped him breathe. He was an old man afraid of dying. Was it the unknown he feared? The loss of daily pleasures? I know he hated giving up control of a life he had snatched back from destiny. Did he fear the Judgment Day, burdened by the guilt of surviving, of returning to a family that had died long ago? Would he recognize them in next world?

The old guy was still a fighter, still a survivor. Released from the hospital he was back in his condo on the 22nd floor with his oxygen machine, though most of the day he was OK without it. He shuttled from doctor to doctor, looking for some pill that would make him better. "I go to the doctor and I ask, 'Please, maybe you can give me something to help?'" This was not so different from his plea to the nurse in the Auschwitz hospital, "Please, can you help me? I am a young man. I want to live."

He was an old man, but still he wanted to live. Dad struggled with his new handicap, frustrated at how quickly he became short of breath. He was eager to leave Florida and go home. With my brother's help, he had made the arrangements. Worried about squeezing his oxygen tank into the coach section of an airplane, he had booked a first-class ticket. I called him a few days before his flight.

"So how are you today?" I asked.

"So, so." It was coded message: Anything less than "good" meant trouble.

"What happened?"

"I fell down," he said.

"Oh my God! How did it happen?"

"I caught my foot in the carpet, and before I know what's happening, I'm on the floor," he told me.

"Are you OK?"

"I fell on the coffee table. You know the one, the marble table. Thank God it has rounded corners." A hint of humor crept into his sad tale.

"Did you hurt yourself?"

"I banged my head. I have bandages on my hands. I put my hands out and scraped them on the table."

"Were you bleeding?"

"No, not much," he said in a low voice. "When I fell, I hit my head and I thought I split it open. I lay there on the ground and called out, 'Christina, please help me!'" His voice sounded like the cry of a wounded child.

After a pause he said, "It's never happened to me before." He was clearly still frightened, perplexed by his loss of balance. It was another milestone in aging, but he was already recovering. He woke up ready to face the next day, still confident he could live at home.

"Yes, now I have fallen, but they say, 'God helps the fallen.' He helped me before; maybe He will help me again."

From his home in New Jersey a month later, he called me on my birthday. I had the flu. "I woke up today," he told me, "and in my mind, I just came from your bris. We are ten men walking from the synagogue to the hospital where your mother was still recovering from her C-section."

Dad called every day I had the flu. He was a sweetie, concerned about my welfare. He was full of advice. "Stay inside! Don't go out! Take Tylenol!" he insisted. He worried about his boys, and he loved getting a chance to be the caregiver after so many years of struggling with his own health.

After recovering, I called him and he said, "I can't talk right now. I have two priests in the house." I tried to get him to explain, but he hung up. Never before had he hung up on me. Flummoxed, I had to wait until my next visit to learn the full story.

Christina was finally preparing to return to her family in Poland. She had arranged for one of her Polish girlfriends to take her place.

The new caretaker, Elle, had a son studying to be a priest in a nearby parish. He had become curious about this old Jewish man who was going to employ his mother. He and the local priest, Father Mario, stopped in to visit. Father Mario was curious about the aging Holocaust survivor, but he also wanted to make sure the young priest's mother was not being exploited.

My father talked about his history and about how dearly he cherished Christina. He explained how he had been uncomfortable having a stranger live in his house when she first came to take care of my mother but that now she was like a mother and daughter to him. Father Mario left reassured that Elle was in good hands.

Two weeks later, Father Mario brought a Catholic bishop who was visiting from Poland to meet my father. The two dignitaries in black robes drove up past the homes of the Hassidim that surround my father's house. The Hassidim had their own black religious costumes. It was these two clerics who had been in my father's house when I called.

The bishop was in the midst of preparing sermons on interfaith issues. He listened with interest to the priest, who extolled Christina's devotion to the church, and to my father's stories of his life first in his small Polish village and then as an inmate at Auschwitz. When the bishop asked about how he had been liberated, my father winced.

"They had us in boxcars. No food, no water. The Allies would bomb the tracks, and we would sit. You live without food for a long time, but water… When the train could go no further, they would march us to another train and we would fall down to drink from puddles on the road. The water was muddy. It smelled of diesel fuel from the truck convoys, but we would drink. We went from one train to the next. One day the train stopped and we waited and waited, until some brave boy opened the door to see what is what. The Germans were gone. The Americans came. It was nighttime. They gave us pajamas and took us to a barracks to sleep. In the morning we had some food, and I went outside to look around. In the center of the barracks, the courtyard was tiled and some symbol lay embedded in the tiles stretched across the courtyard. We didn't understand what it was at first, but someone said, 'Oh my God, it is a swastika!'"

My dad paused. "Not to believe. It was a Hitler Youth camp at Feldafing, near Munich." Eisenhower and later Ben-Gurion visited the camp. There is a rumor that Joseph Ratzinger, Pope Benedict XVI, may have stayed there as a 14-year-old Hitler Youth."

The conversation moved on to Dad's life in the States and his relationship with Christina. They took photos. Dad laughed. "The bishop put on his red yarmulke, and I put on my black one." I am not sure how long the bishop spent at my father's house, but Dad smiled as he talked about their good-byes. "The bishop thanked me for inviting him into my home. He shook my hand, and I thanked him for visiting; then I told him, 'Make sure to tell the Pope I slept in his bed.'"

When I told him I wrote about his wisecrack, he was embarrassed. "No, don't write about this. It's not nice," he said. He did not want to offend millions of Catholics, who might mistake humor for invective.

Christina had gone back to Poland, and Elle had taken over as Dad's housekeeper. I called to check in on him, and he told me about going to *shul*, a good sign. When he did not go to synagogue, it usually meant that he was sick or feeling particularly antisocial. That Sabbath after services there was a kiddush. Someone in the synagogue had a daughter whose marriage was imminent. Drinks and tidbits were laid out. My father drank a toast and was shuffling out the door when the bride's mother cornered him. "We are having a lunch, too. Please come." He demurred, but when she persisted, he joined them. "It was very nice, kugel, fish, very nice. When I was ready to leave, this same woman takes my hand and insists on walking me to my car. Nice woman."

He was a sweet thing, an old man with his *kalyekeh* shoes and his cane, walking arm in arm with the mother of the bride. They stopped for a moment as other guests wished her mazel tov and thanked her for the lunch. Someone he didn't recognize at first approached. He couldn't quite hear the conversation. Was it in Polish? Who was this guy?

Elle had waited for him with lunch. A man with regular habits, he was almost two hours late. She was anxious. What had happened to him? Was he OK? She had called her son and sent him out looking for

Godel. He was the mysterious fellow who approached Dad near the synagogue.

In a world full of terrors, of loss and despair, for a moment, I felt lighter. My heart lifted with the joy of hearing a story about kindness. My dad was a little embarrassed that he had made Elle anxious, but he delighted in telling the story. He was fond of his Polish caregivers, touched by their loyalty and concern. It was a story of three generations. An old Polish Jew, a survivor, and a Polish woman from a different faith and her son, the seminary student sent out by his mother to make sure my father was safe. It was a story of compassion that reached across tribes, kindness treasured by a survivor…and his son.

Jewish Mafia

∞

My father came out of the camps naked.

No home.
No country.
No parents.
No sisters.
No brother.
No cousins.
No nothing.

They gave him pajamas and took him to a Hitler Youth barracks. There were five boys in the unit and one of them was in bad shape, his bones showing through, sick with dysentery. A couple of days later they took the boy to the hospital, but he died. One of the other boys, Felix Messer, would become my father's partner in Munich and a lifelong friend.

Lynn and I were sitting in Dad's kitchen filming him with a little digital camera as he told us the story. It was the day before my father's 92nd birthday. Seven years had passed since Ronnie died.

I asked Dad to take off his glasses, and he looked back and forth between us with his one good eye. He was wearing a dark blue cardigan buttoned to the top with a polo player wielding a mallet just above his heart.

"I had a $20 bill that I had been hiding for months, carried in my belt or wadded up in my mouth. We were still wearing rags. When we finally got a chance to go to town, I thought to buy me a suit. I asked my friend should I buy a suit and he told me, 'No, buy something you can sell. You must begin again!'

"I don't remember what I bought first, coffee, cigarettes. I start to *handel* (trade). I used to travel from country to country to buy and sell. To Italy, Switzerland, but I was unlucky and I thought I must stop."

His ears were even bigger than mine, and when he raised his shoulders to grimace, the earlobes touched down onto the collar of his shirt.

"Coming back from Italy, Felix and I and some other guys came to a German town. It was just an hour before curfew and we were looking for somewhere to sleep. We asked people on the street, but no one could tell us where we could find lodging. I asked an MP (the military police where everywhere) and the MP said go to the local police station and they will tell you. So we went there.

"Some Polish boys had ransacked a nearby village and killed some people. The police looked at us and thought we fit the description, so they locked us up. The next day they took us over to the village, and one of the young men looked at Felix and yelled out, 'You killed my father!' It felt like my soul left my body. How could this happen? We were nowhere near the town. How could this be? Hadn't we suffered enough? They put us in jail. The area was still under American military control, and a few days later an American soldier (I think he must have been Jewish) came to visit us and asked about our situation. We had no lawyer. We had nothing. He went with us to the American commander, and we explained that we were DPs who had never been to the village. The commander believed us and let us go. He told the Polish policemen they had no jurisdiction over us."

Americans were usually the good guys in the stories my father and his friends told about postwar Europe. Their images of American GIs contrasted sharply with the grim reports about American troops in Vietnam and the Middle East. In postwar Europe, the Americans had a refreshing naïveté. The Europeans were morally exhausted after the war. Guilt clung to them whether from their actions or inactions. They still had a siege mentality. Spared the ravages of war in their homeland, the Americans were shocked when they encountered evidences of atrocities. They still held on to a sense of justice and compassion.

"You find some good people and some bad ones. It was like that for me. It was like that for your mother. Your mother was hiding out in the woods, and she saw a woman with a basket of potatoes cutting them up for her pigs and asked if she could take a potato. She reached toward the basket, but the woman pulled the basket away and told her: 'If you put your hand in this basket, I'll cut it off.'"

I was reminded of an encounter I had with a Russian woman at Costco. The wholesaler had stations where treats were dispensed in an attempt to ameliorate the anomie of shopping in a warehouse. At our store most of the stations were staffed by stout older women with Russian accents. One of them was hawking pizza bagels. She was cutting them in half with a menacing knife and setting them out in small fluted white paper cups. I reached out to take one from the pile she was working on but flinched when she stabbed the knife into the cutting board. "Not from here!" she warned. "You wait to take from other side." Sitting in my father's kitchen, I felt guilty, not for reaching in to take the treat but for comparing my little scolding with the traumas my parents had faced to stay alive.

"Later on, in the woods," my father continued, "the Jewish resistance fighters would stop in at night begging for food from the farmers." Dad paused briefly. "There's a Jewish saying 'Hunger breaks steel.' A few of the farmers were charitable and would give them some food, but others would threaten to shoot them or report them to the Nazis. For the ones who reported them to the Nazis, the resistance fighters looked for a chance to get revenge, and if the opportunity arose, they would visit them again, but this time to burn down their barns or their houses.

"Even Mom's girlfriends turned against her. The Germans put her with the Jews in the ghetto in a nearby town. She was supposed to wear a white paper bracelet with a Star of David on it. She knew some Polish people in the town. She had worked for them as a seamstress. She took off her bracelet and was walking down the back streets to see if they would give her work and hide her, but she ran into some Jewish girls that knew her. She had gone to school with them. They had been her playmates, but they told her: 'You cannot be here. We will report you. You must go back to the ghetto.'

"We have so many tragedies as a people: the slavery in Egypt, the exodus wandering in the desert. But it wasn't so bad as what we went through in the war. The Spanish Inquisition was bad, but if you pretended to believe in their religion, they would leave you alive. In my time they killed everyone."

I was surprised that he mentioned the Spanish Inquisition. Mostly he spoke as an eyewitness to history. Conversations about older Jewish history were usually about the legends associated with Jewish holidays, stories of Passover or Hanukkah.

"I was in my town in 1939 in November. This German caught me and put me on a work gang. I ran away back home, but he caught me again. He beat me and he beat me until I told him, 'Shoot me. I can't take anymore.' I said, 'Shoot me!' A year later, he would have just killed me. After they invaded France, they thought they were gods. Instead, he took me into a barn and made me crawl on my knees and collect horse manure with my hands."

The stories spilled out of him like a container overflowing. Some were new. Some had been instruction for his rebellious son who could be a *lobos,* someone who was intemperate or cavalier and unconcerned about the consequences of his actions. I had always thought that assessment was a little harsh for a kid who was on the honor roll at school and spent most of his spare time working on the chicken farm, but my father knew that the schoolwork was easy for me and that I worked begrudgingly, jealous of the kids who had their weekends free. My father's stories were part of his "trying to make me a mensch," a responsible person who has a sense of right and wrong, someone whom other people will look up to. I had heard most of Dad's stories more than once. Sometimes I tried to build a timeline for the stories, but now I did not want to interrupt him. He was pleased that we were trying to capture his story on video. "You make your way through life. It's not easy. They put me to all kinds of work: cutting stones for masonry, breaking stones for roads. You go through a lot. As a young boy I was indentured to a shoemaker for a few years, but later, when I was 20, I became a businessman." He smiled. "I worked for my father in the winter selling caps and long underwear, in the summer, fruit from the orchards at the market in Lodz, the big town nearby. I wanted to rent orchids, too: some pears, some prunes. I went to Warsaw to try to borrow some money, but I could not find anybody who would lend it to me. It was four weeks before the war started, and they knew trouble was coming and no one wanted to lend me money. I went to Lodz and a guy lent me 300 zlotys. You run into some good people. I was hoping to find him after the war. I would have been a real pleasure to pay him back, but he never survived. I asked about him everywhere, but he never survived.

"We had worked hard, and I had saved some money. The war came, and I was crushed. The war started, and I had 700 or 800 zlotys. Like a few thousand dollars today. But when the war came, they became worthless. I lived in the German zone, and they used German marks. The border to the Russian zone was 14 miles to the east where they still used zlotys."

He put his left hand down on the table to mark the border, and with his right hand, he showed us that you could use zlotys only on the other side.

"I finally got a little back. I took a trip to Warsaw and managed to use the money to buy some thread for my father's hat-making business."

I asked him to talk about the time, after the war, when he and Felix were partners and lived in Munich. He described himself as a "bursar." Most people would say he was working in the black market.

"The war was almost over when they marched us out of Auschwitz. We walked the whole night. My partner and I had $46 from our business, and we split it. I got $23, and he got $23."

"How did you get money?" Lynn asked.

"How did we get the money? We would sell stuff and bring back a dollar or two or some marks or money from other countries. Even in the camps you could find a way to trade currency. We traded it all for dollars.

"They threw us out of Auschwitz. *'Raus, raus!'* The whole camp was lined up and marched out. Each night we walk 25 miles. They were marching us to another camp closer to Germany. The first night I was going good. The next night I was asleep on my feet. I was always a good sleeper. You are a good sleeper, too."

He used the same words, *"Raus, raus"* when he tried to wake me as a teenager. He was amused and chagrined that I was so reluctant to give up my warm repose. He might grab my toe to shake my foot, careful because my first reaction would be to kick out and groan.

"I was walking like this." He closed his eyes and leaned over out of his chair pretending to fall over. "If you couldn't keep up, they would shoot you. They would shoot you and leave you lying there. This guy, the one I help after he was castrated, he held me up. He kept me going. If not for him, they would have shot me.

"We were marching to a camp called Groz Rosen (large roses). When we got there, we slept on the floor. They grabbed me for some work. I'll never forget. We carried dead people to the crematorium, four boys carrying a ladder with a dead person on it.

"Then Flossenbürg, Lehrenberg, Mildorf, and then Dachau, the last few places we were not working. They took me from place to place, and they didn't kill me. These camps were not death camps.

"In the biggest camp, in Buchenwald, they didn't have gas chambers. Only in Poland did they have the gas chambers. But if you died or they killed you some other way, they burned you up.

"In Flossenbürg, I ran into a fellow from my hometown who worked in the kitchen. I said, 'Shulim.' His name was Shulim (peace). I said, 'Shulim, you bring me a pot of soup and I'll give you a dollar.'" Dad's eyebrows shot up imitating Shulim's reaction.

"'You have a dollar?'

"'Yes, bring me some soup and I'll give you a dollar.' He would bring me a two-liter pot of soup for a dollar. Three times he brought me a pot of soup and I gave him a dollar. Listen. It helped me to survive. It filled me up. It helped me survive those ten days, and I still had $20." (I think my father could always give you a good estimate of his daily net worth.)

"The last camp was maybe ten days before the end of the war. I was in one of the Kaufering subcamps of Dachau. They were hiding us in underground bunkers. We were buried underground like potatoes. They dug us up and put us on train to take us to the Alps, to the Italian or Austrian mountains, I didn't know which, but I was sure that there they would kill us. They didn't want to kill us in Germany. The train wandered from station to station. The railroads were cut here, there, everywhere. Half the people died in the trains. No food, no water. They just lay there."

Lynn gasped.

"Listen, you get used to, you get used to everything. They were trying to stay out of the way of the Americans, but the Americans found us. The Americans came and they took us to a camp from the Hitler Jugend, where they had trained the Hitler Youth. In the middle of the camp in the square there was a huge swastika. They took our old clothes and burned them, and gave us pajamas. We wore pajamas for three days. We were five boys in a block. One lasted only a few days. A nice kid, he was maybe 18 years old. He had dysentery. One guy was an electrician. All kinds of people, and one of them was Felix Messer."

"Felix? Did you know him before?"

"No, I met him there. He became my partner in Munich.

"One guy told me about an abandoned shop, and we went over and stole some stuff: linen, pillowcases. I went down there and took away as much as I could carry. I sold it, made a little money, and I wanted to go back to my hometown. No one then dared dream we could go to America. In the camps, I never thought I would see my town again. I had to go back. I had three watches and three gold pieces from selling the linen. I had already started to deal with all kinds of merchandise. I came to Poland, and I got to the border.

"Some girl had given me a letter to give to her sister, and they searched me when I crossed the border and found the letter. In it she wrote to her sister: 'Leave Poland, leave this bloody land. Run from this terrible place!' They said I was going to do sabotage, to make trouble. They threw me in jail.

"In my cell, in a basement, this big guy, a criminal, a bandit, he looked at me and said, 'Give me one of your watches!' The wall behind him was stained with blood. He said, 'You see all the blood on the walls. Give it to me or I'll kill you.' I told him, 'Who do you think you are dealing with? I've seen more dead people than you have seen live ones.' I had been a prisoner for almost five years. 'You want me to be scared of a little blood?' He got quiet and he looked away.

"They took me up out the cell to question me and asked me where I got the gold pieces and the watches. I told them I got it from Auschwitz, from Canada. They didn't believe me that I could have this stuff from the camps, but I was lucky. There was a guy in the police station, a Polish guy who had lost a hand in the war. He had been in Auschwitz, and they asked him, 'Could this be true? Could he have this stuff from the camps, from Canada?' And he said, 'Yes. It could happen.' They gave me back my stuff."

"That is amazing," exclaimed Lynn.

"They let me out of jail, oy. It was a long story until I came to my town. It was still 40 or 50 kilometers. I would walk. Sometimes I would get a ride in a cart behind the horses. They would take me for a piece, and I would walk a piece. I got to within eight kilometers of home, and I started to recognize the neighborhood. I saw a farmer I knew, Mr. Klosz. He had a cart with two horses. We used to go to the same markets in Warsaw. I asked him if there were any Jews still here. He pointed me toward an old farmhouse in the valley. 'You got a few Jew boys living there.'

"I came to the place, and there were six boys. One had a bed in the front room, and the others were sleeping in the straw in the barn. I asked them, 'For this we survived, to live like this?' I had been in Germany for six months, and it had opened my eyes. They had indoor plumbing, cars. I borrowed a bicycle, and I went down to the guy whose orchards we rented. I got to my hometown and I stayed just one day.

"I sold the watches for German marks. In Poland, German marks were worthless, but I could take marks back to Germany. I sold the stuff I had and took the marks back to Germany."

My father in Germany circa 1950

That was the beginning of my father's adventures in currency trading. I am in the world because my mother and father met when she needed to exchange some money.

"Tell us about Felix," I said, turning to Lynn. "I knew Felix my whole life, until he died a few years ago."

"A few years?" my father responded. "It was 33 years ago. He died a young man. Felix was like a brother to me. I came back to the Hitler Youth camp to pick up some of the linen that I had stored there, and Felix came and told me, 'You know what they did? They stole it from you.' They left me a little bit, but most of it was gone. We started to talk, to hang out together and he became my partner.

"When we first went to the DP camp near Munich, I got a package of coffee and chocolate from the Jewish organization. I took the coffee and went to sell it on the black market; there was already a black market. I went there and saw a watch, a gold watch. I never owned a watch. I thought it was gold. So I bought it. Felix told me it wasn't gold. It looked like gold. What did I know? It wasn't gold. It was worthless." He laughed.

We asked him about what kind of merchandise he and Felix had bought and sold.

"What did we deal? We dealt everything. We traded in army scripts, everything. I shared a room with Felix for while until I got my own room. In 1946, I found these watches that had come from France, cheap watches. Felix was used to better stuff. He told me, 'These watches are no good.' He was a watchmaker from a Polish town not far from Auschwitz. They were cheap stuff, but I said, 'Felix, there are people here who will buy them.' Russians, they never saw a watch before, a watch was like a diamond, a rich man's jewel. We sold them, the cheap watches, for a few dollars each. Then people started to bring us all kinds of watches. Felix knew which were good and which were cheap. We would buy 30 or 40 at a time.

"In Munich, our market was on the street. I was always well dressed: a nice hat, a suit. We had a currency exchange, and we bought and sold gold, watches, cameras. It was an open market, buyers, sellers, and the prices and exchange rates changed from day to day. The Swiss were short of German marks, and the price went up. Bad news about some country, and the price of their currency went down.

"One day, I was out on the street. One guy asked me for gold. Another asked about gold, another one, everyone was looking for gold. I asked around: 'What's happening, everyone wants gold?' The Korean War had started.

"Most of our customers were DPs. There were maybe ten DP camps all around Munich. The DPs would buy silverware or watches, before they emigrated. We had all kinds of stuff. I had one time cuff links, maybe a kilo of cuff links.

"I worked the street sending customers up to Felix. If things got busy and more than two or three customers went upstairs, I would run up the stairs to help out. I would scramble up those stairs three or four steps at a time." He pulled the watch off his wrist to demonstrate.

"This was our merchandise. Felix would take the mechanisms out of cheaper watches and put them in fancier cases. We had a German guy who would put a brand stamp on them. I would get 50 watches and go see this guy. When I saw him, I introduced myself as Max. I had a different name for each of these guys. We made hundreds of these watches."

My father was proud of his work but also embarrassed. When I asked him later about the details of which brands they put on the watches, he said, "Don't write about that. It's not nice. It's not legal.

"We usually sold them to Russians. They would take them back through Berlin and the border there. They would take along a couple of bottles of vodka for the guards. They never had any problem.

"But it was a risky business. We had these guys from Romania; they wore stiff hats with points sticking up." He held his forefingers up next to his ears.

"They brought us a couple of loads of watches. We were stupid. We trusted them. They said they could bring us a special bunch of watches. The watches would only be available for a little while. They were bringing stuff from Switzerland. They had to act fast, but they needed some cash to buy them. We gave them a $3,000 advance, but they never came back. I found out later they had bought a turpentine factory in Romania. We never saw the money or the watches.

"Felix and I used to go to a local restaurant, really a large house whose living room and dining room had been converted. Some of the clientele were Jewish wise guys; they were like Mafioso. The lady who ran the place liked us. We left a decent tip. She pointed us out to these gangsters as good guys who ran a business that was a good place to get watches. Some of the guys we met at the restaurant stopped in to see us, to buy watches. It turns out, they were looking us over getting ready to rob us.

"A couple of days later, Felix and I were going to a speech by David Ben-Gurion, the Zionist leader. Felix had an apartment where we ran the business. My apartment was one block away.

"I forgot something, and I went back to Felix's apartment. The door was broke down, and stuff was scattered everywhere. Someone had stolen our stuff. I ran down to the street, and they were still there. Five young men were stashing the loot, getting ready to go back for more. I went up to them, and I told them, 'You a stealer, and I am the loser. Give me half of it back and I will leave you to go.'

"They laughed at me, and I grabbed one of them by the collar. I told them, 'You don't give me half, you won't get away from here.'"

He grabbed the lapels of his own shirt to demonstrate.

"I held him like this, and I told him, 'You not go anywhere.' I didn't know what I was doing. They were five of them, and they started to fight with me. I'm a small guy. I don't know how to fight. One guy comes at my back, and he put two knives in me. He gave me those two wounds, and I didn't feel it at first, and then I felt something warm spreading on my back. I reached back and looked at my hand. Blood was running. Before I understood what happened, I fell down and then I called out, 'Help, Help,' and someone took pity on me and helped me to the hospital. The wound was so deep, it had touched my lung. I was six days in hospital, and when I came out of the hospital, I said right away, 'I must get married.'"

"Why did you suddenly need to marry?" I prompted.

"I was weak. I had nobody. Nowhere to go, no one to take care of me. Your mother came and sat with me in the hospital.

"Not everyone on the street was a bad guy. We had just been robbed. We were short on cash. One of my suppliers, when he heard I had been robbed, he told me he could wait to get paid and he said, 'Godel take off $1,000 from what you owe me. I will share your loss.'"

"Tell us about meeting Bronia," Lynn asked from behind the little flip video camera.

"She came to Munich in 1946. She was looking for someplace to live, and at the Jewish agency she met a young woman and they became roommates. This girl recommended us when Bronia needed to change some dollars for marks. 'They are good boys. They give you an honest deal.' She came to us to change $20 into marks, and she looked at what we were selling: gold, silver, and diamonds. She thought we were millionaires. We started to go out to the movies, dinner. We talked sometimes, Should we get married, not get married?

"After I got stabbed, four weeks later, we got married. We went to the rabbi and got married. We had a little party afterwards, maybe 20 people. We lived at 96 East Meininger Strasse near the Jewish Center." He paused briefly.

I sat staring at him: a small old man with big ears and large hands. I marveled at the twists and turns that led to my birth. The dollars my mother had kept tucked into her bra that led her to my father, the stabbing that convinced my father it was time to get married, and all the day-to-day wonders and horrors that my parents had encountered in their struggle to survive.

"I should finish the story about the guy that stabbed me. It didn't end in Germany. I didn't know him, but someone later told me who he was. His nickname was Yagdelele (Blueberry). Fifty years later, in the 1990s in Miami, I was going to a party, a memorial for Ben-Gurion, a Zionist fund-raiser, and who should be there but this guy. I looked at him. 'Do you know who I am? You remember me. You remember your good, good friend. You remember what you do to me?'"

"So you were yelling at him?" I asked.

"No, I couldn't yell. I could barely speak. I tell you, I didn't know what to do. He took his wife and ran away. All I could do was cry....'"

"Did you see him after that?"

"Yes, but what could I do? He would sue me for slander. I had no witnesses. Whenever he saw me, he ran away."

The irony of the Ben-Gurion connection passed by unremarked: the Ben-Gurion speech he was about to attend when he was stabbed, and the Ben-Gurion fund-raiser 50 years later that led to his confrontation with his attacker.

Dad returned to his postwar Munich narrative. "It was a dangerous business. Someone had paid me with traveler's checks. I tucked them away in a little pouch I carried under my shirt, but the pouch was stolen. Two weeks later, some guy came to me and tried to sell me the same checks. I'll never forget. Daniel Beck was the name on the checks. I wanted to take him to a rabbi to try to get a judgment, but the man with the checks said, 'You give me trouble, you won't be in business. I'll send the police after you.'"

Eventually, someone did send the police after my father. The mention of police stirred his memory, and the story came spilling out.

"You were a baby. It was the fall of 1950. Two cars full of customs police came and marched into Felix's apartment. 'Put your hands up

The currency trader fifty years later

where we can see them. Where have you got the watches that just came in from Switzerland?' We used to go in and out of the apartment 20, 30 times a day; customers coming in and out, but the Germans never complained. I think a Jewish guy, one of our customers, sent them after us. The customs guys put Felix in handcuffs. They took 800 watches, maybe $20,000 in merchandise: watches, silver, everything they could find. Felix got arrested, but I was not arrested because I told them I was just visiting. It wasn't my apartment. I had a pocket full of receipts, bills, markers for business we did in the street, and as they were walking Felix to their car, I tossed them into a basement window. They said, 'What did you throw away?' I said, 'Nothing.' They already had Felix, so they didn't bother to try to find a way into the basement to look for what I threw out.

"That time, we were lucky. The lawyer guy who came to represent Felix had just bought a car from the customs guy and he worked out a deal. We went before a magistrate, like a military judge in a small town. We were people without documents, homeless people, not Germans, not Poles. The judge asked us where we were from, and we told him our story and he looked at the prosecutor. 'You picked these guys to harass. Are we trying to bring back Hitler's times? You come into his house with guns? What are you, the Gestapo? What are you guys, storm troopers?'" Mimicking the judge, Dad waved his index finger across his chest.

"'You don't have jurisdiction over these people. Out!' He let us go. The lawyer came out with two bags of stuff that they had confiscated. He took some, the custom guys took some, but we got almost all of it back.

"We lived near a streetcar. The market where we ran our currency exchange was across the street from the streetcar line. Someone had just given me $4,000, and I had wrapped it in a paper bundle. I had a wad of singles in my other pocket: $280. Some American MP had spotted me making a deal on the street and came after me. I went to run away and was climbing a fence, but he was going to catch me, so I tossed the big package over the fence and I pulled the wad of singles out and turned to the American waving it saying, 'Money, money, money...' It was one of the few words I knew in English. I took out the singles. He took the money and let me go." In his New Jersey kitchen, father illustrated, reaching into his pocket to pull out some cash.

"My beloved son, it wasn't so easy." Dad seemed a bit wistful, but you could tell those times still thrilled him. He had been a man about town, cash in his pocket, when a lot of people were still in DP camps.

"I had a pillowcase full of currency, francs, marks, Israeli money, Australian money, all kinds. Our German cleaning women saw it one day and her eyes got wide, but she never stole anything." He was smiling, laughing, thinking about the pillow stuffed with cash and the irony of finding himself with a German lady cleaning his house after working for years as a slave to the Germans.

"Listen, I tell you a story. After Israel was established, Felix went to Israel. He had an old girlfriend who was a capo, a boss, in the camps. He went to her house, and he was standing outside."

"He didn't go in?"

"No. He didn't have the heart to go in. In Munich, people had come to us and told us bad things about her, how she treated people in the camps. How she beat them and stole from them so she could be comfortable. He stood outside. What would you do?

"Felix had a sister in Israel, and we shipped two pianos full of contraband to her husband: silver, dinnerware, gold, jewelry, cameras. Felix's brother-in-law was going to sell it in Israel. He got the stuff, sold it. He took the money and bought a house, and we never saw any of the money. A couple of years later he sent us a few hundred dollars, but the stuff was worth more than ten times that.

"It was $7,000 or $8,000 we sent to Israel. How much money is it now? It is at least ten times more now." He looked away, bemused. "We lost a lot of money in those days.

"In Munich, all my neighbors were German, but they were good. They never sent the police after us. It was some damn Jew who sent the customs police."

"Did you talk to your neighbors?"

"No, just, 'Hello, good day,' not much."

"Did these folks know about the camps?"

"Yes, they knew. By then they knew. But no one talked about it."

"How did you come to buy a chicken farm?" Lynn asked.

"Henry Rosenswieg was a relative of Felix Messer's wife, Sally. He had a chicken farm. Other guys I knew had farms. That was what gave us the idea. I didn't want to go at first, but I didn't speak English." He paused. "And I went [a longer pause] and so for 20 years we had chickens.

"In the early 1970s, I was looking for some other business, and Meckler, whose farm I rented when he gave up farming, had a laundry. He thought I should build a dry cleaning business next door. I put down $2,000. But my other friends talked me out of it. This is not a business for you. Eichenbaum told me, 'You are a businessman. How come you want to run a laundry?'

"Rosensweig, Eichenbaum, Weinberg, Tykchochinsky, all became builders. They all build, maybe I can, too. I tell you, it was a miracle I became a builder. Chamick Rosensweig said, 'Come, be partners with us and we build 30 houses.' I waited to hear from him. He promised, but nothing happened."

Chamick is Henry's Jewish name. I remembered him as a savvy guy, smoking cigarettes and drinking scotch. He always won money when the men got together to play poker. All of them survivors, the women would play rummy and the men would play poker. Now the men are gone, and Dad plays cards with the women.

"One of my egg customers came in and had two lots for sale. I went to Farmingdale the next day and bought the lots. I didn't know much about it. I found some guy to clear the land. I went to another friend, and he gave me the architecture plans to build a house. I found some contractors, and I built those first two houses in 1972 and sold them for $29,000. I still had chickens while I was building until I got the money from the house sales. But after I sold the second house, I gave up the chickens.

"I had some partners for some projects, but I built 40 houses on my own. I built here. I built there, and then I made a development. We put in roads, electric. There is a Godel Drive now in Howell. I went into the neighborhood last year. I asked this guy working on his lawn, 'You aren't the first owner, are you?' He said no. He was the second tenant, and I asked him how the house was and he said: 'It's a good house. You build good houses.' After 33 years it was still a good house."

∞

The next day was my father's 92nd birthday, and he told us more stories, stories about survivors. The English word "survive" probably comes to us from the Latin *supervisee,* "live beyond, live longer than." The Japanese survivors of Hiroshima and Nagasaki feel the word insults those who did not survive. Instead of survivor, they call themselves sufferers. In Yiddish, survive is usually translated *iberkumen* which can also mean overcome, and survivor is rendered *leben geblieben,* or remained alive. My father would mash the two together and speak of those that *uberge-lebt dem krieg,* those that "lived over the war."

We were back at the kitchen table while the coffee brewed and my father talked about prewar Poland.

"Meltzer was one of our New Jersey neighbors. Back in Poland they had caught him distributing communist literature. There were five of them that got arrested together. They locked them up. The jail keeper lived on one side, and the jail was on the other side of the building. The communists had a fund for helping people who were arrested. They paid off the jail keeper. Those five guys survived. One went to Spain to fight the fascists, one to Belgium. All five survived. Once in France, they hid in an area where it was hard to identify Jews, especially if they were communists.

"Kazmin (one of the boys arrested and now another Jewish farmer) was a communist, too. He came to his brother Itzchik after the war. He would say, 'My friends, the communist party surprised us.'" Not a happy surprise. Among other disappointments, the communists turned back Jews trying to escape to the Soviet Union.

"One of the guys, Berkowitz (also a farmer), was nuts. I wanted to buy some property from him, but the guy wouldn't deal with *greeneh;* he thought they were too smart. I asked an agent to buy it for me. The guy was crazy. The electric company had a right of way behind his property, and they came with this huge machine chopping up the underbrush getting ready to put in electric lines. Berkowitz sees them and goes wild. He ran right at that machine. The driver couldn't stop it in time, and it chopped him up. He survived the war, but he died there behind his own fields."

We took a break when the coffee was ready, and I gave my father his birthday card. He liked big cards, and I had picked out the largest Hallmark card I could find.

He began reading the card aloud:

Thank you for helping me to become the man I am today.

"Really?" he asked me.

"If not for you, I wouldn't be here today." I smiled.

My father continued reading:

What more can I say to you about your wonderful guidance and love.

Happy Birthday Liebe Tata (beloved father)
Until 120 years,
Maier

"Is it true?" he asked.

"Yes, it's true."

"You didn't want to go to work at first. But I hollered at you. You didn't want to see what work is. You drove a taxi. You moved furniture. Then you see. The nicest was when you worked here in Howell by the telephone poles." He looked over at Lynn and smiled. "He had a good job. He sprayed kerosene, no, not kerosene, what you call it kreeo, kero."

"I forgot about that job," I said. We struggled for a moment to remember what the stuff was called. "It was creosote! The same stuff we sprayed as a preservative on the walls of the chicken coops."

"Yes, creosote. He spread it around the base of telephone poles. He came home. It was so stinky. I thought: He got a good lesson."

"I had a few stinky jobs. Working in the chicken coops full of manure was pretty stinky," I chided him.

"Later, he wanted to go up to Boston. I gave him a nice winter jacket. A nicer jacket than I had in my 50 years."

"You bought it for him?" Lynn asked.

"No, I bought it for me, but I gave it to him so he could look good for his MIT interview. I said, 'Take my jacket.' He came home. No jacket. I almost fainted. He was wearing a *shmate,* a piece of junk. I tell you, I ask him until today if he sold my jacket for narcotics."

"They were sure I sold the jacket for drug money." I turned to Lynn.

"What happened to it?" Lynn asked.

"I lost it. The truth… I don't remember. I was a space cowboy. I probably went to a party, and I came away with a different jacket."

"Thank God he found his way to MIT," said Dad.

"The things you put up with," Lynn offered, sympathizing with Dad.

Dad asked if we were filming, and I told him we were.

"We dealt gold, silver. This is some of our merchandise."

It was Friday night and Dad pointed to a silver plate that sat beneath our Sabbath candles in the middle of the table beside a two-liter bottle of Diet Pepsi. It was a silver candelabrum that held three candles. The stems rose up from round bases, almost like a person, delicate arms reaching out to hold the two lower candles; a single candle rose above them where the head would be.

"Dad, let's stop now. It's time for your dinner."

Father's Day

∞

A year later, on Father's Day 2010, Lynn and I were once again in New Jersey. Dad was happy to see us, but, at 93, his health was failing. The fear in his eyes betrayed the smile that greeted us. We hugged and kissed. After he sat down in his favorite chair in the living room, child-like bewilderment took over his countenance as he sought to explain the most recent symptoms: His chest would become tight after he ate; sometimes there would be pain, and sometimes he would pass out. His cardiologist was nonplussed. Dad was scheduled to see him again for more extensive tests on Tuesday.

"I would like to live a few more years." At 93, he knew the end was near. Was it too much to ask to live a bit longer?

"Dad, don't be foolish. You'll be OK." Was I in denial? He was still at home, still moving around on his own.

He wanted us to stay until he saw the doctor. Ben would be with him, but he wanted me there, too. We stayed for a couple of extra days, but Lynn and I were scheduled to leave for Europe in a few days and were eager to return home and make our final preparations.

"Ben will be with you. He will explain if you don't understand what the doctor says."

When I thought about leaving Dad, lines from an old blues song rumbled through my brain: "You might as well get ready." I think it's a Blind Willie McTell song, but I heard Mississippi John Hurt sing it in concert at the Philadelphia Folk Festival back in the 1960s or 1970s. An old black man shriveled, hunched over his shiny guitar, long fingers picking out a sweet tune with a somber message. He would sing a racy song like "Candy Man" ("He's got a piece of candy. It's nine inches long"), too shy to look at the audience, or he would sing a sad song and look up with a startled smile.

You just as well get ready you got to die.
You might as well get ready you got to die.
You just don't know the minute or the hour.

Nowadays my dad often looked startled when you approached him, eyes a bit wider, the skin on his head and face lifted, raising the ears. Was he startled, wary, or just curious and attentive? Did it trace back to the camps, or did it begin in his childhood with all those older sisters teasing him? It was so easy to forget that he had had a family, since his family, my family, was exterminated before I was born. On the day of his appointment he was anxious. He may have sensed how much trouble he was in, but I couldn't see it yet. We made our farewells and headed back to Massachusetts. Four hours later were driving through Hartford, with an hour and a half left to go, when I noticed that my cellphone was off. I turned it on immediately and found Ben's voice mail. He was distressed, weeping? As I listened to the message, I received a call from his girlfriend, Lucille: Dad had passed out in the car on the way back from his MRI. They thought it was a heart attack. He was in the emergency room.

Should we turn around? Was he stable? We decided to continue home and get some sleep before returning. The next day we packed some clean clothes and headed back to New Jersey.

It was the summer solstice, and the morning sun crept over the horizon as we approached Paul Kimball Hospital in Lakewood, New Jersey. This was where I had my tonsils removed, where Ben was born.

We called for an update.

"What?"

"Oh my God, code blue! How could it be?"

There was no time to wait for the surgeon. Dad's cardiologist, who rarely does the procedure, had snaked a temporary pacemaker into his chest praying that the Lord guide his hands. The heart started beating again.

When we arrived, he was in a coma. The doctors all spoke in measured tones.

"He is 93 years old. His vital signs are stable, but he is an old man."

I was in shock. I hugged my brother, who was sobbing. My eyes were wet and unfocused. I tried to assess the situation, looking for some way to be useful. What could I do to make sure my father got the best care, the best chance? Time lost its meaning. Day and night blurred in the hospital corridors. The respirator clanked along: bump, bump, bump, shoooooo…. His chest rose as the oxygen pressed into his lungs, the exhale a labored sigh as though someone had sat down gently on a cushion pressing air through the fabric.

Dad underwent surgery to install a permanent pacemaker. We stood guard in shifts waiting for him to regain consciousness. His housekeeper joined us. She was one of a troika of Polish women who had been caring for my father, visiting the United States in six-month shifts. It was the "Small Elle's" turn. A nice lady, but she was not as smart or worldly as the "Big Elle," not as much a part of the family as the saintly Christina had been. Each day, when I arrived at the hospital, I received a status update in Elle's limited English.

"Father no good." (His eyes would not open. His face was a mask of pain.)

"Father good today." (A smile acknowledged your presence, a delicate squeeze when you held his hand.)

Even in the hospital, when he was conscious, my father acted as the translator for his Polish caregivers, filling in the gaps between "good" and "no good." When Dad was sleeping, we struggled to communicate. Often we needed to wait until visitors could translate: Dad's old Polish *greeneh* friends or Elle's son, the onetime seminary student, or Father Mario, the local priest.

The days seeped one into another. Was he still with us? Would he open his eyes? Did he recognize me? Would he be able to breathe on his own? Could the doctors deal with the fluids in his chest, or would his lungs give up pushing against the flood? Was it five days or ten when he had first come off the respirator? Could he speak that first day, or was it the next when he finally had the strength to say a few words?

He grew a bit stronger. He was breathing on his own, speaking, the words muffled by his oxygen mask. Could I let myself hope for another miracle? Looking back, the soup of fear, hope, and despair congealed. Recurring events still held some shape: the commute from Ben's house to the hospital, the visits of Izzy and Sally Bauer also stood out, sweet people, dear friends, but also two people desperate for an audience.

When Izzy and Sally visited, I felt as though I were sitting between two radios tuned to different stations: simultaneous broadcasts of monologues, each talking deliberately, ignoring the other. They told stories from the war, or about their neighbors or their children. Cascading one atop the other, Izzy, six feet tall and still robust for a man in his eighties, might pause occasionally to make sure you noticed when he made a joke. Sally, a foot shorter and a bit frail, would squeeze my hand, a sign of compassion, but also confirming that she still had my attention as she transitioned from one stream to the next. The breathing tube reminded Izzy of a tapeworm. He started in on the story of the worm that came crawling out of Sally's mother's gut while they were hiding from the Nazis.

She had been weak, in pain, losing weight faster than the others in their band of runaways. No one could diagnose her illness. They could not camp near streams or rivers because German patrols focused on those areas. They had to carry water with them. Finding containers was a problem, and they settled on some kerosene cans they found near an abandoned barn. The women in the group complained about the stink, but for Sally's mother it had an unexpected benefit. Izzy explained that the kerosene in the water was just enough to dislodge the parasite. He held up his thumb to show how thick it was. "The whole thing comes crawling out, maybe six feet long."

We waited and we prayed, each in his own way. I stayed at my brother's house. For decades my commute in Cambridge had been on foot or on my bicycle, but now I drove the ten miles to the hospital each day. The trip began under the basketball hoop in Ben's driveway. I usually parked there because it was far enough from the three-car garage to let my brother and the boys get in and out without too much trouble. Forty-five years had passed since I had spent this much time in New Jersey. Many things had changed. Working chicken farms had all but disappeared, but it was still a place filled with images and icons from my youth.

I started down Partner's Lane, the road my brother had built for his subdivision of expensive homes. After the first week I started using my GPS to try alternate routes, but most days I passed Turkey Swamp Park, the Wawa convenience store, a few farms, old houses scattered between new developments, County Line Road, the Lakewood Golf Course. I usually took Forest Street to avoid Route 9, across town to the lake. I had to drive around the lake. Which side today? The lakeshore has a small beach, geese, a crane, and men, all dressed in black suits, heading for prayers. I remember the first time I swam all the way to the other shore, a milestone near the end of puberty.

Ben almost always went in early, still trying to keep his business running. I called my brother to check for a status update before I pulled into the hospital parking lot.

Preparing myself for the worst, I still hoped that the survivor might once again escape death. The drugs were working. The fluid was draining slowly from around his lungs. When his eyes opened, his first impulse was to pull the tube out of his throat. When we were there, we held his hands to comfort him and keep him from yanking out the breathing tube. Getting him to understand the situation took some time. The mood-control drugs they gave him to calm him down and the morphine that helped relieve his pain had left a film over his eyes.

Did he understand me when I spoke to him? Was he trying to talk or just grimacing with discomfort? "Squeeze my hand if you understand." One day he did. He tried to speak but could not. The job of asking the right questions fell to me and my brother so that "yes" or "no" hand squeezes could help him express his needs.

"Do you understand where you are? Do you know what happened? Do you know who I am? Are you in pain? Did the doctor talk to you?

Do you want your eyeglasses? Did they tie you down last night so you wouldn't pull out the breathing tube?"

The syncopated rhythm of his breathing machine marked time, a hapless conductor trudging through a sad symphony. We watched my father's chest rise and fall. I didn't know what to hope for. Should I pray for a peaceful end, a dignified exit? He seemed so frail, but he was still an amazing fighter. His oxygen levels went up, and the doctors decided to let him try to breathe on his own. The tube came out, replaced by an oxygen mask. His eyes were brighter, but he still had trouble speaking. His vocal cords were raw from the breathing tube, and he could barely generate enough air to form words.

The fog was thinning. You could see him gathering himself like a pole-vaulter getting ready to start his run. Then he'd try to move the mask away and squeeze out a few words.

"I want to die in a Jewish place."

"Dad, you are in Lakewood. There is no more Jewish place in the United States."

"This is not a Jewish hospital."

Paul Kimball Hospital is part of the Saint Barnabas Hospital System, started by the Ladies Society of Saint Barnabas from the Episcopal Diocese of Newark. It has been nondenominational for a century. Half of my father's doctors were Jewish, but, except for visitors, most of the other people who walked into his room were not Jewish, the nurses and the rest of the staff.

Like Saint Barnabas, my father was happy to see the gentiles who visited him. Father Mario came nearly as often as Dad's rabbi. Bill and Barb, his office manager and construction foreman, were dear friends and welcome guests. Still, my father held on to dying as a Jew "in a Jewish place"; that was his new mantra. He wanted to go to the Jewish recovery center that his primary care doctor and cardiologist ran just a few blocks away.

Amid misgivings, we waited for the doctors to approve having him moved to the Jewish recovery center. It was nightfall before the ambulance was ready. Dad was anxious and eager. All day he had been asking, "Is it time to go yet? Is it time?" As we rolled him through the halls in his new lodging, I regretted the decision. Perhaps we should have waited for morning. The place was dark and disheveled. Soiled bedsheets and medical bric-a-brac littered the hallways. His room was OK, the bed a bit larger than his hospital bed. There was more room for visitors. We settled him in and headed back to Ben's house.

It was a short stay. Before we set out for our morning visit, we received a call to tell us he had been taken to the emergency room. He was in a coma again. Did he panic when he woke up in new surroundings?

They stabilized him, and the next morning he was back upstairs in the cardiac wing. He was agitated, delirious, in restraints; he tried to speak, but his words were inchoate. I leaned closer trying to pick out the words and piece them together, but it took me a while to make sense out of them.

"This is an *upgenarrt gesheft*."

He was complaining about some kind of swindle, a trick, a cheat. A *nar* is a fool. A *gesheft* is a business. *Upgenarrt* means to fool or to cheat.

"Who cheated you? What happened, Dad? It is OK. We are here now."

"This is a fake."

"What's a fake?"

"The whole thing; it is all a trick."

He was getting even more agitated, and I stopped asking him questions and tried to make soothing sounds as I held his upper arms to stop his thrashing. He calmed down for a bit, but then started up again.

"This is not me. They killed the real Godel last night."

I was flummoxed. My father was the most cogent, coherent, rational man in my small world. When my mother became delirious on her hospital bed, convinced the nurses were trying to kill her, that I could accept, but my father… Was this his way of accepting death, or was it a cry for help?

"Dad, don't give up. You are still alive. We want you to live." He slowly shook his head. It was a dismissive gesture. "Do you know who I am?" I asked.

He knew, but he was not eager to admit it. I tried to pretend that he had been making a joke, but he refused to waver. "This is not Godel. It is a trick, a fool's business."

I held his hand waiting for him to calm down. A monitor above his bed showed his heart rate. Every so often his blood pressure cuff inflated and new systolic and diastolic readings appeared. When his heart rate slowed, I asked him what it would take to convince him he was wrong.

"If I bring you three witnesses to swear you are still Godel, would you believe me?"

The Talmud requires three witnesses for a capital crime, but Dad shook his head. They may just be pretending, conspirators, paid to bring false witness.

"What if I bring you ten? A whole minyan."

He still resisted, but eventually conceded that ten would be enough to shake his belief.

So much of life is surreal. Did the hallucinatory drugs I took as a youth prepare me for these events? I took each new visitor aside and explained as best I could the requirement that they bear witness. One was amused, one distraught; most were confused, but they gamely approached the bed and leaned over to look carefully at my father and assure him that he was still Godel. And eventually he gave up his complaint.

The days crept by, and hope for recovery faded. Were we acting on his behalf praying for him to live, or would we serve him better by letting him pass on to the next world? Memories of my wife's death haunted me. Her agony manifested as the morphine lost ground to the cancer that tortured her. Dad seemed more at peace, or perhaps I was more resigned to the death of a 93-year-old. Resigned and bereft I watched helplessly as my father, one of the last survivors, slipped away.

At the funeral I looked out at the hundred or so people who had gathered and tried to make eye contact, losing the struggle to hold back tears.

Memories

∞

Are memories an inheritance, a carefully husbanded wealth that supports us in our declining years? Are they like a coral reef that builds a barrier around a sinking island? For many of us, as the years pass, memory becomes a fickle friend hiding in shadows just out of reach. I pray that my memories will be like the reefs that Ronnie and I explored in the Caribbean, whose wondrous architecture hosted a colorful diversity of life in a lucid and ever-changing sea. But sometimes I feel as though I am staring into a muddy lake. The clear streams of memories grow murkier as the years go by. The plankton and algae cloud the water until all I can see are the wind-driven ripples shimmering on the lake's surface.

Part of writing this memoir was a fight against the darkening gloom hiding in the murky depths. Telling stories keeps our memories alive and helps us understand ourselves and find compassion for the people who share our world. In these pages, I have focused on my father in part because he was a wonderful storyteller. Even at 90, he had an extraordinary memory. My mother and father worked hard to keep their memories alive.

For me their stories (and memories) were a burden and a wonder, a source of pain and solace. I did not truly understand the weight my parents carried until cancer killed my wife. When my mother died, my relationship with my father changed. We were grieving widowers trying to comfort each other. Now my father, too, has passed, and I feel like part of my memory died with him.

I recently stumbled upon an old birthday card in a desk drawer. My wife, Ronnie, made it for me the year before she died. On a background of fireworks and confetti, a bird of paradise appears atop a drawing on an envelope addressed to me. A butterfly dances among flaming hearts. In one of the hearts, she wrote: "To my one true love." Holding the card now, delight and anguish surge through me. I want to keep her alive in my memory, but I also want to escape from a life of perpetual mourning.

I have trouble believing in an afterlife. I have trouble taking comfort from the ideas of eternal recurrence or reincarnation. I go to synagogue occasionally to say prayers for the dead. I do yoga and meditate, but for me they are comforts for the living body and mind that do not transcend the material world. While I am skeptical about humanity, mindful of the horrors one generation after another inflicts upon its peers and the planet itself, I also marvel at the beauty and majesty of living things. The human creature is one of those wonders.

That my parents held on to their zest for life and their senses of humor—after all the losses and pain that they had suffered—seems miraculous. My father had a bumper sticker on his car that said *Ich bin a pushiter yid* (I am a simple Jew), but he was an amazing man. I have tried to share some of his stories and some of mine. Writing has helped me hold on to the people that I loved most dearly. It has also helped me let them go. I have tried to learn from my father and his determination to live a full life after his liberation from Auschwitz.

In my sixties now, I am still searching for love. Am I an old man, too old for romance? "Old" is a slippery word. Recently, while I was waiting for our salsa class to begin at the local YWCA, a woman sat down next to the instructor and complained that she was getting "too old" for this. She was in her early thirties, chagrined at the energy of the twentysomethings as they pranced about getting ready for the dance class. If she was too old at 33, then at 63 I must be... When my father was 60, he sometimes complained that he had one foot in the grave, but as the years went by, his perspective changed. When he was 91, we were chatting as we walked on the boardwalk along Hollywood Beach. "Sometimes I feel like an old man. And then some days I feel like I'm 80." He delivered this line in a wistful deadpan. I laughed out loud, and a smile sneaked across his face. He looked up like an innocent child, pretending not to know why what he had said was so funny.

My father took joy in living. Even at 93, as death crept closer, he tried to bargain with God for a few more years, but there is only one way for our journeys to end. The Jewish chicken farms have all but disappeared from central New Jersey. The last Holocaust survivors are dying. The section of greenhorns in my father's synagogue is now all but empty, but the survivors live on in their children and in the stories they left behind.

Godel's Eulogy

$$\infty$$

This book was a work in progress when my father died,
and I used some of the stories from earlier chapters
in the eulogy that I delivered at his memorial service,
on Friday, August 6, 2010.

My father was an amazing man who led an amazing life. In Yiddish we would say he had a *yiddisher neshume,* a Jewish soul; a *tiereh neshuma,* a dear soul; a *zeese neshuma.* He had a sweet soul. He was a survivor, and now he is dead. How can I talk about Godel and do justice to the man? He lived for 93 years, through horror and hope, happiness and misery. So much struggle and *tsuris,* until yesterday he overcame every hurdle. His *yiddshkeit,* his family and his friends, were his greatest joys.

Dad was from Wyszogröd, a town on the Vistula River in Poland, where Jews lived even before Columbus set sail for America. Wyszogröd had a famous synagogue; built of stone in the 18th century, it stood for 200 years. My father spoke with awe about the synagogue, the biggest building he ever saw in all his youth. The Nazis destroyed it in 1939.

He was a survivor. His inner circle was that small group of Jews that stayed or were stuck in Europe and somehow survived Hitler's war. They called themselves *greeneh*, greenhorns, newcomers trying to learn the language and the ways of these United States. Even the Jews that arrived before the war were grouped in with the *Americana Teychaster,* people who did not know how bad things could get, people who took things for granted, things like being able to eat or find drinking water. The inner circle is drying up now. My father had complained of how few were left to sit with in synagogue on *Shabbos.* Now another seat is empty.

∞

When I talked with him, it felt like he had many different lives. In each one he shone like a light from heaven.

My father was the water carrier for his family; two pails on a wooden stick slung over his shoulders, a trip down to the stream. He told me of the day when walking back he began spinning and the bottom of the buckets began swirling outward like those rides that my nephews take at Great Adventure that turn sideways at high speed, pressing your bottom into the seat while your legs dangle in open air. *Kleine Godela* spinning around and around, spinning faster and faster, giddy, laughing, boisterous until he looked up to see his father, who looked at the pails, almost empty, and with stern words, sent him back for more water. You could tell my father thought the fun he had was worth the scolding he got from his father. He was a little like my brother that way.

As a young man he worked making hats with his father. He worked for a while as a shoemaker, but he hated it. He wanted to be outside with people. He preferred tending the orchards his father rented. (Yes, there were *Kirschbaume,* cherry trees.) He liked riding on a cart, taking the fruit or hats to the market, but he loved being in the market among the people, the news.

And then Hitler and the war, a life some of you lived and some of us can barely comprehend: dragged from his home to the ghetto, and then the boxcars, the camps. Liberation and a second start in Munich after the war, the chicken farm, his success as a builder.

Let me pause for a moment to send special thanks to Bill and Barbara. Their kindness and support in the last weeks have touched me deeply. Their warmth helped to make a difficult time sweeter and gentler. Also, so many of his friends, Izzy and Sally, Martin, Herman, and others who showed devotion and caring that warmed my heart.

Places bind you and the people near you shape your life. I was bound to our chicken farm and our farmworkers, to Lakewood, where, from kindergarten through eighth grade, I went to Bezalel Hebrew Day School. I was also tied to relics from a terrible massacre, to the history of my grandparents and aunts and uncles, people I never met, people who died before I was born, people exterminated in the cold fury of a madness that my parents survived, a history that drove me to hide in the linen closet when the survivors gathered in our house to tell their stories.

When I finally got the courage to ask my father about the tattoo on his arm, he explained about the selection process and how those chosen to work were lined up and had their clothes and undergarments removed and their heads and pubic area shaved. Those who were to die immediately went elsewhere. He went to the tattoo area where a man took his arm and in a couple of minutes put a triangle in his flesh to mark him as a Jew followed by the number 83193. Just yesterday it peaked out from beneath his paper hospital bracelet. All the nurses in ICU at Paul Kimball commented on it. They remembered the number as much as the face. The number and the man speak for a lost generation.

Godel was a wonderful storyteller. So many stories, I am writing about them in a book, a memoir. It is *Kibud Av,* a Jewish mitzvah, the honor due to a father. If you will permit me, I want to share a few of his stories.

One story is of surviving slavery to make a new life. When we had Passover Seder, we read the Haggadah, but I often thought my parents should abandon the story of the exodus from Egypt and tell their own stories.

My mother hid in a snowbank with no gloves and torn socks in the dead of night, listening to the German patrols that were searching for the partisans. The Germans were close enough so she could hear every word: *Wenn ich euch finde Juden, werde ich euch totschlagen!* (When I find you Jews, I will kill you dead!) Death lurked in every doorway, in every shadow. Each day was a test.

In Auschwitz, Dad stole small items and bartered them. He combed the garbage for anything that seemed remotely edible. Somehow he lived from day to day.

One day he was marching out to a work. The capo, the foreman, a criminal who had been pulled out of prison to become a boss at Auschwitz, would throw stones at the feet of those who walked too slowly. He called out someone else's name and threw a rock at the man, but it struck my father instead. It hit his ankle. He started to limp immediately, but still he went out into the fields. After a day of digging drainage ditches, his ankle was so swollen, he could not stand on it.

The next morning, he was limping badly and they pulled him aside. They set him down under guard to wait for the ambulance truck. My father was desperate. His brother had been "selected" for death because he had open sores on his feet and now his own foot was injured and he could not work. There was no way out. He was sure his hours were numbered.

He got into an ambulance, a panel truck with wood benches and a red cross painted on the side. It was taking him from the work camps to the border of the extermination camps. He shook his head as he told the story. There were some young men in the truck. They were German Jews, nice boys, 80, 90 pounds. Gaunt, their muscles withered, their eyes bulging in their heads. "I am finished," he thought. He took out a small crust of bread and some saccharin he had hidden in his clothes. He wanted to have a sweet taste in his mouth before he died. He sat praying with his whole body shaking forward and back on the wooden bench. "God help me. God help me."

An SS officer stood over him and told him he would need to strip and take a shower before entering the hospital. My father knew about the gas chambers. When he heard the word "showers," his hair rose up on the back of his neck.

As he and the others on the ambulance truck waited their turn, my father made his peace with God. I can still see his face when he first told me the story, eyes moist, eyebrows lifted, and the rumor of a smile on his lips.

"They took all our clothes and we went in, naked, just like the day we were born. I was so skinny, you could see my ribs poking out. They painted my number on my chest with a grease pencil. They closed the door behind us. I stood for a long time waiting to die and then just to see what would happen I reached for the faucet and turned the handle..."

He paused to shake his head slowly.

"I turned the handle ... and water came out, *wasser*, ... cold water."

As he told the story, his hand went out to his sides, palms up as though testing for rain. He looked up with a glassy-eyed smile. "I thought, 'I am still alive.'"

∞

Somehow he lived.

He came out of the camps naked. No home. No country. No parents. No sisters. No brother. No cousins. No nothing.

Well, as it turns out, Godel did have something. He had a $20 bill that he had been hiding for months, carried in his belt or wadded up in his mouth.

"We were still wearing rags. When we finally got a chance to go to town, I thought to buy me a suit. I asked my friend should I buy a suit and he told me, 'No, buy something you can sell. You must begin again!'

"I don't remember what I bought first, coffee, cigarettes. I start to *handel* (to trade). I used to travel from country to country to buy and sell. To Italy, Switzerland, but it wasn't safe for a DP (displaced person) to travel, and I thought I must stop." So he and Felix Messer, a man he met in a DP camp, set up a business in Munich.

"In Munich, our market was on the street. I was always well dressed: a nice hat, a suit. We had a regular currency exchange, and we bought and sold gold, watches, cameras.

"But it was a risky business. We had these guys from Romania, they wore stiff hats…" He pointed his forefinger up next to his ears. "…with points sticking up. They brought us a couple of loads of watches. They were bringing stuff from Switzerland. We were stupid. We trusted them. They said they could bring us a special bunch of watches. The watches would only be available for a little while. They had to act fast, but they needed some cash to buy them. We gave them a $3,000 advance, but they never came back."

He found out later they had bought a turpentine factory in Romania. He never saw the money.

"Felix and I used to go to a local restaurant. Some of the clientele were Jewish wiseguys; they were like Mafioso. The lady who ran the place liked us. She pointed us out to these gangsters as good guys who ran a business that was a good place to get watches. Some of the guys we met at the restaurant stopped in to see us, to buy watches. It turns out, they were looking us over getting ready to rob us.

"A couple of days later Felix and I were going to a speech by Ben-Gurion, the Zionist leader, who was talking at a fund-raiser. Felix had an apartment where we ran the business. My apartment was one block away.

"I forgot something, and I went back to Felix's apartment. The door was broke down, and stuff was scattered everywhere. Someone had stolen our stuff. I ran down to the street, and they were still there. Five young men were stashing the loot, getting ready to go back for more. I went up to them and I told them, 'You a stealer, and I am the loser. Give me half of it back and I will leave you to go.'"

He was always a practical man.

"They laughed at me, and I grabbed one of them by the collar. I told them you, 'Don't give me half, you won't get away from here.'"

He grabbed the lapels of his own shirt to demonstrate. "I held him like this, and I told him, 'You not go anywhere.' I didn't know what I was doing. They were five people, and they started to fight with me. I'm a small guy. I don't know how to fight. One guy comes at my back and he put two knives in me. He gave me those two wounds, and I didn't feel it at first and then I felt a warmth spreading on my back. I reached back and looked at my hand. Blood was running. The wound was so deep, it had touched my lung. I was six days in hospital, and when I came out of the hospital, I said right away, "I must get married."

"Why did you suddenly need to marry?" I asked.

"I was weak. I had nobody, nowhere to go, no one to take care of me. Your mother came and sat with me in the hospital.

"Not everyone on the street was a bad guy. We had just been robbed. We were short on cash. One of my suppliers, when he heard I had been robbed, he told me he could wait to get paid and he said, 'Godel take off 1,000 dollar from what you owe me. I will share your loss.'"

My mother, Bronia, came to Munich in 1946. She was looking for someplace to live, and at the Jewish agency she met a young woman and they became roommates. This girl recommended Godel and Felix when Bronia needed to change some dollars for marks. "They are good boys. They give you an honest deal."

"She came to us to change $20 into marks, and she looked at what we were selling: gold, silver, and diamonds. She thought we were millionaires. We started to go out to the movies, dinner. We talked sometimes, Should we get married, not get married?

"After I got stabbed, four weeks later we got married. We went to rabbi and got married."

They were married for over 50 years, and today we will take Godel to lie down next to Bronia.

He made some money in Deutschland, in Germany, and he came to this country mostly because my mother's father, Simon Winderbaum, was here. I grew up on the chicken farm my father bought a few miles north of Lakewood. Some of you have been in that farmhouse to play cards. Maybe you came to my brother's *bris?* The chickens, *oy gevalt,* another chapter another world…. He could be a stubborn man, and he held out on the farm longer than most and then when he was just my age today, when he was 60 years old, he began a new life as a builder and moved into Lakewood, to his house on 14th Street.

He loved that house, and I want to take a moment to thank the Polish women who made it possible for him to live at home after my mother died: Christina and, as my father called them, the *big* Ella and the *little* Ella. Christina came to help when my mother was dying and for years was like a daughter to my father. She was an angel, a saint. He still called her every two weeks after she returned to Poland. Ella is also sent from God. I also want to thank Ella's son, Martin, and Father Mario, who were both so kind and respectful to my father.

∞

Last year my father called me on my birthday. I had the flu. He told me, "I woke up today and in my mind, I just came from your *bris;* we were ten men walking from the synagogue to the hospital where your mother was still recovering from her C-section."

Dad called every day I had the flu. He was a sweetie, concerned, full of advice. "Stay inside! Don't go out! Take Tylenol!" He worried about his boys, and he loved getting a chance to be on the other side, being a caregiver, after so many years of struggling with his own health.

Recovered, I call him and he said, "I can't talk right now I have two priests in the house." I tried to get him to explain, but he hung up. In my whole life he had never hung up on me. Perplexed, I had to wait until my next visit to get the whole story.

Christina, my father's Catholic caretaker, was finally preparing to return to her family in Poland. She had arranged for one of her Polish girlfriends, Ella, to come take her place. Father Mario became curious about who this old Jewish man was. He stopped in to visit. My father talked about his history and about how dearly he cherished Christina. He had been uncomfortable, at first, having a stranger live in his house, but now she was like a mother and daughter to him. Two weeks later the priest brought a Catholic bishop who was visiting from Poland to meet my father. The two dignitaries in black robes drove up past the Hassidim that surround my father's house. The Hassidim had their own black costumes serving a different religion. It was these two clerics who were in my father's house when I called.

The bishop was in the midst of preparing sermons on interfaith issues. He listened with interest to the priest who extolled Christina's devotion to the church and to my father's stories of his life in his small Polish town and his life as an inmate at Auschwitz.

When the bishop asked about how he was liberated, my father winced.

"They had us in boxcars. No food, no water. The Allies would bomb the tracks, and we would sit. You live without food for a long time, but water... When the train could go no further, they would march us to another train and we would fall down to drink from puddles on the road. They were muddy. They smelled of diesel fuel from the truck convoys, but we would drink. We went from one train to the next. One day the train stopped and we waited, and we waited, until some brave boy opened the door to see what is what. The Germans were gone. Soon, the Americans came. It was nighttime. They gave us pajamas and took us to a barracks to sleep. [His partner Felix Messer was one of his roommates.] In the morning we had some food and I went outside to look around. In the center of the barracks, the courtyard was tiled and some symbol lay embedded in the tiles stretched across the courtyard. We didn't understand what it was at first, but someone said, 'Look, it is a swastika.'"

He paused.

"Not to believe. It was a Hitler Youth camp at Feldafing, near Munich." Eisenhower and, later, Ben-Gurion, visited this camp. There is a rumor that Joseph Ratzinger, Pope Benedict, may have stayed there as a 14-year-old Hitler Youth.

The conversation moved on to my father's life in the states, his relationship with Christina. They took photos. Dad laughed, "The bishop put on his red yarmulke, and I put on my black one." I am not sure how long the bishop spent at my father's house, but Dad smiled as he talked about their good-byes. "The bishop thanked me for inviting him into my home. He shook my hand, and I thanked him for visiting. Then I told him: "Make sure to tell the Pope I slept in his bed."

When I told him I wrote about his wisecrack, he was embarrassed. "No, don't write about this. It's not nice." He did not want to offend his Catholic friends, who might mistake humor for ill will.

More recently, I called to check in on him and he told me about going to *shul*. It was a good sign when he went. One Sabbath, after services, there was a kiddush. Someone in the synagogue had a daughter whose marriage was imminent. Drinks and tidbits were laid out. My father drank a toast and was shuffling out the door when the bride's mother cornered him. "We are having a lunch, too. Please come." He tried to say no, but she persisted, and he joined them. "It was very nice, kugel, fish, very nice. When I was ready to leave, this same woman takes my hand and insists on walking me to my car. She was a nice woman."

∞

He was a sweet thing, an old man with his *kalyekeh* shoes and his cane, walking arm in arm with the mother of the bride. They stopped for a moment as other guests wished her mazel tov and thanked her for the lunch. Someone he didn't recognize, at first, approached. He couldn't quite hear the conversation. Was it in Polish? Who is this guy?

Elle had waited for him with lunch. A man with regular habits, he was a very old man still driving his car. He was almost two hours late. What had happened to him? Was he OK? She had called her son and sent him out looking for Godel.

In a world full of terrors, burdened with loss and despair, for a moment I felt lighter. Was it my heart lifting? The joy of hearing stories about kindness. He was a little embarrassed that he made her anxious, but he delighted in telling the story, fond of his Catholic housekeepers, touched by their loyalty and concern. An old Polish Jew, a survivor, and a Polish woman from a different faith who sent her son to make sure he was safe. Three generations. Compassion that reached across tribes. Kindness treasured by a survivor… and his son.

That was my father. He had seen the worst horrors that man can inflict, but he still looked for the good in people. He found so much of that goodness in the community he lived in and helped build in and around Lakewood. He treasured his family…and his rabbi, his congregation, his landsman and all the *greeneh,* who were like a family to him. He cherished them. Godel is from the Hebrew *gohdol,* which means "big" or "great." He was not that tall, but he was a great treasure, a spirit that enriched our lives. We will carry him with us forever. His wisdom, his love and kindness, his generosity and good made me proud to be his son.

About the Author

Michael Kirschenbaum was born in Munich Germany in January of 1950, the son of two Polish Jews who were holocaust survivors. He came to the United States as a toddler and grew up on a chicken farm in New Jersey.

Mr. Kirschenbaum earned a degree in History from the University of Pennsylvania and went on to study Computer Science at M.I.T. His career followed the emergence of high tech, first, writing systems software used by NASA including some bits that crashed into Jupiter onboard Galileo. In the nineties, he shifted to marketing and management consulting working at the Lotus Development Company and then became a partner in The Jacobson Group, a groupware consulting company in Harvard Square.

In 2001, Ronnie, his wife and soul mate for thirty years, died of lung cancer. Struggling with grief Mr. Kirschenbaum found comfort in his family and developed a new relationship with his parents. He wrote this memoir to explore what it means to be the child of survivors growing up in one of the few Jewish farming communities outside the state of Israel.

www.ingramcontent.com/pod-product-compliance
Lightning Source LLC
LaVergne TN
LVHW051451080426
835509LV00017B/1738